"Josephine Ross has blessed us with a high and frisk from the perspective of its survivor. provocative mash up in which #metoo meets #blacklivesmatter and makes the world a better place."

"A compelling critique of the indignities of routine police stops. Using feminist principles such as the need for bodily integrity and consent, Ross exposes how the criminal justice system weakens the constitutional rights of all of us."

"Josephine Ross has written a book that is stunning in its originality in applying the principles of feminist theory to the issues of policing and especially the law of stop and frisk. Through many interviews, Ross is able to show what police actually do and the harms it causes. She offers great ideas for changing the law."

"*A Feminist Critique of Police Stops* is a critical book for these times."

"This compelling examination of how law and the reality of police stops and frisks is essential reading for anyone interested in restoring the integrity of our Bill of Rights."

"What if every young person of color knew, when stopped by police, to say (and to believe), 'With all respect, I do not consent to searches?' Read this book to imagine a different and better world."

"As someone who advocates for intersectional approaches to equity, I was moved by Josephine Ross's recognition of how our current system of policing further marginalizes already underrepresented communities. Her thoughtful analysis uses a feminist framework to skillfully carve a path forward."

A FEMINIST CRITIQUE OF POLICE STOPS

A Feminist Critique of Police Stops examines the parallels between stop-and-frisk policing and sexual harassment. An expert whose writing, teaching, and community outreach centers on the Constitution's limits on police power, Howard Law Professor Josephine Ross, argues that our constitutional rights are a mirage. In reality, we can't say no when police seek to question or search us. Building on feminist principles, Ross demonstrates why the Supreme Court got it wrong when it allowed police to stop, search, and sometimes strip-search people and call it consent. Using a wide range of sources – including her law students' experiences with police, news stories about Eric Garner and Sandra Bland, social science, and the work of James Baldwin – Ross sheds new light on how police use stop-and-frisk to threaten and marginalize vulnerable communities. This book should be read by everyone interested in how Court-approved police stops sap everyone's constitutional rights and how this form of policing can be eliminated.

Josephine Ross is a professor of law at Howard University School of Law, Washington, DC. She was a public defender in Massachusetts for seven years, then served as an interim executive director of Gay and Lesbian Advocates and Defenders before beginning a teaching career at Boston College Law School. She has published numerous law review articles, first on marriage equality and then on topics involving criminal (in) justice. For two decades, she supervised law students in the criminal trial courts of Boston and Washington, DC.

A Feminist Critique of Police Stops

JOSEPHINE ROSS

Howard University School of Law (Washington, DC)

CAMBRIDGE
UNIVERSITY PRESS

CAMBRIDGE
UNIVERSITY PRESS

University Printing House, Cambridge CB2 8BS, United Kingdom

One Liberty Plaza, 20th Floor, New York, NY 10006, USA

477 Williamstown Road, Port Melbourne, VIC 3207, Australia

314–321, 3rd Floor, Plot 3, Splendor Forum, Jasola District Centre, New Delhi – 110025, India

79 Anson Road, #06–04/06, Singapore 079906

Cambridge University Press is part of the University of Cambridge.

It furthers the University's mission by disseminating knowledge in the pursuit of education, learning, and research at the highest international levels of excellence.

www.cambridge.org
Information on this title: www.cambridge.org/9781108482707
DOI: 10.1017/9781108697477

First published 2021

A catalogue record for this publication is available from the British Library.

ISBN 978-1-108-48270-7 Hardback
ISBN 978-1-108-71087-9 Paperback

To my wife Chris Guilfoy, our son Sam, and daughter-in-law Jameela

Not everything that is faced can be changed, but nothing can be changed until it is faced.

James Baldwin – *I Am Not Your Negro* (a film)[1]

Contents

Acknowledgments

Before I turned my ideas into a book proposal, my good friends Phyllis Goldfarb and Anthony Farley encouraged my early forays into mapping the connections between policing and feminist subjects like sexual assault. So did Margaret Johnson, who invited me to present at the Feminist Theory Conference in Baltimore back in 2009 where the questions from members of the community differed dramatically from those posed by law professors. As these worlds came together in one conference, I knew that I wanted to work on projects that would keep me at this intersection between the legal profession and black communities affected every day by the Supreme Court's decisions. After speaking at a conference at Western New England School of Law, transgender rights activist Jennifer Levi told me that the parallel I made between "consent" for sex and "consent" for police searches worked on more than a theoretical level. Look at how police sexually abuse people, she advised. I didn't have the guts to do this until advocates, social scientists, and journalists started finding and publishing data that backed this up.

It took me ten years to learn to write like a law professor. How long would it take me to stop writing like one? I was lucky an old friend retired just at the time I was searching for someone to give me feedback on early drafts. After reading what I sent, Sue Herz was aghast at the way police behaved and how the Supreme Court ruled – surprised she didn't know what was going on despite her work as a disability rights lawyer. Sue and Stacey Colino helped me to find a voice to tell stories and talk about case law that would make sense to readers who never stepped foot in a law school classroom. My goal was to write this book for all the potential readers, like Stacey or Sue, who can't tell a "search" from a "seizure" but know that when officers taser a person's genitals, that's ugly and wrong. Whether I succeeded in making law accessible to all will be for you, the reader, to decide.

My Feminist Reading Group read the first draft of the book and challenged me to better articulate what I mean by feminism. Martha Ertman, who keeps the book group humming, encouraged me at every step of this process and it was Martha who persuaded me to share my work with the group. I owe a debt to Jane Aiken, Marley Weiss, Naomi Cahn, Ashwini Tambe, Leigh Goodmark, Joanna Silver, and Martha and to three book group members who doubled as experts in constitutional criminal procedure – Cynthia Lee, Jenny Roberts, and Phyllis Goldfarb. It was Phyllis who gave me the closest read (several times) and she writes so beautifully that I often stole her comments, typing them verbatim into my text. Thanks to Phyllis, I was able to synthesize the contradictory feedback that one would expect from a group of feminists and come away energized. Sociologist Celine-Marie Pascale also plied me with ideas and books to expand my concept of feminism. Near the end of this process Phyllis and Judy Appelbaum closely read the manuscript and met me in my now favorite coffee shop in Takoma Park, where they gave me tremendous feedback,

I owe a debt to the Howard law students who allowed me to use their stories in this book and to the many students that spent their Saturday mornings in DC Superior Court training teenagers in how to preserve their rights during police encounters. This includes Koryn High and Dwight Draughon, who ran Youth Court sessions when I could not attend. Thanks also to all the law students who volunteered in other venues across the DC metro area. The genesis for the *Know Your Rights* trainings at Youth Court began with Howard law students Raven Radley and Stanley Tate, who worked with me to create a script that would explain the Fourth Amendment to Chicago middle school students through interactive means. It was my brother Harry Ross, a professor of education at National Louis University, who brought my law students into Chicago classrooms and challenged us to think creatively about how to present constitutional rights to middle school and high school audiences. I thank the Andrew Rankin Memorial Chapel at Howard University for sponsoring my Alternative Spring Break Trips to New Orleans shortly after Hurricane Katrina and then to Chicago.

Danielle Holley-Walker, the dean of Howard University School of Law, threw her support behind this book. I never could have completed the manuscript had she not graciously allowed me to switch from supervising students as they represented clients charged with crimes to teaching Criminal Procedure and Evidence instead. This gave me the space to write. Research assistants Pajah Williams, Malik Baker, and Kaiwan Tresvant deserve the most credit – with special thanks to Pajah, who continued to work tirelessly on endnotes to the last moment. Thanks also go to Howard law librarian Victoria Capatosto, who always turned around my research requests in a heartbeat.

I started writing this book in London, where Birkbeck University offered me a fellowship during my sabbatical year. There, I gained perspective as well as friendship from Maria Aristodemou, Sarah Lamble, and other new colleagues. Barrister Niamh Eastwood, from StopWatch Project in London, took time out from running the advocacy project and I enjoyed learning from her and others about UK parallels to my admittedly US-centered research.

Here are some other wonderful friends who critiqued a chapter or took time to discuss what I should do when I ran into dead ends: Frank Rudy Cooper, Katherine Macfarlane, Val Vojdik, Catherine Grosso, Dea Birkett, Marsali Craig, Kim Thomas, Zina Makar, Valena Beety, and Eric Miller. I am a big admirer of Bennett Capers' writings, so I was on cloud nine when he agreed to read the whole manuscript once it was completed. I'm grateful for his usual brilliant insights and relieved that most of his suggestions fell within my reach, given the short turn-around time. I'm indebted to editor Matt Gallaway of Cambridge University Press for cheering on this project and providing sound advice throughout. Then there's the editor I'm closest to, my wife Chris, who suffered throughout some terrible drafts and didn't leave.

This work was made possible by several summer research stipends provided by Howard University School of Law.

Introduction

In March of 2011, Howard University sponsored an Alternative Spring Break trip to Chicago where law students worked with me to create several lessons in constitutional law for middle schoolers. The lesson on policing teaches civilians the constitutional limits on police power. Sometimes referred to as "Street Law," I call the training *Know Your Rights*. It was a huge hit with middle school students and teachers, and became the genesis for *Know Your Rights* trainings in other venues. I will never forget Raven and Stanley, the two Howard students volunteering in Chicago who wrote the first drafts of skits we performed, and found ways to connect with the middle school students we taught. When another teacher brought her class to hear the two firebrands, doubling Raven and Stanley's class size, Raven even stood on a chair to be heard.

Sitting in a crowded middle school classroom in Chicago that spring, I watched the two of them command the classroom.

"You are our next volunteer," Stanley announces to a small eighth grader sitting at one of the round tables near the front of the room. Handing the kid a backpack, Stanley sets the scene: "You are walking home from school and I am a cop," he explains. "Remember your job is to avoid getting arrested and avoid getting searched."

During the skit, Stanley, who weighs twice as much as this kid does, booms, "Where are you going? I see you have a backpack ... Any knives or weapons in there? Any drugs?" (The kid shakes his head no.) "No? Well then you don't mind if I take a look?" Stanley intones as he holds out his hand. The kid hands him the backpack.

"Cut! Okay," says Stanley, "Let's do it again and this time say to the officer: 'I never consent to searches.'" The kid performs the skit again but with the same result.

Even running the skit through a third time, the young teenager once again quickly passes the bag to Stanley as if there were gravitational pull on the fabric.

This teenager is hardly alone in waiving his rights. More than 90 percent of searches in the United States are consensual. Watching a skit unfold, many of the teens can't tell the subtle difference between an *order* (that must be obeyed) and a *request for consent*. It's even harder for the teenager who has been "volunteered" to perform, and harder still in real life. But this teen can't later complain that police lacked justification to search his bag; according to the law, it's his own fault for consenting.

Consent is "an acid that has eaten away the Fourth Amendment," wrote Rutgers University law professor George Thomas, because it allows police to search people without a shred of evidence against them.[1]

This is the state of our constitutional rights. We have an absolute right to say no when police request consent to search our bags or pockets. But if it's impossible to exercise this right, then the right is more of a mirage. Or, as I argue in these pages, the consent search is one of several consent devices constructed by the Supreme Court to blame the victims of police encounters when officers violate their rights.

As a white law professor who teaches Criminal Procedure, a class devoted to the constitutional limits of policing, I hoped my law students could explain the Supreme Court's complicated regime to middle and high school students so they might exercise their constitutional rights during future police encounters. Instead, *Know Your Rights* lessons revealed a failure of translation. The Bill of Rights was adopted specifically to protect us from government overreach. In reality, these teenagers won't be able to exercise their rights during police stops, even if they understand all the Supreme Court's complex rulings. Adults, too. These trainings reveal a schism between *"law on the books"* and *"law in action."* The fault lies not with my law students nor with participants in these trainings, but with an aggressive police culture and Supreme Court decisions that are based on a fantasy in which police officers and civilians are equals.

STOP-AND-FRISK

Throughout the United States, thousands of individuals who are otherwise going about their business are stopped and questioned. Many are ordered against a wall and touched in ways that would be considered sexual harassment or even sexual assault if performed by civilians instead of police officers. We're talking about the police practice commonly referred to as "stop-and-frisk," also referred to as "Terry stops" after the name of a court case that sanctioned the practice.

The chapters that follow offer a fresh look at the costs and benefits of stop-and-frisk, applying feminist insights and new data. Ultimately, the new perspective reveals that the Supreme Court got it wrong in the 1968 case of *Terry* v. *Ohio* – that approved stop-and-frisk – when it concluded that society's need for this policing tool outweighed any harmful ramifications. On one side of the scale, Terry stops are supposed to make communities safer, but it turns out that they don't and they may actually increase crime. On the other side of the scale, numerous harms flow from stops and frisks, including the loss of bodily integrity, stress, anxiety, and poor health outcomes. Beyond the people stopped, the harms flow outward, creating psychological damage to friends, families, and whole neighborhoods. Even when police don't violate the law, the practice saps the Bill of Rights when the courts approve Terry stops and "consent" stops based on legal fictions.

This book argues for the end of so-called consent stops and consent searches and the abolition of stop-and-frisk. The *Know Your Rights* trainings showed me the interweave between these two areas of law.

Gabriel, an outgoing Latinx born and raised in New York City, told me of the day he fell victim to stop-and-frisk. Gabriel was twenty at the time. Years later, he came to study at the Howard University School of Law, where I teach. That's how I came to hear his story which begins in a similar fashion to the way George Zimmerman profiled and killed Trayvon Martin, sparking the Black Lives Matter movement:[2] Gabriel was walking home from a corner market. Luckily for him, this turned out to be just a garden variety stop-and-frisk – nothing you would end up reading about in outraged posts online.

> This was back in March of 2012. It was maybe 8 or 9 p.m. I was with a friend. We had bought groceries and I was returning to my fiancé's house. I walked out carrying two bags of groceries, one on each side. The cop came up between two cars. He came up really quickly and began frisking me. He had no uniform. No badge. He told me to put the bags down and started patting me down the length of my body to my socks. He did it fast, with both hands. Now, there's no way I was carrying a weapon. I had on shorts and a tank top. If I had anything on me, there would have been a bulge. And the bags were see-through, so this was crazy. "Who the fuck is this guy?"I remember thinking. For a minute I wasn't even positive he was a cop, although he looked like one.

Gabriel's frisk was quick but invasive.

> With both hands, the cop came all the way from my socks up to under my armpits. "How are you doing? Do you have any plans tonight?'" the cop asks. What's he asking? I mean even he knows my plan is to put these groceries in the fridge.
> The cop did each leg individually. When he got to the waistband of my gym shorts, he ran his thumb all around the circumference of the shorts. He pulled on my underwear, which felt weird. He pulled up on my gym shorts. Then he pulled the elastic out and let it snap into place. He did that a couple of times while I just stood there. I mean it was like wearing a bathing suit and being frisked. I had almost nothing on. He quickly finished with me. Then did the same thing to my friend. I knew it was over when he jumped into an unmarked police car (a Crown Vic) with three white undercover detectives wearing sweats.[3]

From New Orleans to New York City and from Ferguson to Baltimore, this aggressive policing tactic victimizes adults and teenagers.[4] Gabriel is among its thousands of victims. It's likely that Gabriel's combined identities (Latinx and male) explain why police singled him out, how police treated him, and how he experienced the stop. Poor neighborhoods bear the brunt of this policing, and officers overwhelmingly target young black and Latinx males.

In its heyday, from 2004 to 2012, the New York Police Department averaged 1,500 stops per day. One statistic says it all: in 2011, the focus on black males between the ages of 14 and 24 years old was so pronounced that the number of stops that year exceeded the total population of black teenagers and men in that age range living in New York City.[5]

Police also unfairly target members of the LGBTQ community, particularly transgender women of color. "Studies from around the country reveal persistent police use of profiling to harass and falsely or selectively arrest based on race and gender presentation." Not only are transgender women more likely to be stopped when they have not violated any laws, they are "more likely to report experiencing inappropriate touching, sexual harassment, humiliation and violence."[6]

Gabriel was angry when police stopped and frisked him. And he still sounds indignant when he talks about it. "I was disrespected," Gabriel told me, and he wants to do something about it. "I cannot wait to become a lawyer." But that's not every person's reaction. Stop and frisk leaves scars. The humiliation does not always – or usually – lead, as it did in Gabriel's case, to the victim becoming vice president of his class and then one of Howard Law's proud graduates. Howard students helped me bridge worlds, and for those who share my original perspective, that's the journey I want the reader to take. The young people I trained – or helped my law students train – also helped me to recognize where my assumptions were wrong.

I thought I understood stop-and-frisk before I came to teach at Howard University in 2005. After all, I had been a criminal defense attorney for seven years and I then spent a decade supervising Boston College Law School students as they represented criminal defendants in Dorchester Criminal Court. But transitioning from a predominantly white law school to the country's preeminent African American law school soon opened my eyes to the difference between the way the law appears in the books and the way it plays out across the country. As the statistics bear out, my black and Latinx students were far more likely to be stopped or mistreated by police or tell me about a family member enmeshed in the criminal justice system. Unlike me, my clinic class seemed to take it in stride when their classmate was locked up for an expired sticker on his vehicle. In the next class, when he explained how police stole his money while he was locked up, I was the only white person in the class and the only one advocating to lodge a complaint. Don't kick the hornet's nest; that was the gist of the students' advice.

My law students and I devote the majority of *Know Your Rights* lessons to navigating Terry stops. Many of these trainings took place in Youth Court, a now defunct diversion program in Washington, DC, where teenagers arrested for minor misdemeanors (such as fighting or truancy or marijuana possession) avoided juvenile court by submitting to a jury of their peers. After a hearing, the peer jury might require the accused to write an apology or attend mentoring sessions. At a minimum, every teenager had to return to Youth Court to serve as a peer juror seven times before his or her charge was dismissed.

What began as a one-time training for at-risk youth turned into a regular event. Every other Saturday morning, three or four Howard law students arrived at DC Superior Court. They set up training in the well of one of the courtrooms, close to the jury box where we would usher the Youth Court participants to sit. My law students and I taught boys and girls, ages ten to seventeen, how to be thoughtful jurors. But *Know Your Rights* was my favorite part of Youth Court training and became the genesis of this book.

One day during a *Know Your Rights* training, I met Jamal, a black teenager from a poor black DC neighborhood. Jamal had been stopped, searched, and then arrested for possession of marijuana. That was what had brought him to Youth Court. I remember his name because at the end of the training I went over to the end of the jury box where he was seated a few seats away from other participants and asked him a couple of questions, including how often he had been stopped that year. He thought for a moment and then answered, "In the last twelve months? About ten times, I guess." With an unhappy shrug he added, "I try not to go out if I don't have to."

Jamal's shrug can't hide the psychological toll of this court-sanctioned harassment. Even on harassment-free days when police let Jamal walk home from school unmolested, the repeated indignities continue to work their magic. Jamal no longer feels free to walk to the corner store to buy candy or meet his friends at a local park. Instead, this 16-year-old suffocates in his family's small apartment, too scared to leave. Police have successfully sent the message that he can be detained by uniformed men and plain-clothed detectives carrying guns; that he's not safe on public streets.

Although Jamal made the best of a bad situation by choosing Youth Court instead of Juvenile Court, I feel bad that he has an arrest record, and guilty because police departments deploy stop-and-frisk so that white professionals like me feel safe. If only *Know Your Rights* training could keep Jamal safe in the future, my Saturday would be well spent. Well, that's what I thought at the time. But now in the cold light of day, I confess that knowing our rights will protect neither our rights nor our bodies. The Supreme Court has quietly gutted the Bill of Rights to support police power, including the Constitution's guarantee to free speech, the right to silence in the face of interrogation, and the right not to be detained, touched, or searched without a good reason. And it's not just people stopped who suffer the consequences, although they bear the deepest scars.

The Fourth Amendment to the Constitution limits police power and (theoretically) requires that police have individualized suspicion every time they stop a person. Those who assume that Terry stops are fine as long as police officers hew to the Supreme Court's constitutional constraints don't realize how easy it is for unfair policing to clear the Court's low constitutional bar.

The first nine times Jamal was stopped, police didn't find anything, so judges never evaluated the constitutionality of their actions. Same for Gabriel's stop-and-frisk; the vast majority of Terry stops never come before a court. We're talking approximately one hearing for every 5,000 encounters.[7]

For those few stops that lawyers challenge, judges hold hearings where they hear the officers' version and occasionally the person who was stopped might also testify. If a judge finds that an officer acted solely to fill a quota or solely to harass, lacking "reasonable suspicion" to believe that a civilian like Gabriel was committing a crime, then the stop violated the Fourth Amendment. But a judge might decide that both the stop and patdown of Gabriel's body were reasonable. And that's pretty much the end of the legal inquiry.

A FEMINIST LENS

Taking a feminist approach to stop-and-frisk means celebrating the insights and accomplishments of feminist scholars and activists in areas that enrich our understanding of how these encounters disrupt safety and security and why courts don't rein in police aggression. Here are three primary ways that this book harnesses feminist principles:

1. **Bodily integrity.** Feminism places a high value on people's right to control their own bodies and helps readers to recognize the ways that police stops can interfere with an intimate sense of self.
2. **Victims' perspective.** Many feminist successes to date began with consciousness-raising methods that illuminated the ways that the law failed to adequately address women's lived experiences.
3. **Consent runs through it.** Feminists have long critiqued laws that blame women for not resisting an aggressor. When a person cooperates with someone who wields power, feminists call that submission, not consent.

This is not an exhaustive list. These and other feminist insights will be explored throughout the book. Let's start with bodily integrity.

BODILY INTEGRITY

Gabriel's anger and Jamal's fear are only two of the many different reactions a stop-and-frisk victim might have. They point to severe consequences and a lack of vocabulary to fully describe how these stops and frisks resonate within the bodies and psyches of men, women, and youth. Nothing in Fourth Amendment law reflects how stops create psychological damage or how repeated stops can compound stress and interfere with quality of life. We need a fuller discourse capable of describing the interactions that Gabriel and Jamal endured. Indeed, a feminist perspective proves quite useful in understanding stop-and-frisk and responding to it.

To protect women faced with verbal or physical harassment at work, feminists successfully pressed for the passage of anti-harassment laws.[8] There are useful parallels between workplace harassment that primarily targets women (although not exclusively) and the policing problem that particularly affects young men (although not exclusively). Anti-harassment laws provide a legal language that parallels Gabriel and Jamal's experiences with the police.

When employees face severe or pervasive sexual harassment, the law calls the workplace a "hostile work environment."[9] Jamal's experience during the police encounters can also be described in sexual harassment terms. For Jamal, Terry stops were pervasive, turning the streets into a hostile environment. Just as sexual harassers send a message that the workplace isn't safe for women or effeminate men, police sent a message to Jamal that walking while black isn't safe.

Current anti-harassment law includes protections against continued victimization. When the workplace environment becomes intolerable, employees can quit their jobs to stave off psychological harm without losing their right to sue. Employment law calls this "constructive discharge."[10] But when police harass Jamal in his neighborhood, how can he quit that? There's no comparable safety valve or remedy against unwelcome and repeated Terry stops.

There's a sexual aspect to Terry patdowns. Even when an officer is simply following his training, people can experience frisks as sexual assaults. When trustworthy officers "frisk" breasts and groins in the manner they were taught, this can feel like a sexual invasion to the men, women, and teenagers on the receiving end.

In Gabriel's case, the officer felt around his waistband, snapping it the way boys once snapped bra straps with impunity, when our society widely considered such playground bravado to be harmless. Even though the officer did what he was trained to do – and didn't make sexually demeaning remarks or put his hands inside Gabriel's shorts – that fact doesn't erase the indignity.

Sexual harassment law recognizes that physical touching, especially sexual touching, increases the severity of the harm caused by unwelcome attention. Naming the sexual aspect of frisks also serves to illuminate their psychological toll. But even without a frisk, aggressive Terry stops create stress and anxiety that's analogous to how women – and some men – respond to verbal taunts, humiliating encounters with creepy bosses, or other forms of sexual harassment that stop short of physical contact.[11]

There's one Supreme Court decision that acknowledged the sexually invasive quality of a search for drugs. Not coincidentally, the case, *Safford* v. *Redding*, involved a white female teen who was suspected only of possessing ibuprofen in school, and nothing was discovered during the search. The school nurse asked 13-year-old Savana Redding to strip down to her bra and underwear to confirm or disprove a classmate's report that Savana had supplied a contraband pill. Even though the search did not take place in public and she was not physically touched, the Court described it as "embarrassing, frightening, and humiliating" from the young woman's perspective. The Fourth Amendment must be interpreted, wrote Justice David Souter, with a recognition that "adolescent vulnerability intensifies the patent intrusiveness of the exposure."[12] Although the Supreme Court ultimately ruled against Savanna – because it's difficult to sue police and school officials for civil rights violations[13] – at least the Court recognized the vulnerability of the person detained and looked at the search from her perspective. In the context of the Supreme Court, and of the judicial system as a whole, the opinion stands out like a sunny day in February. But it's my belief that this is the consideration courts should give to all victims of stops, frisks and full-blown searches, approaching victims with empathy, but, unlike the *Redding* decision, not ending there.

Many generations of feminists prioritized women's bodily integrity and articulated the harms that flow from interference with autonomy. From Andrea Dworkin to bell hooks to Patricia Hill Collins, these theorists investigated unwelcome attention and violence by men and the lack of legal recourse for victims. Feminist subjects such as sexual harassment, domestic violence, and sexual assault provide useful parallels into the harms that flow from stop-and-frisk and illuminate the legal gaps in how courts treat police encounters.

My feminist critique of stop-and-frisk focuses on the power to control our own bodies rather than letting others control them, the power to inhabit public spaces without fear of harassment, and the right to be free from unwanted touching.

VICTIMS' PERSPECTIVE

Feminist methods of consciousness-raising and telling stories about women's lives helped expose the law's deficiencies when it came to harassment and violence against women. Starting in the 1970s, feminists described a methodology that begins with storytelling as a means to challenge cultural assumptions and discover where laws failed to protect women. When women started sharing their stories in consciousness-raising sessions in the late 1960s, it led to a recognition of how legal rules privileged male power. US feminists exposed laws that favored husbands over wives, that devalued single women, and that provided impunity for violence against women. Even the term "sexual harassment" derives from this method.[14]

As Catharine A. MacKinnon wrote in 1979 about sexual harassment, "I envision a two-way process of interaction between the relevant legal concepts and women's experience." Done right, women's experiences "begin to shape" the law "so that what really happens to women, not some male vision of what happens to women, is at the core" of what the law allows or prohibits.[15]

My colleague Lisa Crooms-Robinson explains how mainstream legislators "use stories to construct a [harmful] narrative" that "places the blame for innercity poverty squarely on the shoulders of poor, Black, single mothers." In response, black legislators should "reassert control over these misappropriated stories" and "infuse the debate, as well as their own narratives, with the protagonists' voices."[16]

Building on these previous efforts, the #MeToo campaign turned a spotlight on power, consent, and sexual abuse. In 2006, black activist Tarana Burke created "Just Be Inc.," a nonprofit to support sexual assault survivors in marginalized communities "through which she launched the 'Me Too' mantra" to make sure poor black women and girls received support services.[17] A decade later, actress Alyssa Milano tweeted an invitation for women to come out as sexual assault survivors and the hashtag #MeToo was born, with millions posting on Twitter, Facebook and Instagram.[18] Together, #MeToo describes a movement in which women and some men share experiences of unwanted sexual aggression from harassment to rape. Whether it's a movement or a moment, the #MeToo success stories – from mounting awareness to the toppling of high-powered men – stem from taking the victim's perspective.

I don't want to overstate the claim. Critical race theorists Devon Carbado and Paul Butler also use a victim-centered perspective in their work that focuses on black men. When Professor Carbado calls for a "victim perspective," he's asking the Supreme Court to acknowledge the "coercive and disciplinary ways in which race structures the interaction between police officers and nonwhite persons."[19] Both blame the Supreme Court for enabling violence and mass incarceration, for giving police what Professor Butler describes as "superpowers," including the power to stop-and-frisk. Both writers build on *The New Jim Crow*, by Michelle Alexander, illuminating our broken punishment system.

Feminism inspires my particular victim-centered approach. My former colleague Phyllis Goldfarb writes how feminist lawyers must "perpetually seek to uncover whose perspectives and interests are represented in a particular law, case, practice or institution, and whose are excluded, and how including excluded viewpoints might reshape the analysis."[20] That's what this book endeavors to do.

The "SayHerName" movement publicizes female victims of police violence.[21] Certainly, feminism demands the inclusion of women in any analysis of life or law, but feminism is not confined to the study of women and girls or those who defy gender categories. Feminist theories that advance women's equality should also protect men. As masculinity scholars point out, male privilege never extended evenly to all men. When the Supreme Court struck down laws that criminalized gay male sex, the ruling was built partly on the feminist-supported principle of autonomy and literally grounded in a legal line of cases that granted some measure of reproductive freedom.[22] And protecting vulnerable men ultimately helps women. As one scholar phrased it, "the world will not be safe for women in frilly pink dresses ... unless and until it is made safe for men in dresses as well." When the Court agreed that sexual harassment law protects gay men against homophobic torment, this benefited female workers too.[23]

Feminism "means different things to its many supporters" as the editors of *Feminist Judgments* wrote, but for me, as for them, "feminism is both a movement and a mode of inquiry. In its best and most capacious form, feminism embraces justice for all.[24]

It's Gabriel and Jamal's perspectives, along with female and LGBTQ victims, that are currently missing from the law. Similarly, whether it's the Youth Court teenagers or others who agreed to share their experiences with me, their stories expose what's rotten within stop-and-frisk. The lived experiences of Youth Court teenagers ultimately led me to recognize the central role that consent plays within the practice and the theory of Terry stops.

CONSENT RUNS THROUGH IT

At first glance, it may seem difficult to see how consent relates to stop-and-frisk. It's not the lawyer's standard view. In most textbooks on criminal procedure, consent makes up a short chapter. And the authors don't connect consent to Terry stops. Textbooks reflect the legal reality: courts and law professors tend to look at stop-and-frisk from an officer's point of view.

The laws that govern stop-and-frisk look different in a law school classroom than they do in Youth Court when my law students and I teach *Know Your Rights*. What civilians need to know is how to preserve their rights. If they submit to a police officer because they are scared, will a judge later say that they consented?

In the law school classroom, students learn the Supreme Court's rules on police stops. Students divide police encounters into three categories and absorb how each of these three categories demands a different justification.

- "Arrests," where police need "probable cause" to believe a suspect has committed a crime.
- "Terry stops," where police need "reasonable suspicion" to believe a suspect has committed a crime.
- "Consent stops," where police need no justification at all.

Searches follow a similar rubric. To frisk during a Terry stop, police need additional "reasonable suspicion," a reasonable belief that a suspect is armed and presents a danger to them or others. Police claim to be afraid a lot. As with "consent stops," when police obtain "consent" for a search, that's all the justification they need, whether it's a patdown or full-blown search of a person's body or possessions. [25]

These categories might work for police and judges, but they confuse civilians.

Let's consider the testimony of an LGBTQ Youth Leader in New York City named Trina who described events that unfolded when she was 17 years old:

> I was going to a kiki ball on a Saturday night in the West Village. I was standing on the street talking with some friends and an officer approached me. She asked me for my ID. I gave it to her. At that time I didn't have my name legally changed. She not only would not call me by my real name, but she kept calling me a man and a faggot. She took a picture of my ID and sent it to the 6th precinct. The dispatcher told her that my record was clear but instead of letting me go, she said she wanted to see in my purse. I didn't know my rights then or I would have not consented to the search. I thought I had to show her the contents of my purse.

When police approach and question people without physically restraining them, the Supreme Court categorizes this police maneuver as a "consent stop." Unless police yell "halt," order Trina to stand against a wall, or touch her, the courts place the burden on her to walk away from an officer's unwelcome advances. Had Trina's case come before a court, a judge might find that she consented in three ways: (1) by submitting to a "consent stop"; (2) by handing over her identification when the officer made this a request (not an order); and (3) by agreeing to let police search her bag (a "consent search").

The "consent search" ended badly for Trina. When the officer looked into the purse, she found two condoms and used them to justify an arrest. Trina testified during a city council meeting about what the police did next. Her testimony was reproduced by the Center for Gender & Sexuality Law at Columbia University in *A Roadmap for Change*:[26] "'Why are you locking me up? I can't carry condoms?' [The officer] replied, 'You are getting locked up for prostitution.' I was taken to the precinct and put in with the men. I was 17 years old. This is my story, but this is also the story of many of my friends.[27]

There's an inside/outside conundrum with Terry stops. Although the law is the same in Youth Court as it is in my law school classroom, the shift in perspective changes everything. Although a court would probably view Trina's encounter as consensual (until her arrest), in Trina's eyes, she was stopped and searched against her will.

Experiencing the discrepancy reminds me of listening to my cousin discuss building a house with her husband. They argued a lot until they finally recognized that he, the builder, was talking about the structure from the outside. Meanwhile she was talking about the inside, thinking about what it would be like to live in the house – no wonder they had trouble communicating.

Courts imagine stop-and-frisk from the outside, from the perspective of the officer. I view the Supreme Court as the original architect when it created the rules in *Terry*

v. *Ohio*. Officers know the structure and can choose to call an encounter a "Terry stop" or a "consent stop" in their reports. If they call it a Terry stop, they know how to write the magic words that allow them to detain Jamal or Gabriel and the special words they need to frisk.

From the civilian's point of view, *Terry*'s legal structure creates a confusing labyrinth. Consider reasonable suspicion, another officer-centered concept. Law school courses discuss how police officers need "reasonable suspicion that crime is afoot." Students need to hear this because that's what the bar exams will test and that's what judges understand. But when I step outside the law school setting to train communities about the limits that the Supreme Court sets on police, a different reality sets in. At Jamal's next stop, he won't know if officers received a radio call about a crime or if they're just fishing for an easy target, hoping he will consent to stop or consent to a search.

Usually capitulation presents the only way out of the maze. But submitting to officers carries its own risks. In Trina's case, capitulation landed her behind bars. As the following chapters will show, *Terry*'s architecture requires civilians to invoke their rights or lose them but fails to design methods where civilians can safely exercise these rights.

Feminist writings analyzed the line between submission and consent. Consent is central "to the entire struggle for women's rights."[28] Scholars denounced traditional rape law for blaming the victim when she submits to an aggressor's unwelcome advances. "New rape laws are needed," urged feminist Andrea Dworkin in 1975, that will "redefine consent to denote meaningful and knowledgeable assent, not mere acquiescence."[29] #MeToo criticizes coercive tactics by men who hold power over their victims – when a woman fears she might lose her career if she doesn't submit to sex, for instance. Police requests for consent are situated in a similarly complex framework of power, aggression, and privilege.

Police can instill fear and command obedience without any outward signs of violence, due simply to the imbalance of power between officer and civilian. Legally, Trina "consented" to stop and talk to the officer. Legally, Trina authorized a "consent" search. But there was no "meaningful and knowledgeable assent." Feminists would describe Trina's consent as "mere acquiescence" to power, what I call "sham consent." Where courts find consensual searches and voluntary statements, feminists will see coercion.

What use is knowing your rights if you can't apply them safely? What happens to stop-and-frisk if the courts were to admit that consent is a mirage? Can the Supreme Court still justify stop-and-frisk without resorting to fictions? They sound like riddles, but these questions guide this book.

ABOLITION, NOT REFORM

There's a misconception that stop-and-frisk only violates people's fundamental rights when police behave badly. After a seven-week trial, a federal judge declared that

New York City's stop-and-frisk program was unconstitutional. Setting quotas for stops and arrests predictably produced stops without proper justification, the judge found in *Floyd* v. *City of New York*. In addition, the NYPD intentionally discriminated based on race when instructing officers on "the right people" to stop.[30] After *Floyd*, two criminologists envisioned stop-and-frisk practices where "discretion is exercised in a fair, just, and constitutional manner."[31] Stop setting quotas for stops and arrests and don't beat suspects, the argument goes, and, once again, Terry stops will become a valid crime-fighting method. But this notion only survives because we ignore the experience of Youth Court participants and other civilians who must navigate the *Terry* doctrine when they walk alone to a corner market or walk home from school with friends. That's where the pure *Terry* doctrine must be tested, if we follow a feminist methodology. Feminists ask how the law submerges the perspective of women and other excluded groups, how to make "legal decisionmaking more sensitive to" the true context in which these situations play out, and they require us to listen to personal stories as "a means of testing the validity of accepted legal principles through the lens of the personal experience of those directly affected by those principles."[32]

Weeks of Youth Court trainings and Supreme Court decisions led me inexorably to the conclusion that stop-and-frisk can't be fixed with small reforms. Even if police officers could somehow be forced to follow the Supreme Court restrictions on police power, this would improve lives but not solve the fundamental flaws addressed in these chapters. That's why this book calls for the end of stop-and-frisk, not just those stops that courts currently recognize as unconstitutional.

There are six main points.

1. Terry stops look very different from the vantage point of Supreme Court decisions than they do from people who must maneuver through a maze of "rights" and either assert their rights or lose them.
2. The Supreme Court created legal fictions about why civilians relinquish their rights during police encounters (such as allowing officers to search them), by treating submission as if it were voluntary "consent."
3. Sexual abuse by on-duty police officers has been hidden from the public for too long.
4. Frisks can feel like sexual assault to those on the receiving end even when officers touch bodies in the way they are trained.
5. Feminist insights about power, dominance, and race illuminate these points and help expose law's deficiencies. So too, feminist methods that emphasize people's lived experiences contradict the ways that courts understand police stops.
6. There's a hitherto unseen connection between Terry stops and the right to silence so that once we admit that civilians can't say no to officers, we must see that *Terry* v. *Ohio* was built on a lie.

Stop-and-frisk should become a feminist issue. Ending the abusive policing practice known as stop-and-frisk connects with other ongoing feminist efforts. Angela Y. Davis and Ruth Wilson Gilmore aspire to rid the world of prisons. Feminist law professor Bennett Capers seeks to broaden the movement against sexual assault to include eliminating male-on-male prison rape.[33] Then there's Black Lives Matter – a black, queer, feminist-inspired organization – that focuses on police brutality. As historian Barbara Ransby writes, "Black feminist politics and sensibilities have been the intellectual lifeblood of this movement and its practices."[34]

Feminists of all racial and ethnic backgrounds should be natural allies in the movement to end racist police practices. Fifty years ago, police raided gay bars and harassed the male and female patrons almost as regularly as they now harass young men like Jamal. Today, people of color within the LGBTQ community continue to face excessive policing and stop-and-frisk. Most feminist groups now embrace LGBTQ equality. In her classic book of essays, *Women, Race & Class*, activist and scholar Angela Y. Davis explains how "racism nourishes sexism" and laments how white women came late to the cause of protecting black women from rape and not seeing how lynch mobs ultimately reinforced white women's inequality as well.[35] *A Feminist Critique of Police Stops* invites readers, feminist or not, to support the abolition of stop-and-frisk. Let's not miss the opportunity to build coalitions this time.

THIS BOOK'S ROADMAP FOR REEXAMINING CONSENT AND *TERRY*

A Feminist Critique of Police Stops is divided into two parts. Part I tells the stories from trainings in the community where Howard law students help me teach teenagers how to navigate stops and frisks. This half lays out the divide between *law on the books* and *law in action*, using feminist tools to investigate the intersection between Terry stops and what the Court calls "consent" (what feminists call submission to those who wield more power). I conclude that *Terry* v. *Ohio* was based on faulty assumptions about people's ability to refuse to do what police ask them to do, assumptions that crumble under close scrutiny. Part II examines the high costs of frisking that law and society ignore. How courts envision Terry stops is quite different from how they actually happen and how people feel when they experience them.

Chapter 1, "Waive Your Rights," explains my theory that a feminist view of consent undercuts *Terry* v. *Ohio*'s sole justification for stop-and-frisk. The Court in *Terry* undertook a balancing test, where it weighed the need to detain people to ask them questions against the loss of personal privacy to those questioned. *A Feminist Critique of Police Stops* chips away at both sides of the scales of justice. Stop-and-frisk fails to prevent crime and Chapter 7 will explain how it might increase criminality, but, against the evidence, courts assume that stop-and-frisk makes everyone safer by solving crimes. I note that there are two theories about how stop-and-frisk prevents crime. One theory holds that police employ stop-and-frisk to control neighborhoods, acting as an occupying army in order to dissuade people from carrying weapons or drugs. Championed by New York City mayors Rudolph Giuliani and Michael Bloomberg, and then praised by President Donald Trump, the method of instituting Terry stops advocated by the control theory violates the US Constitution, as one court found, and most scholars agree.

The second theory comes directly from the *Terry* case, where the Supreme Court imagines that a few questions can ripen into probable cause for an arrest without resort to police coercion. As one Justice explains in *Terry*, when officers detain someone and pose questions to confirm or dispel their suspicions, "the person stopped is not obliged to answer, answers may not be compelled, and refusal to answer furnishes no basis for an arrest."[36] That's the theory that bears more investigation. Implicitly, the Court in *Terry* envisions that some victims of unwanted stops will "voluntarily" answer questions and those answers will provide the basis to arrest and prosecute. But that's the very justification for stop-and-frisk that crumbles when we admit that what the Court calls "voluntary" should be renamed "coerced speech." In reality, civilians feel compelled to answer an officer's questions during Terry stops, fearing arrest or other forms of retaliation, and there's justification for such fears. *Terry* v. *Ohio* was built on a lie.

Chapter 2, "The Most Dangerous Right," covers the Fourth Amendment right to walk away from police officers during so-called consent stops. When I represented clients as a defense attorney, they always believed they had been detained by officers; judges, however, often ruled that my clients had been free to walk away, rendering it a so-called consensual stop. When police officers don't order someone to stay and don't frisk, civilians are legally allowed to walk away from officers who are questioning them, but this right to walk away is pure legal fiction. Although the "free to leave" right is engraved in Supreme Court opinions, my Howard law students warned me that I would endanger the teenagers if we taught this. A pristine example of *law on the books* versus *law in action*.

Chapter 3, "Consenting to Searches," describes how the Supreme Court excuses a range of unwelcome searches, even strip-searches, because the victim did not resist. Feminist critiques of rape law shed a bright spotlight onto the deficiencies in the Court's analysis of consent to search. In 2018, New York State recognized that any sex with an on-duty officer is inherently coercive. Under the new law, police officers can't argue consent when they're accused of on-duty rape. The law was inspired by a rape allegation against uniformed police officers. Before the alleged rape occurred, one of the officers asked the woman to lift her shirt to see if she was hiding drugs: Was this a consensual exercise? Eliminating the consent defense for sex recognizes that police hold all the cards. That's an excellent step, but then why should the law allow that officer to claim that the civilian consented to a search of her body or purse? The situations involve the same unfair power differential. In both situations, police have the power to let you go or charge you, what to charge, and whether to be rough or gentle. Ultimately, civilians submit to police because it's the safest thing to do. Consent within the Fourth Amendment suffers from the same legal myopia as consent within rape law. In both instances, courts often blame the victim for their fate as a way to support dominance by the group that holds power.

Chapter 4, "Punishing Disrespect," bemoans the loss of free speech. Here's another constitutional right that I dare not share with the young people at risk for police stops: their First Amendment right to tell an officer what they think about his harassment. If the Supreme Court was right when it stated that the "freedom of individuals verbally to oppose or challenge police action without thereby risking arrest is one of the principal characteristics by which we distinguish a free nation from a police state," then stop-and-frisk threatens our very republic.[37] Despite all the lofty words by the Supreme Court about our right to voice opposition to the government, police routinely punish disrespect. Coercing respect lies deep within police culture, and punishments range from arrest to brutality.

Chapter 5, "Beyond Miranda's Reach," examines what's left of the right to remain silent during Terry stops. While the law governing pre-Miranda silence remains murky, the reality is clear: the teenagers we train can't successfully invoke their right to silence during a stop-and-frisk without risking retaliation. Court-sanctioned lies compound the difficulty in navigating police stops. When I train teenagers, my law students and I tell them that police are allowed to lie during Terry stops and at the police station. This fact confuses the teenagers we train. "If the officers will lie and say that I consent, why should I bother telling the officer that I don't consent to searches?" Why learn one's rights at all? As one teen put it, "The cop will just say I waived my rights no matter what I do."

Some courts don't recognize a right to silence during Terry stops. It's legal in some jurisdictions for police to arrest individuals for refusing to answer their questions. This is court-approved retaliatory arrest. As Chapter 1 established, *Terry* v. *Ohio* justified stop-and-frisk on the basis that police would use these stops to gather "voluntary" statements. But statements are not "voluntary" when made under threat. Once we acknowledge this, we see that *Terry* was built on a lie.

Part II lays out the hidden harms of stop-and-frisk and how the Supreme Court undervalued the costs of frisking when it decided that the benefits of Terry stops outweighed their harms.

Chapter 6, "The Frisk," lays out a continuum from lawful but awful frisks to sexual assault. I'll never forget the male teenager who told me during a training that the last time he was frisked, "it felt like rape." Sexual abuse of women and girls targeted for stops constitutes an enormous problem that's rarely addressed. Likewise, police sexual misconduct is a huge hidden problem for men and boys. Courts mostly avoid mentioning the sexual aspect of patdowns, although the Supreme Court noted in *Terry* v. *Ohio* that a police training manual directed the officer to "feel with sensitive fingers every portion of the prisoner's body. A thorough search must be made of the prisoner's arms and armpits, waistline and back, the groin and area about the testicles." This chapter illuminates the challenges that flow when courts categorize certain police actions as sexual abuse while omitting most sexual indignities from that category. If it feels like rape, it's even more troubling when training manuals call for the maneuver and the Court approves it.

Chapter 7, "Invisible Scars," lays out the mounting research documenting the negative consequences that flow from aggressive policing methods such as stop-and-frisk. While it's uncontroverted that these stops increase distrust between police and communities, there are many additional harms. Researchers connect stops and frisks to lasting psychological distress, including anxiety and post-traumatic stress disorder. There's even evidence to suggest aggressive stops will encourage some innocent victims to become offenders. In balancing the harms of these stops on one side of the scale in *Terry* v. *Ohio*, the Supreme Court makes two mistakes. First, Terry stops don't merely fail to reduce crime; they increase the likelihood of future law-breaking. Second, most of the harms that flow from Terry stops never enter into the Court's calculation. In fact, we now know that stops and frisks create trauma and the trauma spreads outward, threatening the health and safety of whole communities.

Chapter 8, "High Court Camouflage," investigates the Supreme Court's role in creating a system in which judges routinely blame the victims of unconstitutional policing for submitting to police requests instead of exercising their rights. The Court mistakes submission for consent by constructing an alternative reality where police behave like the proverbial "Officer Friendly."

These fictions camouflage police aggression and racial profiling and allow it to thrive.

The Supreme Court should review *Terry* v. *Ohio*'s balancing act, admit that the case was based on the false premise that people can choose not to cooperate, and this time include what we now know about the harms that flow from stop-and-frisk. But that's not what happened in 2016 in *Utah* v. *Strieff*. There, the Supreme Court again weighed the benefits and harms that flow when police stop people without probable cause (although in that case, the officer also lacked reasonable suspicion for the stop). Instead of overturning *Terry* v. *Ohio*, the Court expanded the government's authority to control our liberty and our bodies. Justice Sonia Sotomayor's dissent in *Strieff* is both lyrical and haunting. Although the case involved an unconstitutional Terry stop, her words ring true for all stops and frisks. This case, she writes, "tells everyone, white and black, guilty and innocent, that . . . your body is subject to invasion." Her opinion demonstrates a true understanding of the depth of harm caused by unchecked police power and could serve as an epilogue to this book.

Because we can't look to the courts to fix this, it's more important than ever that readers recognize that stop-and-frisk leads the way in sapping constitutional rights. Chapter 8 suggests that legislators and progressive prosecutors, with the support of the public, can effectively abolish the "consent" excuse for violating the Constitution and end stop-and-frisk as we know it.

A *Feminist Critique of Police Stops* makes the case that the practice of stop-and-frisk ultimately tramples the freedoms and dignity of some and the rights of all. Racially suspicious stops like Gabriel's will reverberate beyond the individual who has been stopped. The harm spreads out to his family, his friends, witnesses to the stop, and even people who merely live in the neighborhood. These stops serve as a funnel for mass incarceration, racial profiling and police brutality. Stop-and-frisk harms white civilians too – or, as Ta-Nehisi Coates writes, "Americans who believe they are white."[38] While people who fit certain demographics are less likely to be stopped than other people, no one should imagine themselves fully immune from a culture that coerces respect from Youth Court participants.[39] When the Supreme Court treats obedience to police as if it were voluntary consent, it guts our constitutional protections. Anyone who thinks the harm is contained, that the damage ends at the proverbial ghetto walls, does not realize that constitutional rights belong to all of us.

PART I

Bye, Bye Bill of Rights

Waive Your Rights: That's How Stops and Frisks Were Meant to Work

Well, if one really wishes to know how justice is administered in a country, one does not question the policemen, the lawyers, the judges, or the protected members of the middle class. One goes to the unprotected – those, precisely, who need the law's protection most!

James Baldwin, *No Name on the Street* (Michael Joseph, 1972)

FROM TERRY STOPS TO POLICE BRUTALITY AND SEXUAL ASSAULT

Let me begin with one of my favorite law students. Whenever I went to Youth Court, Richard, a third-year law student, would offer to carry the large poster board and other props I brought. His gentlemanly style seemed a throwback to an earlier era. When he wore jeans, they appeared ironed. When he spoke to me, he started each sentence with my title, as in, "Professor Ross, today we are in a different room." Among many dedicated law students, Richard stood out with his quiet drive to make each training session better than the last.

One day I discovered a primary source of his motivation:

Before Richard became a law student at Howard University in Washington, DC, he lived in New York City and worked at a restaurant. One evening when he was 18, weeks away from graduating high school, he became a victim of stop-and-frisk. About seven years before we spoke: Richard leaves his job as a dishwasher in Brooklyn at 9 p.m., he begins his mile-long walk home. Although this is known as a bad neighborhood, Richard knows it well, and is comfortable navigating its streets. As he strides purposefully down the sidewalk, he notices three uniformed officers walking toward him. For the first time, Richard feels unsafe in his own neighborhood. The officers block his path, while one demands, "Where are you going at this time of night?"

"I'm going home," answers Richard, trying to keep the fear out of his voice.

"Identification," barks the same officer.

As soon as Richard complies, the second officer, who is barely older than Richard, orders the college-bound senior to stand against the wall, feet apart, hands up on the wall for a frisk. The young, second officer methodically pats down Richard outside his clothing, from head to groin and from groin to toe. No one wanders by. Richard is scared. That is a "by the book" frisk, but they don't stop there. Breaking the rules, the officer digs his hands into Richard's pockets then digs his large hands inside Richard's underwear. When Richard feels the young officer digging around beneath his underwear, his fear turns into anger. "Why are you doing this? This has to be because I'm black," he blurts out, but the three white police officers just laugh and tell him to "shut up."

"This is ridiculous," Richard says. "I know my rights. You can't do this."

Because Richard doesn't shut up, the second officer grabs Richard by his shirt and shoves him into the wall. Before Richard can finish the sentence "I'm going to report . . ." the second officer throws him to the ground and pulls out a collapsible baton. As Richard tries to protect his ribs, he realizes that now all three officers are taking part. He sees fists and batons flying about, and then sees more officers arrive in a squad car. Police grab his arms and handcuff him in front of his body, beating him while they yell at Richard to "stop resisting."

Eventually the police stop the beating and inform Richard that he is under arrest for assaulting a police officer, resisting arrest, and disorderly conduct. It turns out that one officer injured his hand after swinging and missing Richard's head, punching the concrete instead. The officer's resulting hand injury forms the basis of the criminal assault charge leveled against Richard.

RICHARD'S STOP DISSECTED

In Richard's view, his treatment by police embodies the connection between court-sanctioned stop-and-frisk procedures and police brutality.[1] He's right. There's direct line from the approved investigative stop to the officers' gratuitous cruelties. When police initiate a stop-and-frisk, this creates opportunities to humiliate and harm.[2] Those who seek to end the killings of the unarmed, the shooting of the mentally ill, and other police violence should start by reexamining stop-and-frisk policing.

What happened to Richard started as a classic stop-and-frisk, although most reported police stops are not as violent as the one Richard experienced that night, and not all stops include a patdown (the "frisk"). Sadly, even with a law degree, it's not easy to discern where Richard's stop conformed to constitutional requirements and precisely where it diverged.

A Primer

Fifty years ago, in a case called *Terry* v. *Ohio*, the Supreme Court decided that the Fourth Amendment allows police to detain people for questioning, even though they lack probable cause to believe the person has committed a crime. Two caveats: the police must have something the Court calls "reasonable suspicion" (meaning facts known to the officers that would lead them to suspect that the civilian was involved in criminal activity); also, the stop should be short, just long enough to ask questions that "verify or dispel the officer's suspicion in a short period of time." *Terry* also allows an officer to frisk people he lawfully stops when "a reasonably prudent man in the circumstances would be warranted in the belief that his safety or that of others was in danger."[3] Once the suspect answers the questions and dispels the officer's suspicions, she will be allowed to go about her business. In theory, the Fourth Amendment protects civilians from police overreach. In theory, *Terry* v. *Ohio* only modestly reduced the Fourth Amendment bulwark against tyranny.

That's the theory. Richard lives where the rubber meets the road.

For Richard's brutal encounter, here's how law students learn to analyze whether it was legal:

1. **The stop.** When police officers initially confronted Richard, was he stopped? The question for a court is whether someone in Richard's position would believe he could decline to talk to the police and continue to walk away. This stop would not even be called a Terry stop if a judge decided Richard was "free to leave." Richard was scared when the police walked up to question him. Nevertheless, in my experience of trying cases in Washington, DC, the officers will testify that there was room for Richard to walk around them (if he dared), and most judges would consider Richard "free to walk away" until officers ordered him to stand next to the wall. (More on that in Chapter 2.)

2. **Was the stop legal?** If police had reasonable suspicion to suspect that Richard was involved in a crime, they had the right to stop him. If the case goes to court, officers will be given a chance to explain the reasons for their suspicions. Was there a recent robbery in the area? Did Richard match a description of a suspect? I imagine that the officers' behavior was motivated by the NYPD quotas for stops and arrests more than any true concern that Richard was engaged in criminal activity. That makes this stop unconstitutional. However, even when a criminal defendant challenges questionable police practices in court, they are routinely upheld. Judges usually credit the officers' testimony and police are notorious for making up reasons after the fact to uphold their arrests. (This is also discussed in Chapter 4.) From Richard's perspective, it's usually impossible for the person stopped to know what the officers knew at the time of the stop. In this, police hold all the cards.

3. **The frisk.** Once the person is lawfully stopped, police may feel all along the outside of a person's clothing if they reasonably fear that the person might be armed and dangerous to them. Frisks are also known

as "patdowns" for weapons. When the officer told Richard to stand against the wall, that's a permissible method of conducting a frisk. But by going into Richard's underwear, police went beyond the scope of a proper frisk. At that point, the police clearly violated the Fourth Amendment's ban on unreasonable seizures. In my opinion, the "frisk" that Richard described should be deemed a sexual assault. Frisks provide an opportunity for such man-handling and woman-handling. (See also Chapter 6.)

4. **The beating.** Police are allowed to use physical force to subdue an uncooperative suspect. It would be up to a judge, or to a review board (had Richard complained), to decide if Richard were truly resisting arrest or assaulting an officer or whether police made that up after the fact to justify the beating. Most likely, the police beat up Richard to punish him for calling them racists and challenging their authority. (See Chapter 5 for more on punishing bad attitudes.) I'm convinced that Richard was a crime victim as well as a victim of an illegal stop. Theoretically, the officers could be charged with criminal assault or even sexual assault, but police are rarely held accountable for their misdeeds on the job, let alone prosecuted.

5. **The arrest.** Police need probable cause to believe a person is committing a crime. Police often use malleable charges like disorderly conduct or refusing to obey an officer's order when they wish to punish a suspect for their attitude or because supervisors want to see "activity," and that includes arrests. When police harm suspects, they commonly charge resisting arrest or assault on a police officer. It's a defensive offense because police know they will have to explain Richard's injuries. These charges may not pass strict constitutional muster, but the Supreme Court refuses to allow criminal court judges to consider the motive for an arrest as long as the police can point to probable cause for at least one misdemeanor offense.

This is how students would analyze Richard's case on an exam – a bloodless exercise divorced from the trauma of real lives. I never asked Richard what it felt like to have a police officer put his hands into his underwear, but I have a realistic sense of how violated he must have felt and the lasting trauma that can result from such an invasive encounter. I can imagine how it has changed his feeling of safety every day since then.

SUPPRESSION – A TOOTHLESS REMEDY

Richard didn't incriminate himself when he answered the officer's questions. He told the officers "I'm going home." Imagine instead that he said something to police that hurt his case; his lawyer would bring a motion to prevent the government from using the statement at trial.

First, his lawyer would argue that police violated Richard's Fourth Amendment rights by stopping him without reasonable suspicion. We don't know what officers will claim, for they control the narrative here. But as you saw above (in #2), defendants almost always lose because police officers can testify to a large range of behavior that they find suspicious and that qualifies for the Court's low bar. So we'll focus on the other two arguments.

Second, we would want Richard's lawyer to argue that officers used excessive force, violating the Fourth Amendment when they shoved him against the wall and then in the way they frisked him. When police violate the Constitution, the government cannot introduce evidence at trial that was found as a result of wrong-doing. That's called the exclusionary rule. Excessive force violates the Fourth Amendment so that means Richard's statements must be excluded from trial, right? Wrong. The exclusionary rule won't help Richard, not if he made the statements before the police brutality. A court won't address the abuse unless Richard files a civil lawsuit; these are notoriously hard to win, and not many lawyers can afford to take these cases. Even when the law is purportedly on his side (against brutality), it's impotent to help.

Third, his lawyer can argue that any incriminating statements Richard made should be kept out of court because the Fifth Amendment prohibits coerced statements from coming into trial. He would argue that Richard was in no position to refuse to answer questions when the police came up to him and asked him where he was going.

For this third claim, again the law is not on Richard's side. The law presumes that statements made during Terry stops are voluntary and can be admitted at trial against him. This presumption becomes important later on, as we consider *Terry* v. *Ohio's* fatal flaw.

In short, the law won't save people like Richard. While police often exceed their lawful power during Terry stops, they get away with it because most cases never see a court, and even when judges do review the stop, most civilians find themselves on the losing end. There's no accountability outside the courts either. And it's not just improper stops that should scare us. The Supreme Court grants so much power to police that even when police follow the law, stops and frisks can still seriously interfere with people's well-being.

TERRY V. *OHIO*'S BALANCING ACT

Readers who object to the abuse inflicted on Richard might still wonder whether to rally around a lawful form of stop-and-frisk. The answer is no. Even when officers put away their batons and refrain from obvious abuses, stop-and-frisk sits rotten at its core. By shining a spotlight on the justifications for stop-and-frisk, I hope to expose its deep structural flaws.

The seminal case of *Terry* v. *Ohio*, from 1968, began on a Cleveland sidewalk. Officer Martin McFadden watched a black man named John Terry hang about a commercial neighborhood, conferring with another black man in a way that raised the patrol officer's suspicions. Officer McFadden was concerned the men might be casing a store for "a stick up," as he later explained to a judge, especially when they briefly conferred with a third man, a white man, on a corner. At that time, even the officer agreed that he had no basis to make an arrest. What the officer did next ushered in fifty years of stop-and-frisk with the Supreme Court's blessing. Officer McFadden approached the men as they walked off together and asked for their names. Receiving a mumble, the officer grabbed Mr. Terry, spun him around and patted him down looking for weapons. Not only did Mr. Terry have a gun, it was unregistered. Jackpot. That allowed Officer McFadden to arrest Mr. Terry, who was subsequently prosecuted for carrying a concealed weapon.[4]

After the defense moved to prevent the government from introducing the gun as the fruit of an illegal search, the case went all the way up to the Supreme Court. Mr. Terry's argument was straightforward: (1) the Fourth Amendment governs "searches and seizures"; (2) police stops are seizures (a person who is detained has been "seized") and frisks are searches; (3) until this point, "probable cause had been the gold standard and the dominant substantive framework for justifying searches and seizures";[5] and (4) ergo, police need probable cause for the stop and for the patdown. Mr. Terry lost. Although the Court agreed that stops were a type of seizure and patdowns were a type of search, *Terry* decided police don't need probable cause. The squishy concept of "reasonable suspicion" was born.

As law students learn, the Court reached its decision in *Terry* v. *Ohio* through a balancing test. On one side of the scale, the Supreme Court evaluated the harms that stops and frisks impose on civilians. On the other side of the scale, the Court weighed the benefits of giving police this crime-fighting tool. Under "harms," the Supreme Court wrote that the stops are short in duration and have a "nonthreatening character." On the other hand, frisks constitute a "serious intrusion upon the sanctity of the person, which may inflict great indignity and arouse strong resentment."[6] Nevertheless, the Court decided society's need for the practice outweighed these concerns. Unfortunately, the Court wasn't thinking about Richard or Gabriel or Jamal when they adjusted their scales. Richard's experience alone suggests that the Court miscalculated how much weight to accord to harms from Terry stops. And that's just the beginning. Later chapters will further explore the collateral damage from Terry stops – harms that the Court has never acknowledged – while this chapter focuses on the Court's mistake on the side of the scale that measured the benefits of stop-and-frisk.

On the benefits side of the scale, *Terry* v. *Ohio* sanctioned stop-and-frisk policing in the name of "effective crime prevention and detection."[7] Crime prevention remains the sole claim to the legitimacy of stop-and-frisk.

There are two current theories for how stops and frisks prevent crimes. I call one the "control theory" of policing. The second theory, hidden within *Terry*, I call the "waive your rights theory." Neither crime-fighting strategy actually reduces crime, according to a research review published in the *Journal of Research of Crime and Delinquency*.[8] Both theories – the "control theory" and the "waive your rights theory" of how Terry stops prevent crime – reveal serious flaws and both help explain how Richard was victimized on his way home from work.

THE CONTROL THEORY FOR HOW TERRY STOPS FIGHT CRIME

Many police departments deploy stop-and-frisk to signal that police officers control the neighborhood.[9] Police are told to detain certain demographics (usually black, brown, and poor) and show them that the police own the streets. This control theory of policing (sometimes known as programmatic stop-and-frisk) became famous in New York, where Federal District Court judge Shira Scheindlin scrutinized the practice during a three-month bench trial in *Floyd* v. *City of New York*.[10] One NYPD officer surreptitiously taped roll calls, including one where a Lieutenant instructed his officers in Bedford Stuyvesant, Brooklyn, as follows:

> We've got to keep the corner clear . . . Because if you get too big of a crowd there, you know . . . they're going to think that they own the block. We own the block. They don't own the block, all right? They might live there but we own the block. All right? We own the streets here. You tell them what to do.[11]

In theory, repeated instances of stop-and-frisk will cause men, women and teenagers to be afraid to break the law. Basically, police use the stops and frisks as a means of managing target populations. As we learned from the testimony in *Floyd*, officers were pressured to make stops even when they lacked reasonable suspicion. The bench trial in *Floyd* v. *City of New York* included testimony from civilians, officers, and experts. Recordings of roll calls helped round out the picture. One Lieutenant admitted she told her "officers to 'go crazy' in St. Mary's Park" to make sure she got five summons or stops from each officer, while another precinct expected a minimum of 20 summons and 1 arrest during 22 days on patrol. While not every precinct gave precise numerical goals, officers learned that their careers depended upon the numbers. The pressure came from above: "supervisors must evaluate officers based on their activity numbers, with particular emphasis on summonses, stops, and arrests, and that officers whose numbers are too low should be subjected to increasingly serious discipline if their low numbers persist."[12]

Boasting that programmatic stop-and-frisk kept guns off the streets, New York City Mayor Michael Bloomberg championed the practice. The data proved him wrong. The NYPD made over 685,000 stops one year, only to find that over 600,000 of the people stopped were innocent of any crime.[13] Police seized guns in roughly 0.1 percent of these stops. Nevertheless, using convoluted control theory logic, Mayor Bloomberg argued that the terrible rate of return – police made 1,000 stops before they found one person with a gun – proved that that this saved lives. Bloomberg concluded that people are scared to carry guns thanks to stop-and-frisk. It works because "the kids believe that the likelihood of being stopped is so great that they shouldn't carry a gun."[14] In a 2015 recording that he tried to keep secret, the mayor was more explicit about the program's racist and violent design: "Ninety-five percent of your murders, murderers and murder victims . . . are male, minorities, 16 to 25" and "the way you get the guns out of the kids' hands is to throw them up against the walls and frisk them."[15]

What happened to Richard represents a classic control theory stop. The model explains why police selected him. The NYPD targeted people for stops based on race, age, and gender.[16] Richard, like Gabriel in the last chapter, fit the demographic. In addition, as Judge Scheindlin wrote in *Floyd*, "the stopped population is overwhelmingly innocent."

Even Richard's beating fits the control theory model. When Richard challenged their authority, the officers showed him who was boss. In cities like New York, that use stop-and-frisk to signal police officer control, any slight or perceived disrespect merits swift retribution.

Control-style stop-and-frisk violates the US Constitution. In a scathing 198-page decision, Judge Scheindlin concluded in *Floyd* that the NYPD policy violated the Fourth Amendment and the Equal Protection Clause by intentionally selecting people to stop-and-frisk based on race.[17]

"I was wrong . . . And I am sorry," Mayor Bloomberg apologized during his run for president.[18] But there are other politicians who did not back down.

When President Donald Trump praised New York's stop-and-frisk program on the campaign trail and recommended it for the whole country, he was talking about using stop-and-frisk to control poor black people. It was classic dog-whistle politics, a way of talking about locking up people of color and controlling them without saying so directly.[19] When Trump told a gathering of police officers: "Please don't be too nice" to suspects, the president advocated rough handling, a logical corollary to control-style stop-and-frisk.[20] Two years into his presidency, Donald Trump urged Chicago law enforcement to ramp up the practice there, making his remarks in the aftermath of a highly publicized jury verdict convicting a Chicago police officer of second-degree murder for shooting a black high school student named Laquan MacDonald sixteen times.[21]

The presidential advice met with suitable skepticism from some because *Floyd* had already struck down New York City's programmatic use of stops and frisks. Moreover, Chicagoans already endured "the most intense stop-and-frisk program in the nation," with four times the rate of stops compared to New York City at the height of its infamous program.[22] And by then the data proved that stop-and-frisk did not make cities safer. In October of 2018, after the NYPD ended its aggressive stop-and-frisk practices, New York – a city of millions – was able to boast that in one weekend there was not a single homicide for the first time in twenty-five years.[23]

But President Trump was right about two things. As his remarks suggest, there's a direct relationship between Terry stops and police killings, and between Terry stops and mass incarceration. Second, these stops are a political question because, in the end, the courts don't have much control over the police. Even the New York City consent decree after *Floyd* did not fully end the system that thrived for over a decade. Five years after the NYPD signed a consent decree agreeing to abide by constitutional constraints, the top brass continues to push unconstitutional practices in the name of public safety. In the documentary *Crime + Punishment*, NYPD whistle-blowing police officers explain how their supervisors still require them to get a certain number of "collars" (arrests) and although much reduced from the preceding decade, there is still an unwritten quota for stops and frisks.[24]

Similar politics play out across the country. After Attorney General Eric Holder's success with court-enforced consent decrees that curtailed unconstitutional policing under President Obama, along came Jefferson Beauregard Sessions. As Trump's attorney general, Mr. Sessions drastically limited the ability of the federal government to enforce prior agreements or to pressure towns to rectify civil rights violations by local police departments.[25] Under the Trump presidency, police departments need not concern themselves with inconvenient constitutional constraints. An election ushered in the successful Department of Justice investigations under President Obama and it was an election that ended them, at least temporarily. The political hiatus on DOJ investigations tells us that it's not the courts but the court of public opinion that can end policing abuses.

Whether police escalate or eliminate stop and frisks will depend upon the voters. It will be the court of public opinion that calls a halt to stop-and-frisk.[26]

TERRY'S PROMISE

When *Floyd* struck down the control theory approach as unconstitutional, the judge left *Terry* v. *Ohio*'s framework in place.[27] Chief Justice Earl Warren wrote the decision in *Terry* v. *Ohio*. He never approved the control theory stops that *Floyd* condemned. Likewise, many members of the Warren Court would have disapproved of the policing methods in Baltimore, where frisks are like a side of fries, served up with every Terry stop.[28] After all, the liberal Warren Court, which decided *Terry*, was the same Court that brought us Miranda warnings and decriminalized birth control. Justice Thurgood Marshall explained four years later that he voted with the majority in *Terry* v. *Ohio* because:

> we were not watering down rights, but were hesitantly and cautiously striking a necessary balance between the rights of American citizens to be free from government intrusion into their privacy and their government's urgent need for a narrow exception to the warrant requirement of the Fourth Amendment . . . It seems that the delicate balance that Terry struck was simply too delicate, too susceptible to the "hydraulic pressures" of the day.[29]

The lone dissenter in *Terry* v. *Ohio*, Justice William O. Douglas, sounded the alarm, calling the Terry decision "a long step down the totalitarian path."

> There have been powerful hydraulic pressures throughout our history that bear heavily on the Court to water down constitutional guarantees and give the police the upper hand. That hydraulic pressure has probably never been greater than it is today. Yet if the individual is no longer to be sovereign, if the police can pick him up whenever they do not like the cut of his jib, if they can "seize" and "search" him in their discretion, we enter a new regime.[30]

Yet the Court's own assumption in *Terry* v. *Ohio*, that stop-and-frisk fights crime, remains woefully unexplored. This chapter argues that *Terry* got it wrong when it assumed that stopping people on mere suspicion could help police to solve crimes without forcing them to confess or searching them without justification. I argue that even in its purest legal form, the Terry stop shortchanges our fundamental rights because the Supreme Court expects people to give up their right to silence or consent to searches.

Terry v. *Ohio* allowed short detentions for officers to pose questions to suspects. In theory, a suspect's answers will either dispel the officer's reasonable belief that there's a crime in progress or confirm his suspicions, enabling the officer to make an arrest based upon probable cause. In other words, the Court approved stop-and-frisk to allow field interrogations; to allow questioning. But what about the suspect's right to silence? Did Richard have a right to silence?

The right to silence is more than a line in the Miranda litany. The guarantee's constitutional roots run deep and wide. It's rooted in the Fifth Amendment right for a person not to be "compelled in any criminal case to be a witness against himself." Then there's the First Amendment's guarantee of free speech that prevents the government from compelling civilians to talk. (See more on free speech and compelled speech in Chapters 4 and 5.)

Building on the First and Fifth Amendment rights to silence, *Terry* v. *Ohio* imbedded the right to silence into the Fourth Amendment law on stop-and-frisk. By right to silence, I mean the right to refuse to answer an officer's questions. In a consent stop, "the individual has no obligation to respond" and "may decline to answer and simply go on his or her way."[31] But the right to decline to answer once extended beyond consent stops. *Terry* also promised protection to the civilian "briefly detained against his will." Even when civilians were not at liberty to walk away, they could still decline to answer questions without fear of arrest.

Justice Byron White explained (in a separate opinion in *Terry* v. *Ohio*) how Terry stops would play out in practice: "Of course, the person stopped is not obliged to answer, answers may not be compelled, and refusal to answer furnishes no basis for an arrest, although it may alert the officer to the need for continued observation."[32]

In other words, silence might mean that police followed you or detained you longer since you did not dispel the officer's initial concerns. Yes, there are some negative consequences for remaining silent, but police can't assume that silence equals guilt. You could not be arrested for refusing to answer questions.

Sixteen years later, the Court again affirmed that civilians retained the right to silence during Terry stops. "Typically," the Court explained in *Berkemer* v. *McCarty*, an officer may ask the civilian "a moderate number of questions" during traffic stops and Terry stops "to determine his identity and to try to obtain information confirming or dispelling the officer's suspicions. But the detainee is not obliged to respond."[33] Thus, it was settled law that police could not retaliate for silence during Terry stops.

Because suspects like Mr. Terry possess the right to remain silent during questioning, that makes their statements "voluntary." That's important, because only noncoerced statements are admissible at trial. *Terry* v. *Ohio* justified stop-and-frisk as a crime-fighting strategy because police questioning could lead to prosecutions. To this day, courts assume that people choose whether to cooperate, and a suspect's answers can form the basis not only for arrest but also for prosecution and conviction.

"WAIVE YOUR RIGHTS" THEORY FOR HOW STOPS FIGHT CRIME

Imagine a lawful Terry stop. Police tell Richard to stop walking because they are suspicious that he has just bought drugs. (I will use drugs as the stand-in for all contraband since the Drug War forms the primary purpose behind non-control theory stops.) Assume that there's no basis to frisk. How can mere suspicion blossom into probable cause by detaining someone a short time to ask questions?

Turning to *Terry* v. *Ohio*'s own thesis that stop-and-frisk solves crimes, the opinion is strangely inscrutable. While the Supreme Court reasons that reasonable suspicion can ripen into probable cause when an officer detains a person a short time while posing a few questions, the *Terry* Court never explains how this actually is supposed to work in practice.[34]

Let's play around with the facts of the 1968 case of *Terry* v. *Ohio* to demonstrate how the pure theory can unfold. As every law student learns, the patrol officer in *Terry* had reasonable suspicion to believe that John W. Terry was casing a store for robbery, and that this allowed the officer to stop and frisk Mr. Terry because there was reason to believe he was armed and dangerous. The officer in *Terry* got lucky; he felt a gun during the frisk that turned out to be unregistered. This fortuitous discovery led to a valid arrest. But what if carrying a gun was legal, as it is now in many states? What should the officer do if the frisk netted no gun at all? What next? What's the Court's plan for police to develop probable cause for an arrest for conspiracy to rob?

The *Terry* decision doesn't explain what should happen if the gun was legal. Under the current legal structure, when police officers discover lawful weapons during frisks, they may hold onto them until they complete their questioning.

Presumably, if the officer in *Terry* v. *Ohio* found a legal gun, he would go back to asking Mr. Terry to talk or to consent to a search, hoping he would give up his rights. Perhaps the Court imagines that after a couple of questions, Mr. Terry might respond, "yes, officer, I was planning a robbery, I was casing this store." Certainly, that would add up to probable cause for conspiracy to rob and justify an arrest. What this demonstrates – and the Court never explicitly admits – is that stop-and-frisk's method of solving crime is premised upon Mr. Terry waiving his constitutional right against self-incrimination.

Implicit in *Terry* v. *Ohio*, there are three ways Terry stops can lead to crime detection:

1. When police lawfully *stop* a civilian and ask questions, the civilian waives his right to silence and incriminates himself. Those "voluntary" *statements* then give them a lawful basis for a search or a lawful basis to arrest.
   – According to the Supreme Court "the person stopped is not obliged to answer," but more on that in Chapter 5.
2. After police lawfully *stop* a civilian, they can seek *consent* to search (and find drugs).
   – According to the Supreme Court, the consent must be voluntary, but more on that in Chapter 3.
3. Alternatively, police can conduct a *consent stop* and seek *consent to search*.
   – According to the Supreme Court, people feel free to walk away from officers who ask us questions like "Where are you going at this time of night?" so courts will say we chose to stop as long as police don't pull out their guns, grab us, or order us to stop, but more on that in Chapter 2.

Notice that each of the methods described above requires civilians to waive or give up their rights. Number one requires civilians to give up their Fifth Amendment right to remain silent. Number two requires people to consent, thereby giving up their Fourth Amendment right not to be searched without probable cause. Number three requires people to give up two Fourth Amendment rights: the right not to be stopped and the right not to be searched without proper justification.

Terry's Original Rationale Versus Fishing Expeditions and Other Cheats

Under *Terry* v. *Ohio's* constitutional scheme, for an officer's suspicion to evolve from reasonable suspicion to probable cause to arrest for the suspected crime, the civilian must give up either her right against self-incrimination or consent to a search of her body or possessions. This will seem strange to criminal lawyers, because, in practice, police use stop-and-frisk in many ways that go beyond *Terry* v. *Ohio's* original justification that stops give police an opportunity to ask questions. The exceptions swallow the rule. Often both the stop and the frisk are merely pretense for a fishing expedition.

Take Richard. He counts as one of the "successful" Terry stops, one of the 6 percent of stops in New York City between 2004 and 2012 that led to an arrest.[35] You may remember that police arrested Richard for allegedly assaulting them during the stop. This is an example of police charging an offense unrelated to the stop (in his case making one up). It's not how the Supreme Court justified detaining people on mere reasonable suspicion in *Terry v. Ohio*. Questioning Richard didn't turn police suspicions into probable cause. Instead, police exploited the Terry stop to bootstrap an arrest for something else entirely. That's a cheat!

Frisking is one of the favorite work-arounds to the pure doctrine. For example, I've watched while DC police officers shake out a young man's baggy pants during a frisk, looking down to see if drugs fall to the curb. That's not a true search for weapons. Stops and frisks often feed the hungry Drug War when police get lucky during patdowns for weapons, feeling a packet they *could immediately tell was cocaine* when they merely touch it with their palms through several layers of clothing.

Frisking for drugs, although widely practiced, should not be mistaken for *Terry*'s crime-fighting theory. Rather, it's how police bootstrap *Terry*. The term bootstrapping comes from an age when men pulled on their boots using fabric straps.[36] When police find drugs when they are looking for drugs, I call that bootstrapping because the frisk was merely an excuse to search without probable cause. Holding a person for a pretextual frisk violates *Terry*. As the Supreme Court explained two decades after *Terry*, police must use "the least intrusive means reasonably available" that can quickly verify or dispel their suspicions during a stop.[37]

In reality, police officers are trained to use patdowns to help them find drugs, although that's not what *Terry* says. *Terry v. Ohio* only allows police to frisk for their own safety. Under the pure *Terry* doctrine, an officer frisks only to make sure he can safely ask a few questions during a stop. And police may legally search a person's pockets for drugs only if the civilian admits she possesses drugs or consents to a search. Although it's widely known that police use the frisk to look for drugs, this distorts the *Terry* justification of short detentions to ask a few questions to allay the officer's suspicions or to confirm the suspicions, leading to probable cause.[38] Frisks have always been misused in this way, and judges generally look the other way as long as an officer testifies that he frisked for safety reasons (*high crime neighborhood, hand in his pocket, furtive movements, in my experience* ... etc.).

A recent Supreme Court case, *Utah v. Strieff*, provides an example of how police bootstrap Terry stops even without the hated frisk. Narcotics detective Douglas Fackrell heard rumors of drug dealing in a house in South Salt Lake City. One day, the detective saw a man leave the house and stopped him. I discuss the case fully in Chapter 8, but what's important here is how the detective got lucky and discovered an unpaid traffic ticket during the Terry stop. This enabled Detective Fackrell to arrest his suspect, search him "incident to arrest," and find a packet of methamphetamine that became the basis for prosecuting Edward Strieff for drug possession.[39]

Warrant checks are another cheat! That's not the pure *Terry* theory of asking a couple of questions to confirm an officer's suspicions or dispel them.[40] Although Detective Fackrell violated Mr. Strieff's rights by stopping him without reasonable suspicion, the Supreme Court took away the remedy, allowing the government to prosecute him with the drugs found during the illegal stop. While the Court decision focused on creating a rationale that would allow Strieff's prosecutors to use the ill-gotten gains, that's not my focus. I'm interested in separating out bootstrapping from Terry's original concept of fighting crime by asking questions. Even for officers whose stops don't violate the Fourth Amendment, the warrant counts as getting lucky, not as a demonstration of Terry's crime-fighting strategy.

Detective Fackrell wants to put his hands into Mr. Strieff's pockets to find out whether his suspicions are accurate. Under *Terry* v. *Ohio*'s original protocol, the detective has few legal options that would allow him to search for drugs because he lacks the probable cause. Implicit in *Terry* v. *Ohio*'s limitations on police, Mr. Strieff cannot be searched unless he admits to carrying drugs or consents to a search. If Mr. Strieff declines to stop or answer questions, the police are supposed to let him walk away. Under *Terry* v. *Ohio*'s initial restraints, good police officers only search for drugs when civilians relinquish their rights.

Terry Was Founded on a Confidence That People Will Waive Their Rights

A majority of Supreme Court justices once believed that courts should encourage civilians to exercise their constitutional rights even if that made it more difficult for police to gather evidence. Now, that sentiment mostly arises in dissents.

"If the exercise of constitutional rights will thwart the effectiveness of a system of law enforcement, then there is something very wrong with that system," the Supreme Court stated in 1964.[41] Justice Stevens quoted this phrase in dissent in 1984, adding that "our system of justice is not founded on a fear that a suspect will exercise his rights."[42] I've shown that *Terry* v. *Ohio* was founded on such a fear, or rather, stop-and-frisk's legality was founded upon the confidence that people will waive their rights.

Know Your Rights Trainings reveal how consent intertwines with stop-and-frisk both in theory and practice. I use consent broadly here: (1) civilians consent to stop when they don't walk away during consent stops; (2) civilians consent to talk to the officer and answer questions; (3) civilians consent to the search of their bodies or their property. It turns out that if we think of consent broadly, it forms the backbone of *Terry's* notion that constitutional stops and frisks will solve crimes.

Teaching the case of *Terry* v. *Ohio*, law professors explain that the Constitution limits what police can do during these "Terry stops." We tell our students that police need "reasonable suspicion" to stop people and "probable cause" to search them for drugs. But that's not really true. Consent law combines with *Terry* so in reality, the person stopped must assert his constitutional right to refuse the search. Under law, the person who is stopped must invoke their right to silence. And when police initiate a consent stop, the person approached must walk away. Police need only sham consent from civilians to stop them, question them, and search their pockets. The constitutional limits on *Terry* have to be asserted.

A FEMINIST PERSPECTIVE ON POWER DIFFERENTIALS

Teaching *Know Your Rights* with my law students in the community gave me the victim's point of view and led me to recognize the flawed reasoning at the heart of *Terry* v. *Ohio*, namely the "waive your rights theory." Law professors generally don't teach how each method allowed under *Terry* v. *Ohio* relies upon civilians giving up their rights. The Supreme Court has never admitted as much. In fact, the Court eschews the word "waiver" because the law usually equates "waiving" one's rights with knowingly, intelligently, and voluntarily giving them up. In contrast, we don't even need to know we have a right to say no when consenting to stop, talk, or submitting to a search. Although the Court has never confessed this, it places the burden on civilians to exercise their constitutional rights or lose them.

Once we recognize that the Supreme Court approved Terry stops because they could solve crimes if civilians "voluntarily" gave up their right to silence and "consented" to speak to police, this calls into question the legitimacy of stop-and-frisk. Are we comfortable assuming that civilians know their rights? Are we comfortable assuming that civilians, even those who know their rights, will be able to exercise them when called upon to do so? Richard can tell you what some officers do when they feel disrespected.

#MeToo criticizes coercive tactics by men who hold power over their victims – when a woman fears she might lose her career if she doesn't submit to sex, for instance. So might a critic of stops and frisks see consent as impossible during Terry stops. Police requests for consent are situated in a similarly complex framework of power, aggression, and privilege. Police have power and authority vis-à-vis civilians. Where courts find consensual searches and voluntary statements, feminists will see coercion.

When Youth Court participants talk about a stop from their perspective, they have many practical questions. "What happens if I say 'no' to the officer?" "Why shouldn't I run?" "Are you telling me that police won't lie in court but they can lie to us?" This is what civilians ask and what *Terry*'s victims need to know. From a civilian's perspective, the constitutional limits on *Terry* are scary. Like #MeToo victims faced with a powerful man who just starts kissing them, these teenagers have to weigh their options at a bad time – a time when they feel vulnerable, a time not of their own choosing.

As #MeToo illustrates, when someone holds power over you, it may not be possible to refuse consent. Supervisors can make life difficult and even fire you. Consider also that failing to submit to an officer might produce the same result. You might also lose your job if you are arrested in retaliation for your refusal to submit to police requests. But police officers hold even more power, for, unlike a boss, once they decide to detain or arrest you, we empower them to use a reasonable amount of force to accomplish these goals. This power makes it nearly impossible to withhold consent, to say no to the men and women who wear the uniforms.

To critique *Terry* v. *Ohio* properly, we must grapple with the fact that requiring civilians to assert their rights represents a weak bulwark against unlimited police power. In reality, *Terry*'s constitutional limits are virtually impossible to assert on the street.

It's difficult to see Richard's stop as in any way consensual, even at the beginning when the officers followed a traditional *Terry* v. *Ohio* script, and that's the point. Nothing about the encounter describes an interplay of equals. Although consent was not an issue in Richard's specific stop-and-frisk, *Terry* v. *Ohio* imagines that Richard could voluntarily choose to speak to the officers or not. What makes the Supreme Court think someone like Richard actually retains a right to silence? After all, suspects retain free speech rights during Terry stops (in theory), but police dishonored Richard's free speech by beating him for calling them racist.

Do we expect Richard to stand up for himself next time the police come knocking? He knows what happens when he dares question a police officer's motives, so he will not risk appearing uncooperative by refusing to consent. And it's not just Richard, but his friends and family and everyone he tells about his ordeal.

Richard's story also illustrates the relationship between the frisk and sexual assault. Here, the frisk literally turns into a sexual assault when police dispense with *Terry*'s rule limiting frisks to touching bodies outside, not underneath their clothes. How about before officers touched Richard underneath his clothing – when they first touched his groin through his clothing as he stood spread-eagled at the wall – did that also feel like a sexual violation? Richard uses the word "brutality" rather than sexual assault. Still, to my way of thinking, the encounter also belongs within #MeToo's category of unwanted sexual touching. Certainly, feminists often demand that society name something "rape" or "sexual harassment" when our culture wants to call encounters by other names, such as drunken mistakes or blurred lines of communication.

One could view Richard's sexualized frisk as a logical extension of the control theory of policing. As feminism teaches, sexual harassment and sexual abuse is often a way of demonstrating dominance. Harvey Weinstein used the sexual massage as part of an overall strategy to control certain actresses. When a distraught actress asked Weinstein why he grabbed her breast without permission, he apologized, explaining that this was just "behavior he is 'used to.'"[43] He was used to getting his way.

Dominance, however, is hardly unique to New York City or programmatic stop-and-frisk. Officers control every stop. Even in jurisdictions where supervisors don't impose quotas for frisks or reward officers for drug arrests, officers still exert power and control when they confront suspects. We teach officers to use command presence; we train police to use body language and words that signal that they have the power.[44] Policing demands this. Moreover, in a masculine profession, what sociologists call toxic masculinity, force, and violence are often celebrated over skills such as negotiation or de-escalation. Masculinity theorist Frank Rudy Cooper explains how police dominate every encounter and sometimes initiate encounters in order to boost their self-esteem. Officers may perceive the refusal to submit to a request as disrespect that must be punished. Sexual degradation must be understood as one tool among many that police employ to prove their dominance, just as hazing rituals in all-male institutions sometimes involve sexual assault.[45]

Even after the stop, the power imbalance continues, making it difficult to complain. Some members of the public seem baffled why Anita Hill and Christine Blasey Ford waited "so long" to complain. Feminists understand why victims fear that their complaints will boomerang and hurt them, while the perpetrators remain untouched. Unsurprisingly, Richard never filed a formal complaint. I'm grateful that he agreed to let me share his story in this book.

A WORLD WITHOUT CONSENT OR *TERRY*

For the most part, our country recognizes that it's difficult for civilians to refuse an officer's request for sex. But when it comes to searches, the courts call them "consensual" and when it comes to statements, courts call them "voluntary." *Terry's* original crime-fighting justification relies upon such fictions. The Constitution forbids the government from introducing involuntary statements at trial, so we must ask whether statements made in response to police questioning should be categorized as "voluntary." If not, then *Terry's* original justification was built on a lie.

Here's what police could do if we abolish Terry stops and consent stops. Police could still stop and interrogate us, but they would need probable cause to believe that we committed a crime. In addition, police could no longer justify stops or searches based on nothing more than people's "voluntary" cooperation, since the "consent" doctrine must simultaneously be overturned. Probable cause was the standard justification before *Terry* v. *Ohio* announced the watered down "reasonable suspicion" justification for stops and frisks. Frank Rudy Cooper, a law professor at the University of Nevada, defined these terms best: police need an educated guess to arrest someone (namely probable cause) but even "uneducated guesses" will suffice for Terry stops.[46] In other words, if police receive information about a robbery or other crime, they may detain and frisk people if "there is a reasonable ground for belief of guilt ... particularized with respect to the person to be searched or seized."[47]

In a world without Terry stops, police will also be able to stop and question potential witnesses (without probable cause) and use that information to solve crimes, but the government will no longer be able to turn around and prosecute the witnesses themselves for drug possession or other wrongdoing that police found during these stops. In emergency situations, the Supreme Court already suspends our constitutional protections, so there will be some exceptions to the probable cause standard, although I will leave it to future authors to hammer out their breadth and depth.[48] Ultimately, while the changes proposed in this book will hamper police efforts to look into people's pockets for drugs, police will still be able to investigate crimes.

Anyone who imagines we successfully fight crime by stopping Richard or hauling him off to jail has not met Richard or the many other Howard law students who have been stopped.

This chapter has shown that *Terry* v. *Ohio* was built on the premise that vulnerable civilians can stand up to police officers and that it is safe to do so. In the chapters that follow, I will show that, in fact, police requests are as coercive as the advances described in #MeToo posts or sexual harassment lawsuits, even when police are simply doing their jobs.

The Most Dangerous Right: Walking Away from an Officer

If an officer stops you, promise me you'll always be polite
And that you'll never ever run away
Promise Mama you'll keep your hands in sight.

> Bruce Springsteen, "American Skin" (41 Shots)

I wonder what path I will take
I hear that there's only two ways out
I see mothers bury their sons
I want my mom to never feel that pain
I am confused and afraid.

> Antwon Rose (poem for sophomore year honors English course assignment two years
> before he was killed running from police)

My law students teach the bulk of the *Know Your Rights* sessions, but, beforehand, I make sure they understand the nuances of Fourth and Fifth Amendment guarantees. One day, I briefly lectured my law school class on the Fourth Amendment concept called "free to leave" to prepare them to teach Youth Court. I explained that when an officer approaches you and asks you questions, unless the officer orders you to stop or physically restrains you, the Constitution grants you the freedom to walk away.

As the Supreme Court stated in 1983, a person approached by an officer *need not answer any question put to him; indeed, he may decline to listen to the questions at all and may go on his way.*[1] This "free to leave" doctrine is a cornerstone of the Court's conception of limited police power under the Fourth Amendment.

Because this Fourth Amendment right is only available to those who actively exercise it, I thought that we should include "free to leave" as one of the rights we teach teenagers in Youth Court. After all, people unintentionally waive their rights all the time. Courts follow the "use it or lose it" policy, placing the burden on civilians to know their rights and to exercise them. How could knowledge be a bad thing?

My Howard law students saw things differently. They explained that in their neighborhoods, if you walk away, "you can get yourself arrested" . . . "or shot." Most chilling perhaps was the comment from the former police officer in the class: "It would be irresponsible for us to tell young people that they can walk away from police." The ex-cop was not speaking lightly. To teach these boys and girls the actual law would set them up for an arrest or physical retaliation.

My law students were right. That was in 2010, before the deluge of online video clips from police body cameras and cell phones. Hundreds of them now show officers using excessive force. Many of them involve civilians who tried to run. This is a stark example of the gap between *law on the books* and *law in action*.

"FOOT TAX"

Fifteen-year-old Dajerria Barnes was among a handful of black teenagers who ran when the police came to investigate a disturbance at a pool party on June 5, 2015 in McKinney, Texas. Weighing about 100 pounds and wearing a bikini, Dajerria was obviously not a threat to the officers. Nevertheless, a video captured one of the twelve officers grabbing Dajerria by the wrist and throwing her to the ground. He grabs her head and shoves her face into the grass, then kneels on her back. Meanwhile, another officer calmly explains to a group of teens, "Don't take off running when the cops get here."[2]

Both officers sent the same message, one verbally and one violently: don't run. Fleeing poses such a high risk of police retaliation that experts have a nickname for the injuries suffered: they call it a "foot tax," meaning that police will punch or beat suspects who flee.[3]

Even walking away can get you hurt. The arrest of Charlena Michelle Cooks in May 2015 provides a chilling counterpoint to the Supreme Court's imagined world. The interaction between a police officer in Barstow, California, and an eight-months'-pregnant black woman is available for all to see, thanks to a body camera worn by the arresting officer.[4] It shows what can happen when a civilian has the audacity to exercise her right to walk away.

It began as the most minor of disputes, an argument between two women in a parking lot as 29-year-old Ms. Cooks dropped her child off at school. The other woman, a school employee who was white, can be seen on camera telling the police that Ms. Cooks yelled at her and threw something that hit the employee's car after she criticized Ms. Cooks's parking. The officer can be heard explaining that in his view, no crime has been committed. At this point of the interaction, the officer lacked reasonable suspicion or probable cause to detain Ms. Cooks. All he could do legally was approach Ms. Cooks and hope for her cooperation. If the officer was lucky, Ms. Cooks would not know that she had the right to decline to talk to the officer and the right to walk away. Unfortunately for Ms. Cooks, she knew her rights, but the officer did not play by the Court's rules.

Ms. Cooks, clearly pregnant, was waiting for the officer and she explained her side of the incident, denying throwing anything at the car and claiming it was the other woman who scared her child. Nevertheless, the officer asked Ms. Cooks for her name. Under the Constitution, the officer may always ask for identification, but if the officer lacks reasonable suspicion to believe a crime is being committed, the officer may not command a person to identify herself.[5] Ms. Cooks refused to give her name, phoning someone to get advice about whether she must reveal her identity, but eventually she gave the officer her first name, even though legally, she need not have done so.

What happens next to this pregnant mother in California deviates from the Supreme Court's vision of police–civilian interactions. Ms. Cooks begins to walk away from the officer, saying "I told you my name is Michelle" and "I'm not comfortable right here," precisely as the Supreme Court allows. With that, the officer gives the signal to begin an arrest. Arrests can be ugly. As Ms. Cooks cries "don't touch me, don't touch me; I'm pregnant," the camera jerks like an old-fashioned movie and it is clear she is being forced to the ground. All the while, the officer can be heard calmly asking, "Why are you resisting?" Officers routinely charge people with resisting arrest as a preemptive strike when they fear they have used excessive force and here the officer sets the groundwork for such a charge by repeating, "Why are you resisting?" In fact, the officer had no reason to arrest Ms. Cooks in the first place. She can't resist arrest if she is not being arrested, so the charge is absurd on its face.

Without doubt, Ms. Cooks was arrested for exercising her right to walk away from the police. To try to make sense of the officer's senseless hostility, we must recognize current racist views toward black women, especially mothers and expectant mothers. Law professor Kimberlé Crenshaw coined the term "intersectionality" in 1998 as a way to explain the particular legal barriers faced by African American women claiming employment discrimination.[6] In her important book, Andrea Ritchie uses intersectional theory to explain police treatment of black, Latinx and indigenous women and *Invisible No More* includes several examples of ugly police violence directed at black pregnant women.[7]

When she was seven months pregnant, Malika Brooks received "fifty thousand volts of electricity" to her body when police tasered her for refusing to sign a speeding ticket and for refusing to get out of her car when ordered to do so. A panel of appellate judges threw out Brooks's federal civil rights claims and split on whether the force was excessive. As one judge explained, when civilians refuse to comply with orders, "police must bring the situation under control, and they have a number of tools at their disposal."[8] The law gives the officer the authority to use force but an intersectional approach to misogyny helps us understand why the officer chose to exercise his discretion in this manner. It's not just the "insufficiently feminine" who are treated badly in the workplace, for example, but pregnant women and mothers too. As Elizabeth Bruenig points out, "the great paradox of misogyny is that its object is womanhood itself." Ms. Brooks's treatment fits under the most virulent hatred, the "eugenic sort, which vilifies the poor, disabled, and nonwhite women who have children for daring to increase the ranks of those whom the elites consider unfit."[9] There's the "trope of the welfare queen who gives birth 'solely to increase the size of her check,'" making her someone "that must be punished," writes political science professor Cathy J. Cohen. Even without pregnancy, black women have more to worry about than white women during police encounters for society views black women as an inherent threat, Cohen explains, as masculine or queered "through projection of non-normative and deviant sexualities."[10] In hurting Michelle Cooks, I see the officer accomplishing two things at once: he punished defiance and devalued her motherhood. I know of no white woman treated this way.

Thanks to the video of Ms. Cooks's arrest, we see what happens when someone knows her rights and exercises them. No wonder my law students thought it dangerous to explain the constitutional free to leave guarantee to vulnerable teenagers.

FOURTH AMENDMENT RIDDLES

Riddle #1 (or exam question): When is a stop not a stop?
ANSWER: When it's a contact.

The Supreme Court makes a distinction between police "stopping" civilians and police merely "approaching" civilians to question them or investigate. Officers, "by merely approaching an individual on the street or in another public place, by asking him if he is willing to answer some questions, by putting questions to him if the person is willing to listen," are not "stopping" that person, intones the Court. It is merely a request for voluntary cooperation that officers call a "contact" and law professors call a "consent stop."[11]

In some jurisdictions, police do not even describe what they do as stop-and-frisk. In the District of Columbia, where my clinical law students represented clients in misdemeanor court, the police pretend that Terry stops are consensual encounters. In their police reports, instead of writing that the undersigned police stopped a young woman, police will write, "I made contact with a young woman." This fine line between a contact and a stop separates bad Terry stops from ones blessed by courts. Police need a reason to "stop" a person – that's a basic constitutional guarantee. Only authoritarian countries allow police to stop anyone at any time for any reason. But what do police need to conduct a "contact" – as DC police call stops when they pretend their suspect was free to walk away? For that, the police need zilch. Nada. Nothing.

The "free to leave" case law draws distinctions based on nuances such as whether the officer used the term "halt" or just began questioning, whether the officer touched the civilians or whether or not there was room on the sidewalk so they could conceivably walk around the officer standing in front of them without having to push the officer away. The Supreme Court bases its decisions on hair-splitting nuances, such as the officer's tone of voice and whether an officer couches demands in request-like language. Thus, "show me your identification" is a command and a judge will demand a showing of reasonable suspicion of wrongdoing. But the judge may view the same encounter differently if the officer testifies that he used normal conversational tones and asked, "Would you mind showing me your identification?" With those details changed, some judges might conclude that the officer has merely made a contact, just a friendly request for voluntary cooperation. Such distinctions are pure fiction, of course. Moreover, these nuances invite police perjury (at least if his body cam is not recording), because how does an officer remember the tone he used when asking a civilian for identification?

The officer in the Michelle Cooks video knows the rules. He never tells Ms. Cooks that she is detained. That way, if she cooperates, he can paint the whole encounter as a voluntary contact. Even as the officer escalates the parking lot encounter by interrupting Ms. Cooks, he's careful not to use command language. He repeatedly says "Ma'am, give me your name please," rather than ordering her to give her name. Phrasing is part of the gossamer nuances that the Supreme Court relies on to distinguish between commands and friendly requests. In addition to throwing in the word "please," the officer used a calm voice, another nod to how courts distinguish a stop from a mere contact.

Had Ms. Cooks not walked away, this would have been considered a consensual contact. As a matter of law, the officer simply approached an individual in a public place and put questions to her and she was willing to stop, listen, and respond. Although the courts don't like to use the language of waivers when analyzing consent stops, in essence, if the case ever got to court, a judge would say that she voluntarily chose to waive her rights by engaging with the officer (and by not leaving). Up to the point that Ms. Cooks walked away, this was a mere "contact." Once she walked away and the officer ordered her to stop, it became an unlawful Terry stop, a detention without reasonable suspicion and then an arrest without probable cause.

The law was on Ms. Cooks's side and she knew her rights, but the law didn't help her. The violent arrest of a pregnant black woman in a school parking lot shows how impossible it is to play by the rules when the police do not. Viewers of the video learned what most black people in this country already know, that in real life it is dangerous to walk away from the police even if police are simply making a "contact." It is dangerous not to give one's name, even though the law allows this. It is dangerous to exercise one's rights.

THE RUNNING AWAY RIDDLE

Freddie Gray would be alive today were it not for stop-and-frisk. The Baltimore man was free to leave, that is, until he took off running. Looking at what the police did to Freddie Gray illustrates how the Supreme Court turned the "free to leave" guarantee on its head.

On April 12, 2015, four Baltimore police officers on bicycles happened to notice two black men who began to run when they spotted the officers. One of the men was Freddie Gray. Up until the point that Mr. Gray ran, there was no Terry stop or reasonable suspicion for a Terry stop. The police did not see Mr. Gray do anything illegal; he was not suspected of any crime before he took flight. Before he ran, Mr. Gray was free to leave.

Police chased and grabbed 25-year-old Freddie Gray (this is legally the "stop"); then they patted him down for weapons (the "frisk"). During the frisk, police felt a knife and illegally arrested him for possessing it – a bad arrest because Freddie Gray's knife was not a switchblade prohibited by Maryland's criminal code.[12] When the officers arrested Mr. Gray for possessing a weapon, regardless of whether their error was deliberate or not, this action flowed directly from the police officers' gratuitous decision to stop and frisk him in the first place.

Quite understandably, the public has focused on what happened to Freddie Gray after he was grabbed and placed in police custody. Police shackled the black native of West Baltimore and dumped him into the back of a police wagon. The ride proved fatal, causing the young man to suffer a severe spinal injury that put him in a coma and led to his death. Although the driver of the van was ultimately acquitted of second-degree murder, prosecutors introduced evidence that the driver intentionally gave Mr. Gray a "rough ride" using sudden acceleration, sudden stops or sharp turns in order to bounce the prisoner around. Baltimore erupted in demonstrations for days, as protesters sought answers and justice. Protesters focused on accountability for Freddie Gray's death, for here was another police killing of a young black man less than a year after Michael Brown was shot by an officer in Ferguson, Missouri. Although prosecutors failed to prove which officer was responsible, the rough ride that proved fatal was a foot tax to punish Mr. Gray for running away.

All the news coverage of Mr. Gray's death and the prosecutions of the officers involved in his arrest and transport missed something: A wider lens reveals that the fault for Freddie Gray's death extends beyond these police officers. Without an aggressive stop-and-frisk policy in place, police could not legally give chase. The encounter shows how constitutional stop-and-frisk is rotten to the core.

Riddle #2: When are you free to leave but police can still stop-and-frisk you for leaving? **ANSWER:** When you're in a "high-crime neighborhood" and you leave too fast.

The Baltimore officers admitted that the only reason they chased, grabbed, and then searched Freddie Gray was because he ran from them. "How can this be legal?" my law students asked me. "Doesn't the Fourth Amendment protect against stops and frisks when officers lack reasonable suspicion?" My law students are not naïve about police aggression, and many have experienced it firsthand, but they reason that the Baltimore police must have violated the Constitution by chasing Freddie Gray. My students are correct that police were required to have "reasonable suspicion" to believe Freddie Gray had committed a crime (or was in the process of committing a crime) before they could legally "stop" him. Next, in order for police to "frisk" Freddie Gray – to pat him down along all the contours of his body outside of his clothing, feeling for weapons – they needed additional evidence that he was armed and dangerous.

But the Supreme Court carved out a running exception to their free to leave doctrine in a case decided in 2000 called *Illinois* v. *Wardlow*.[13] In the aftermath of Wardlow, civilians could be incarcerated or not, depending upon how they exercised their free to leave rights. Run, jog, walk, walk too fast? Odd as it may seem, Freddie Gray's stop was legitimate – and probably his frisk, too – because the Supreme Court watered down the concept of reasonable suspicion to the point where merely running from police in a "high-crime neighborhood" is enough to justify a stop-and-frisk. *Wardlow* severely undercut *Terry*'s free to leave guarantee.

Notice the hidden racial dynamic at play in a Supreme Court's ruling that flight plus a high-crime neighborhood equals reasonable suspicion. The concept of high-crime "can easily serve as a proxy for race or ethnicity." Examining data from New York City, researchers found that for many officers, a "suspect's race predicts whether an officer deems an area" to be high-crime.[14] That means that most white people can legally run away from police, while police are encouraged to tackle black men, women, and children in urban communities. Yet blacks have more reason to fear police, and therefore more reason to run. Although the rough ride was an illegal foot tax exacted on Freddie Gray, the chase and tackle were constitutionally permissible thanks to *Wardlow*. This can't be good policy. Freddie Gray was free to leave, except he left too quickly.

Remember the Supreme Court's language that when an officer approaches a civilian to ask questions, the civilian *may decline to listen to the questions at all and may go on his way*? Ever since the Supreme Court decided *Wardlow*, judges are expected to distinguish between "headlong flight" that allows police to give chase, from quickly walking away, when they must not retaliate. But no one seems to have told the police.

I once supervised a Howard law student in DC Superior Court who argued that our client was constitutionally entitled to "evade the police" by walking away. The police officer believed that he could stop our client when he evaded him. That's probably what he was told in training, that evasion equals suspicion. That's how it works in practice – see Michelle Cooks's story above. The decision came down to the speed at which our client walked away. Determining freedom based upon the speed at which civilians evade police questioning is almost as silly as distinctions based upon an officer's tone of voice. It's not only teenagers who might have trouble grasping these Supreme Court nuances. One can almost forgive officers for believing my client had no such right. I remember this case because it's one of those rare instances when my student won a motion to suppress. Both our client's case and that of Charlena Michelle Cooks point to the failure of police to appreciate what's left of the free-to-leave guarantee, whether based on ignorance, a police culture that coerces respect, or both.

This book wants readers to critique the trap set by courts and seek changes that will shore up rights. In contrast, when training Youth Court participants, our focus becomes navigating the law as it currently exists and trying to apply it to the world as it currently exists. Although we considered teaching students to pull out cell phones and ask permission to film the officers who stop them, some of us were worried that this would provoke retaliation, too. For those readers who want to teach *Know Your Rights* themselves, I recommend learning about the culture of policing in that particular jurisdiction. When teaching *Know Your Rights*, we can all start with the assumption that police will not respect the right to walk away.

LESSONS AND RIDDLES FOR YOUTH COURT

Riddle #3A: If it's too dangerous to tell people their rights, then how will they exercise them?
ANSWER: They won't.
Riddle #3B: And if people don't know their rights, then can they waive them?
ANSWER: Sure. (Unlike other contexts where waivers must be knowing, intelligent and voluntary, people can give up their Fourth Amendment rights by accident.)

Given the crazy quilt of Supreme Court rules, and the stories of police abuse and killings, it is virtually impossible to explain the free to leave doctrine in a way that won't leave civilians confused and vulnerable. Because the right to walk away is the most dangerous right, how can we inform Youth Court participants of this right without encouraging them to waive their rights? We must explain to them that police officers need "reasonable suspicion" for a stop but admit that they will have no way to know if the officer has any justification for the stop. We might help them decipher the language that denotes an "order" that will trigger an arrest if the teenagers disobey. We must find a way to explain the dangers inherent in running away without appearing to be clueless to their plight.

When I rented a car in Yellowstone National Park for a short hiking trip, the car came with a can of bear spray. Teaching the free-to-leave doctrine is like the instructions for bear spray. The man behind the rental counter was explaining when to use the spray during a hike: "If the bear comes upon you suddenly, then back up slowly. But get ready to use the spray if the bear has been tracking you. Just make sure you are downwind of the bear or else it will end up in your eyes and not the bear's. Sometimes it is better to just drop to the ground and try to protect your stomach. Whatever you do, don't run." The paper he gave us emphasized this: *You shouldn't run or make any sudden movements as this could startle the animal, triggering a chase response and you cannot outrun a bear.*[15]

I left the rental counter more worried than I entered and certain I wouldn't know whether the bear I saw had been tracking me or whether it wished me harm.

Similarly, the teens at Youth Court won't know if the officer has received a radio call about a robbery (giving the officer a reason to detain them) or whether he is just trying to find a reason to arrest that will provide overtime pay. Has the officer been tracking them or did he just come upon them? In addition, these teens won't know the officer's personality type. Does this police officer understand the constitutional rules? Is he willing to obey them? Is he prone to violence? Will he retaliate if they assert their rights? As my law students grasped, a *Know Your Rights* training on "free to leave" could be misinterpreted by a high school student, to deadly results.

Then there was the clash between our views and the voices that students hear at home. Parental advice to black children about police violence is so widespread that it is often referred to as "the talk." Many Youth Court participants have been told to always "keep your hands in sight" and to do everything an officer asks. If followed, this means waiving their rights. My students and I try to teach methods to preserve rights without clashing with loving parental advice, but that's not always possible.

Instead of telling teenagers that they have a right to leave when an officer approaches them, we teach them to ask, "Am I free to leave?" The question forces the officer to make a choice. If the officer has reasonable suspicion, he will tell the teen she can't leave. But if the officer lacks reasonable suspicion, he either violates the Constitution by keeping the teen against her will (and she can complain later) or ideally, the officer follows the law and tells her she may go.

We write on the flip chart in big letters:
LESSON: "Officer, Am I Free To Leave?"

Youth Court volunteers memorize this language. We make several points when we teach this lesson in *Know Your Rights* trainings:

1. Our goal is to keep you safe and help you walk away as soon as possible without being arrested or searched.
2. You have to obey orders, so if an officer tells you to stop, you must stop. Otherwise, police can arrest you for failing to obey an order.
3. It is almost impossible to know if the officer is stopping you or just hoping that you will give up your rights. That's why you should ask, "Am I free to leave?"
4. The question forces the officer to make a choice. Either he has reasonable suspicion and he will tell you to stay. Or he does not have reasonable suspicion and he should tell you it's okay to leave.

5. If the officer refuses to let you go or refuses to answer your question, then you can complain later to DC's Office of Police Complaints (an agency independent of the police).

6. Or if they claim they found something illegal on you, such as a pill without a prescription, it will be difficult for the officer to later claim that the stop was consensual (especially if the officer's camera is running).[16]

7. If you think the officer violated your rights in any way, make a note of this in your phone as soon as you are out of his sight. Remember as many details as you can about what happened. This will be like your own police report to refute anything he says.

8. The words "Am I Free To Leave" come from a Supreme Court case so the officer will recognize that you know your rights. That's much better than saying "I know my rights and you can't do that to me." That will just piss off the cop.

9. Whatever you do, don't run!

In Youth Court, the teenagers loved to run away during the skits where a law student pretended to be a police officer asking questions. This is particularly true for the male teens we taught.

When we sought volunteers for the first skit, before we offered any instruction, our male volunteers took off running almost every time. Even after we explained that running gave the police a reason to stop them, some still ran. I understood why they did so. One reason is that they are teenagers and that's normal teenage behavior.

Another reason they run is to survive *jumpouts*, a method of fighting open air drug markets in many cities.[17] In the District of Columbia, three or four officers cram into a vehicle that screeches to a halt at a location where drug dealing is rampant. As the title suggests, officers jump from the vehicle, and everyone scatters. Usually buyers and dealers throw their bags on the ground as they run. Officers grab up the drugs and have to guess where they came from. Sometimes there are as many as four vehicles involved. It's chaotic.

In the first jumpout case I supervised in DC, our client foolishly thought that his innocence would protect him, so he didn't run. Officers found a bag and pinned it on him, someone they could cuff without any exertion. He told us he was innocent, just walking through on the way to the bus. Even if the judge acquitted our client at trial, he was afraid he would lose his job because of all the times he missed work for court, so my student pushed hard to get the case resolved earlier. Running is actually a rational response to jumpouts. If my memory's accurate, our client took a deal where he didn't have to admit guilt, but had to pay fines and adhere to certain probationary conditions for six months. Next time, he too will run.

My colleague Lenese Herbert views running as a form of protest that should be protected by the First Amendment. Running expresses disdain or distrust of the police, a form of protest. Moreover, this might be the only way people can express this sentiment.[18] Similarly, post-structural feminists might see running as "performative," the refusal to be branded a criminal.

Youth Court teens have given me more prosaic reasons. When we told the kids at Youth Court some of the dangers of running, some of them thought we didn't know the deal. "They can only beat me if they catch me," one responded. "How do you know they won't beat us up anyway even if we don't run?" asked another.

A FEMINIST LENS ON FREE TO LEAVE

#MeToo collides with the Fourth Amendment free to leave doctrine in Monica Decker's 2004 lawsuit, illustrating how a feminist critique works well for both.

Monica Decker went for an evening ride-along with Officer Tinnel because she was contemplating a career in law enforcement, but the officer had other things in mind. About forty minutes into the ride, while stopped to run radar on a bridge, the officer leaned over from the driver's side, pushed his face against the eighteen-year-old's (whose race is unknown), tried to kiss her and then "forced his hand between her closed thighs, coming within an inch of her vagina." The officer stopped when she yelled "no," but then redoubled his efforts a short time later, grabbing her chest as well as trying to kiss her again. After the second unwelcome grab, Ms. Decker canceled the mentoring opportunity and the officer brought her back to the station.

Ms. Decker fought back in the courts, filing a federal civil rights lawsuit that claimed that Officer Tinnel violated her Fourth Amendment right not to be physically seized without just cause.[19] One might expect her to win because the Fourth Amendment protects us against unreasonable "seizures," a word that includes physical touching by police. Officers on duty can violate civil rights through an unwanted grab as surely as if they perform a Terry stop without reasonable suspicion. Here, Officer Tinnel lacked reasonable suspicion or any law enforcement justification for grabbing Ms. Decker. But the judge threw out her lawsuit, ruling that Ms. Decker was free to leave, making this a "consent stop" or consensual contact.

"Upon due consideration, this Court believes an objectively reasonable person would have believed she could have terminated the encounter," writes the judge in the Decker case. To get there, he points to various factors that are familiar to criminal lawyers: "Decker voluntarily entered Tinnel's police car," and "Officer Tinnel did not brandish his weapon" or make verbal threats. Overall, the officer's conduct communicated to a reasonable person that she was "free to decline his requests, or to otherwise terminate the encounter." Unfortunately, this troubling ruling is well grounded in Fourth Amendment case law. Ms. Decker got the criminal defendant treatment.

Notice that the judge doesn't ask whether Ms. Decker consented, whether she felt fearful, or consider whether there is a power imbalance between Ms. Decker and the officer. Instead, the judge must decide how a "reasonable person" in her situation would view it. Who is this reasonable person who thinks she can stop this uniformed officer from kissing and touching her?

The judge's disturbing decision illustrates why the law on sham consent stops needs a #MeToo correction: Under current law (1) consent stops don't turn on whether an actual victim felt fearful, (2) the courts willfully ignore the power imbalance between the parties, and (3) the courts blame the victims for their predicament.

"When Monica Decker was asked why she did not leave earlier in the encounter, she responded, 'because he's a big guy – Tinnel is a big guy, and he has a gun. And I was afraid he was going to chase after me. I didn't know what he was going to do, so.'" It's the victim's perspective that matters in #MeToo. In contrast, Fourth Amendment law intentionally ignores the victim's actual experience. Legally, guns won't cause fear in the reasonable person who is groped or questioned, not unless police brandish them. While to Ms. Decker, Officer Tinnel was a man with a gun, that's not what the mythical "reasonable person" would think according to the Supreme Court.[20]

To reach his conclusion, the judge endows certain facts with outsized significance. Why should it matter that the officer didn't pull the gun out of his holster? He was armed. Why should it matter that Ms. Decker voluntarily entered the cruiser? That doesn't mean she wanted to be grabbed. This reads like outright sexism, blaming the victim for her predicament.

Unfortunately, the judge in *Decker* v. *Tinnel* didn't make up the law. He faithfully followed a pair of Supreme Court drug interdiction cases where police board interstate buses and question each passenger without any individualized suspicion, looking for their "cooperation" to search.[21] In those cases, the men voluntarily got on a bus just like Ms. Decker voluntarily got into the cruiser. The Supreme Court faced an inconvenient hurdle: How can it rule that civilians on interstate buses are "free to leave" when they're not? In real life, when agents board interstate buses, passengers find themselves stuck, waiting while police finish questioning and searching bags so the bus driver can resume the journey. The Court circumvents the impasse by changing the test (for bus passengers) from "free to leave" to "free to decline the officers' requests or otherwise terminate the encounter."[22] Even though bus passengers are not actually free to walk off the bus, the Court still labels these drug interdictions as consensual "contacts."

Don't blame the police, explains the Supreme Court. Passengers voluntarily got on the bus themselves. Police cannot be blamed for taking advantage of a situation where civilians are confined, in the Court's view. But if it's not the officers' fault, that begs the question, who's to blame for the fact that the passengers can't exit? By a process of deduction, the reader must see that the Supreme Court blames the men on the bus for their own predicament. When the federal judge blames Monica Decker for voluntarily entering the cruiser, he's just following the Court's lead.

Whenever the Court finds Fourth Amendment consent – this is true in all its forms – it's a victim-blaming maneuver. Sometimes the blame game is subtle. In Ms. Decker's case, because she wasn't a suspect, victim-blaming becomes visible.

Voluntarily entering the cruiser seems to have turned an unwanted grope into a consensual touch. Paraphrasing a famous line from Donald Trump, "you just kiss them," and the Fourth Amendment lets you do it.[23]

THE DOUBLE-BIND

The law puts Charlena Cooks – and anyone approached by police officers – in a lose–lose situation or "double-bind." Ms. Cooks had only two choices: cooperate with whatever the officer wanted, or stand on her rights. We saw what happened when she walked away. What would have happened if she had cooperated? Bad consequences befall those who submit to police authority when a court thinks the civilian should have felt "free to disregard the police and go about his business."[24] Courts won't throw out incriminating evidence seized from you if a court decides that you cooperated when you could have walked away. You cannot later complain that the police lacked a reason to stop you. But you exercise your rights at your peril too, for, if you refuse to stop, you may be beaten up, arrested, or worse. Law professor Margaret Raymond likened the civilian's choices in sham consent stops to the "heads I win, tails you lose" game. Stay or leave, the officer always wins.[25]

The law protects people from double-binds in some contexts. In *Price Waterhouse* v. *Hopkins*, the Supreme Court considered whether a senior manager at a large tax and consulting firm could be denied partnership for not acting sufficiently feminine. The feminist court decision ruled in favor of Ms. Hopkins because she was in a double-bind. Assertiveness and competitiveness, traditional masculine behaviors, were essential for success in her field. To advance, she must violate traditional gender norms but she was fired for those same "strengths," for not acting "nice."[26] Damned if you do; damned if you don't.

The Supreme Court corrected the sexist double-bind of some working women but has never noticed how its own *Terry* rules create a double-bind for civilians accosted by the police. Civilians must be sufficiently meek to please an officer while, at the same time, sufficiently assertive to walk away from an officer. As the Court recognized in *Price Waterhouse* v. *Hopkins*, what's "too assertive" lies in the eyes of the beholder, with stereotypes playing an outsized role. So too with policing, where race, gender, and class contribute to how officers respond to assertive civilians. Police may fear black men more than white men or may expect black women to act subservient and therefore interpret their behavior as more aggressive than if a white woman or a man of any race behaved exactly the same way. Implicit bias research documents that race often plays a role in how officers view resistance.[27] Court rules trap every civilian in a double-bind when police make contact, but the bind wraps tighter for some people.

We've seen various ways that courts blame victims for their predicament; it was Ms. Decker's fault for getting into the cruiser. For Freddie Gray, it was his fault for running. But at the heart of the rules on sham consent stops lies a different form of blame: the "free to leave" rule from *Terry* v. *Ohio* blames civilians for not walking away even though it's dangerous to leave.

DOMESTIC VIOLENCE PARALLELS

When I was a public defender, most of my clients were not as brave or well informed as Charlene Cooks. They stayed put and cooperated fully. "Why didn't you leave?" That's what I used to ask my clients to prepare them for motion hearings. Judges must answer this question under current rules to figure out whether the stop was a "consensual contact." The implication of the Supreme Court cases is this: If the officer didn't threaten you, didn't order you to stay, you should have walked away. If you stayed, it was your own fault.

Judges used to ask the same to victims of domestic abuse: "Why didn't you leave your alleged abuser?" If you were so scared of him, why didn't you move out? Even today, some women and men who survive abuse and don't leave their partners must defend themselves to skeptical judges or others who question their credibility or blame them. Still, feminism has wrought an evolution in our understanding of domestic violence. We would do well to consider importing many of those lessons into our analysis of policing. While the issues are different, the two situations share unhealthy power dynamics, coupled with the law's refusal to acknowledge them.

First, researchers proved that leaving an abuser can be more dangerous for domestic violence victims than staying put. And judges now more often recognize that leaving is dangerous. This applies to police stops. Just as it's risky to leave an abusive domestic partner, it's likely that a person is most at risk of violence if he tries to leave when police officers question him. This is particularly apt for those who flee. Combining justified and unjustified shootings together, the numbers tell the story: almost one in three deaths at the hands of police belong to those who run or drive away.[28]

Second, courts recognize that when jurors decide whether a victim's fears were reasonable or not, they often do so based on sexist narratives. That's why courts sometimes allow an expert to educate jurors about the psychological effects of long-term coercion and explain the reasons why victims don't leave. Courts should apply this insight to police stops where the mythical "reasonable person" doesn't act like a real flesh-and-blood civilian. Instead, it's the Supreme Court that created this fictitious reasonable person, and the current Court appears unmoved by social science that proves that civilians feel coerced when police ask for their "cooperation".

Third, many courts now recognize that victims of domestic violence are in the best position to know whether or not it's safe to leave. For our Youth Court teens, parents are probably in a better position than the courts to know whether their child can safely walk away from officers who want to question him. Police have the guns. Police have the power to arrest. And if that weren't enough, many black parents know best because they have heard stories of bad police encounters all their lives.

WHEN A RIGHT EXISTS ONLY ON PAPER

Many of the most publicized cases of police brutality belong to black men who flee. The Miami riots of 1980 were a result of Arthur McDuffie's death and the acquittal of the officers who killed him. After running a red light, the 33-year-old black insurance salesman led police on a high-speed chase on December 1979. Mr. McDuffie was on a motorcycle and although he finally stopped and shouted, "I give up," at least four officers beat him hard enough to crack his skull and put him into a coma from which he never recovered. Five officers were charged with manslaughter, then acquitted. Although the law does not endorse deadly force as punishment for evading arrest for nonviolent offenses, police culture doesn't follow the law. The punishment meted out for running from the police in that case was death.[29]

Similarly, the Los Angeles riots of 1992 erupted after a jury acquitted the officers who surrounded and clubbed Rodney King. Mr. King's beating was gratuitous and brutal, though not fatal. People my age remember the astonishing video of a dozen officers surrounding and hurting one unarmed man and remember when the jury cast aside the visible proof to find them all not guilty. Forgotten in the excitement of the trial was the fact that the beating was a foot tax. When police first tried to pull Mr. King over for speeding, he led them on a chase with speeds estimated up to 115 miles per hour. The beating served to punish him for the high-speed chase.

Walter Scott's death is a high-profile example of how video changed the response to police shootings. On April 4, 2015, a North Charleston, South Carolina, police officer, Michael Slager, pulled Walter Scott over on the pretext that his third brake light was out. When Mr. Scott ran away, Officer Slager shot the 50-year-old man in the back. Unfortunately for Officer Slager, an onlooker filmed the shooting on his iPhone. The video also showed the officer moving his stun gun close to the body of his cuffed victim to support his claim that Mr. Scott had tried to grab his gun. Although Walter Scott was not actually legally "free to leave" when he ran, his death validated my law students' fears. As Mr. Scott's brother later asked, "How do you lose your life at a traffic stop?"[30]

The high-profile beatings scare some people into giving up their rights. For others, ironically, the way police punish people for running actually makes them more likely to run. On June 19, 2018, as 17-year-old Antwon Rose fled from a car stop, an East Pittsburgh officer opened fire. This was a Terry stop of a car that turned deadly; the officer had reasonable suspicion to believe the car and its occupants were involved in a shooting from earlier that day, though it turned out that Antwon was unarmed and not the shooter. Antwon was absolutely not free to leave; he died because he fled. After Antwon Rose was killed, his childhood friend explained that

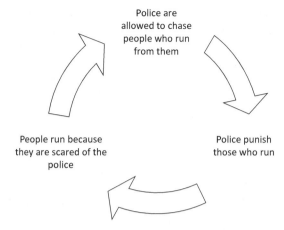

FIGURE 1 How a Supreme Court ruling produces more police violence and more fear.

Antwon ran "out of fear." "If I was in Antwon's shoes," the 18-year-old said, "I would have ran."[31]

Figure 1 shows there's a circular quality to how the foot tax operates.

- Police are allowed to chase people who run from them➔
- Police punish those who run ➔
- People run because they are scared of the police➔
- (back to the top).

Kendrec McDade's death is a classic example of why we urge teenagers not to run during Terry stops. This black college student with no criminal record left his father's house in Pasadena, California, to walk to a friend's house a couple of blocks away. The 19-year-old teenager was unarmed and totally innocent, but police thought he was armed and dangerous because another man nearby had reported his laptop was stolen by a man with a gun. When Mr. McDade ran, the police chased him in their cruiser and then on foot before finally shooting him seven times and cuffing him while they waited for an ambulance. Mr. McDade died within hours of the shooting. Police failed to activate their lights, which would have automatically triggered the camera to record.[32] We will never know why Kendrec initially ran away, and whether he even knew that the car chasing him into a dark alley was a police cruiser.

White people may not imagine this could apply to them. We don't hear the stories of Kelly Kenneth Sutton, Daniel A. Fuller, Dustin Odom, or Alan Greenough, all unarmed white men killed in 2018 after they fled from police.[33]

Two things are true: police kill white people, too, and the numbers prove that racist policies saturate policing.[34] Tracking fatal police shootings, the *Washington Post* determined that white deaths represented 50 percent of those killed since the

Post began tracking in 2015; black deaths made up 26 percent; and Hispanics accounted for 19 percent of those killed. Half the men and women killed that year by police were white, not insignificant yet revealing racial privilege when one considers that black people are killed at twice the rate of their percentage in the overall population.[35] The racial slant becomes even more pronounced when the data are sorted by whether a civilian carried a weapon when shot. An unarmed black man is four times more likely to be killed than an unarmed white man.[36] When the *Guardian* examined all police-involved deaths in 2015, including non-shootings, it found that young black men between the ages of 15 and 34 were five times more likely to be killed by police than white males in that age group. Looking at the number of black men and teenagers in that age group who died in 2015 of any cause, the *Guardian* concluded that "about one in every 65 deaths of a young African American man in the US was a killing by police."[37]

We don't solve policing problems by pretending that only people of color are targets. The invisibility of white victims might make it harder for some members of the public to care about police violence; they are not practicing empathy that would allow them to see these confrontations from the point of view of the victims or their families. Should parents give their white children "the talk"? Everyone has lost the right to walk away from police during consent stops and everyone who runs is at risk.

If a right exists only in a Supreme Court opinion, is it really a right at all? According to the law books, we are free to walk away from police who don't tell us to stop, but don't try this out; don't try it, ever.

Feminists saw how the courts' hands-off approach to domestic abuse enabled violent men to control women, and there's a parallel for policing. The Supreme Court invests in a view of police–civilian encounters that ignores the mounting proof of excessive force, brutality, and killings in order to maintain a system where police can stop people without one iota of justification, call it a "mere contact," and then blame the victim for leaving too quickly or for staying.

It's time for courts to evolve their thinking about the reasonable person in the Fourth Amendment context as they did for reasonable DV victims. When police seek cooperation, people should be afraid. There is no freedom to leave. You may or may not be stopped by an officer in your lifetime, but, either way, those rights are supposed to form a protective shield for all Americans. It's time to free ourselves from the double-bind.

3

Consenting to Searches: What We Can Learn from Feminist Critiques of Sexual Assault Laws

The problem ... is that a man can force a woman to engage in sex against her will without resorting to violence as the law understands it. Power will do.

Real Rape, law professor Susan Estrich's groundbreaking 1987 book on the shortcomings of sexual assault law[1]

Consent is an important concept in rape law, yet most people don't realize that consent also plays a major role in police searches. Just as the last chapter showed how police don't need any reason to stop people on the street when courts label the stops "mere contacts," the consent doctrine creates a constitutional bypass for frisks or full-blown searches. Ordinarily, the Fourth Amendment requires police to have "probable cause" before they may search a person's pockets or their belongings. But police who obtain "consent" need no justification for the search at all. It sounds easy: *just say no.*

Feminists have hurled critiques at sexual assault laws for the past century. There are striking parallels between what's wrong with the laws on consent for sex and what's wrong with the consent to search exception. In both settings consent should be an honest choice, not the mere submission to power. This chapter will unpack the parallels between "consent" for sex and "consent" for searches.

When Lawrence answered a question during my criminal procedure class, I knew I had to interview him for this book.

In 2013, I had an internship with an online radio network. They were having a hip-hop holiday party at the studio in Brooklyn. I had a cup of – literally – water. I was walking with a cup of water. Just walking outside for a minute – had to take a phone call. It was right around Jay Street, by the water. It's a neighborhood that's gentrified until it's not. There were two cars, two officers. They told me to stop. They started to ask me some questions, asked for ID, and asked if they can search me. "Can we search you right quick? We are looking for somebody."

Lawrence was twenty-one. This is not a story about a high school student who needed a *Know Your Rights* training. In addition to his work at the radio station, Lawrence worked for a solo attorney. "It's because of him that I'm here in law school. I had some kind of basic knowledge because I worked for a lawyer." Nevertheless, that day the police ran his identification, patted him down and "searched through my stuff" because he gave them permission. Why didn't he say no?

> At first, I was hesitant, but you know, when two officers walk outside and come around you, you start to think okay, I may not have many options here. [2] They asked me something about a chicken coop robbery. I knew they were joking around because they were laughing in the car as they ran my ID. [The chicken joke] was because I was so scared, I was shaking. I had my hands in the air as soon as they came up to me –I had them up the whole time. They patted my pockets. They went into one jacket pocket. Nothing is there, that's the whole tap, tapping on my stuff. I think they looked in my wallet. The police wrote a summons for "open container violation" even though it was water. The ticket got dismissed even before we went to court.

In only twenty seconds, the officers felt his crotch, putting their hands between his thighs over his jeans. Of course, even as Lawrence consented, he never imagined they would go that far. I asked Lawrence what went through his mind when the police asked to search.

> My mind was completely cluttered. I had no idea what I did. I had no idea how the outcome was going to go. I said go ahead. I was shaking. I'm not going to lie. I was scared. No matter how much education, and no matter how much you know of the law, as a black man you are always going to be scared of law officers. Because you know through experience, through history, you know that anything can set things off the wrong way. Anything.

The law recognizes that Lawrence must submit when the police told him to stop but imagines that he then voluntarily chose to be searched. That's the opposite of how Lawrence experienced his Terry stop.

> I understood the stop because of the red cup even though it was 95% empty and I threw it away before they told me to stop. They must have been watching me. [But] when they asked to search … it felt like they were violating me. It felt like they were taking advantage of me. That's when they crossed a line.

As Lawrence thinks back the "consensual" frisk, one 20-second patdown was traumatic. "If they weren't police officers, somebody definitely would have said it was sexual assault," he agreed. "My experience at work was really never the same after that."

Consent to search serves as an exception to the Fourth Amendment's requirement of probable cause and warrants. Readers and law students may be forgiven for confusing the "free to leave" doctrine (explained in Chapter 2) with "consent to search" because they are similar. Although "free to leave" applies to police stops while the consent doctrine applies to searches (and the Court created two separate tests that law students memorize), both rules take advantage of civilians who don't know their rights or who don't feel safe enough to invoke them. Sometimes these two exceptions to the Fourth Amendment work together, as they did in a case my student handled in the DC Superior Court, which fleshes out how both issues might arise during the course of a motion to suppress evidence.

COURTS CONFUSE SUBMISSION WITH CONSENT

Several years ago I supervised Brad, a white law student in the Howard University Criminal Justice Clinic.[3]

Brad met his client for the first time in a holding cell where the defendant, Gerome Thompson (a pseudonym), was milling around with fifty or so other men, almost all of them black. After calling out his client's name, Brad had introduced himself and promised to try to convince the judge to let Mr. Thompson go. This was an older client – in his fifties, with prior drug arrests – who faced a new charge of possession of heroin. Brad was relieved when his client was friendly and content to let a law student represent him. The government did not seek to keep Mr. Thompson locked up, so Brad actually had to do very little at the arraignment, but when the two walked out of court together side by side, I am not certain who was more elated.

One week after court, Brad came into my office for a weekly meeting weighed down with files, including this new case. He was self-assured and hardworking, the type of student who was going to succeed at whatever law he decided to practice. After the briefest of hellos, he carefully stacked all his folders on the small round table, sat across from me, and launched into the details. Mr. Thompson's case had him flummoxed.

Mr. Thompson told Brad that police "stopped" him and a friend. Mr. Thompson explained that a cruiser was driving by and when the driver saw him, the cruiser quickly changed direction and drove toward the curb, pulling next to the sidewalk at an angle. Both officers hustled out. The two officers stood directly in front of the two pedestrians, an arm's length away. One officer started questioning Mr. Thompson. It never occurred to Mr. Thompson that he could walk away or refuse to let the officer frisk him. Mr. Thompson had been searched half a dozen times before, and he explained to Brad that he thought saying no would make the officer angry. So when they asked to him to stand a certain way for a search, he said "okay." Defense attorneys have often heard that police get angry when they are stuck by a needle, so woe to the man or woman who doesn't tell them about where to find "the works" before officers discover it. Mr. Thompson also possessed "drug paraphernalia," but fortunately, the government never added that charge. Based on Mr. Thompson's past experiences, our client felt sure the officers would search him no matter what he said.

Mr. Thompson demonstrated precisely how he stood when the officer told him to put his hands behind his head, fingers interlaced, legs three feet apart. This fact ended up being important to the outcome of the case during the hearing when the officer conceded that he conducted the search just as our client had described it to us. (This didn't sound like a consensual experience to us and it turned out that this didn't sound consensual to the judge, either, although the Supreme Court said that merely lifting your arms for a frisk when asked can prove consent).[4] Our client showed us how "the cop put his hands on my shoulders" patting him on the outside of his clothing and then began moving his hands down his body, "down to my socks." Our client told the arresting officer about the drugs and where to find them.

Mr. Thompson's friend was also frisked by a second officer, but that officer let him go after coming up empty-handed in his search. Our client was arrested for possession of heroin, a misdemeanor that carried 180 days in jail.

Remember the riddle in Chapter 2, when is a stop not a stop? The report did not even use the word "stop." Instead, the officer wrote that "Mr. Thompson and an individual were walking in a high-crime neighborhood in Washington D.C. when officers made contact with them." DC police use the term "contact" to signify consent stops, so the report implied that someone in Mr. Thompson's situation would have felt free to walk away. The police report gave no reason for the officers to suspect criminal wrongdoing. That meant that the government would probably argue that both the stop and the search were consensual affairs.

Notice how smoothly the free to leave doctrine flows into the consent to search doctrine. The two doctrines don't need to go together, but, when they do, police don't need a shred of evidence to justify the stop and search. It's enough that the two men looked like they could use a hot shower and didn't say no to the officer.

To decide cases, judges listen to live testimony; they don't read police reports. Still, reports are good indicators of how officers will testify. As Brad predicted, at the hearing the prosecutor tried to convince a judge that the whole encounter was a voluntary consensual affair, from the confrontation on the sidewalk to the search of our client's body.

Motions to suppress, routinely submitted by defense attorneys, seek to keep out evidence from the trial by alleging that the police violated the defendant's constitutional rights. If Brad successfully showed that the police should not have stopped our client in the first place or should not have searched him, then the judge would keep out the evidence the police found. In other words, if Brad could show that the police violated Mr. Thompson's constitutional rights, it would spell the end of the government's prosecution. Gerome Thompson, a long-time heroin user whom Brad quite liked, would be a free man. But if we lost the motion, Gerome Thompson would serve time behind bars because he stayed to talk to the officers instead of walking away or because our client "consented" to a search. Brad couldn't see how locking up a person with an addiction helped anyone. It would just make it less likely that Mr. Thompson would be able to address the underlying issues that made him numb his pain in a way that cost him jobs and family. "Professor Ross, I am trying to write a motion to suppress for Mr. Thompson, but I don't see how I can win."

I'll reveal how things turned out for Mr. Thompson later in this chapter. Initially, Brad was pessimistic about his chance of winning because the law went against us. It's obvious that Mr. Thompson did not want to stop walking and that he did not want the officer to search him. But that didn't matter much under the Supreme Court case law, as we will see in the next section.

BAD CASE LAW: THE CONSENSUAL STRIP SEARCH

No one wants to be stopped by Drug Enforcement agents (DEA), and most of us cannot even imagine getting strip searched, but what could Sylvia Mendenhall do? In 1976 she was 22 years old, flying from Los Angeles and changing planes in Detroit. After the passengers fanned out onto the concourse toward bathrooms, baggage claim, and the sad airport shops that predated Starbucks, two burly agents blocked her path. Flashing a badge, one of them said something like "Let's see your ticket and identification," and Ms. Mendenhall dutifully handed him both.[5]

Supreme Court Justice Potter Stewart described the power differential plainly in his 1980 opinion: Sylvia Mendenhall was "22 years old, had not been graduated from high school, and was a Negro accosted by white officers."

"Come with us," the agent said, handing back her ticket and driver's license, and taking Ms. Mendenhall to an isolated room off the concourse known only to drug agents and people who fit their profiles. Soon, a female police officer came and led Ms. Mendenhall into an even smaller room and asked her to take off her clothes.[6]

According to the police, Ms. Mendenhall fit one of their drug courier profiles. This time, racial profiling worked and the police hit gold. When the female officer asked Sylvia Mendenhall to disrobe, she complied, taking off her blouse, brassiere, skirt, pantyhose, slip, and panties as directed. Thanks to the strip search, the officer emerged triumphant, carrying two small packages of heroin. Sylvia's lawyer moved to prevent the prosecution from introducing the drugs at trial because the DEA agents did not have a good enough reason to stop her or to search her.

The case went all the way to the Supreme Court, where Sylvia lost. The Court (ignoring the racial implications of drug profiles) agreed with the prosecutor that the police had reasonable suspicion, based on a drug profile. The Terry stop was valid. As for the search, police didn't need a good reason, the prosecutor argued, because Ms. Mendenhall consented to take off her clothing. Again, a majority of the justices agreed.

The justices who called the strip search "consensual" finessed some key facts. During the hearing, the female officer admitted: "She kept saying she had a flight to catch," even though she began to undress under the officer's directions.[7] That sounds like a 22-year-old's timid request to please let her go. But the trial judge chose his own interpretation that most of the Supreme Court justices adopted. Sylvia's words were "simply an expression of concern that the search be conducted quickly," and they did not indicate any resistance to the search.[8] In other words, if Sylvia had wanted to leave, she would have said something like "No way!" or "Get your hands off my body!"

You don't have to be a feminist to think that women don't want to be strip searched. You don't have to be a feminist to think there's something seriously wrong with case law that claims that a woman consents when she takes off her clothing because a police officer tells her to. Nevertheless, feminism helps us understand what's wrong with cases like *United States* v. *Sylvia Mendenhall.*

APPLYING FEMINIST CRITIQUES TO FOURTH AMENDMENT CONSENT

Feminism has a great deal to say about consent, although, before now, these critiques focused on consent for sex. The consent to search doctrine bears striking similarities to the way common law twisted the notion of consent to make it exceedingly difficult for victims of sexual assault to prove they did not consent to sex. Both use the word "consent," but the similarities go far beyond word choice. Broadly put, feminists have argued for over a century that rape laws should protect female autonomy and self-determination, not men's right of access. This is the same overall problem with consent to search rules.

"One of feminism's most dramatic contributions to legal culture has been expanding society's perception of what constitutes rape," writes law professor Dorothy Roberts.

Rape laws vary state to state, and I use the past tense for traditional common law because every state reformed their codes to some degree in response to feminist critiques.[9] Nevertheless, despite the reforms, vestiges of the common law requirements described here remain on the books or in practice in some jurisdictions. Under common law rape, proving that a woman didn't want to have sex was not enough to prove rape. The law required force, and courts interpreted that to mean that a man must overpower a woman or threaten her with death or physical injury. If a woman submitted to more subtle coercion, the law would view her submission as consent. In addition, common law courts required rape victims to resist unwelcome advances "to the utmost." This resistance requirement put victims in danger of physical retaliation by the aggressors. Victims had to choose between giving up their ability to prove rape and their safety.

There's recent disagreement, especially in college campuses, over whether consent should always be explicit and whether the party that initiates sexual activity can rely on nonverbal or ambiguous communication. Despite continuing debate at the margins, feminists fundamentally agree that consent should be a subjective question that asks simply whether a person was a willing partner or not.[10]

There are four areas where Fourth Amendment consent echoes the way courts traditionally burdened women who claimed they did not consent to sex.

1. Consent to search case law requires extra police coercion, mimicking the force requirement in common law rape.
2. Consent to search case law requires resistance. Civilians who are too timid to tell the officer they don't want to be searched "cannot later complain" that they didn't want the officer to search them, mimicking common law rape's requirement that victims resist even when they feared it was dangerous to do so.
3. Consent to search case law treats people who possess contraband as unworthy of constitutional protection, mimicking common law rape's determination that people with bad reputations were incapable of refusing consent. This might also be called a credibility problem for victims.
4. Consent to search case law blames the victims of unconstitutional searches for their own predicament.

Each of these parallels will be explored in turn.

THE FORCE REQUIREMENT

Everyone agrees that it's not consent for sex when a woman says yes to a stranger who jumps out of the bushes with a weapon. Feminists criticized traditional rape laws because they only recognized obvious forms of force and ignored subtle forms of coercion. "Imagine a continuum that ranged from a mutually consensual sexual act, to one in which a man persuaded an ... unwilling woman to engage in sex through verbal coercion ... to a purely physical coercion (or conquest) despite verbal resistance, to a violently aggressive sexual assault."[11] In the nineteenth century, only the last category would be viewed as nonconsensual. Feminists draw the line between consent and coercion at a different place along this continuum than traditional rape law.

Rape statutes required prosecutors to prove force or threat of force. Law professor Catharine MacKinnon argued that even if one accepts that force is an element of rape, courts created a higher burden for rape victims than for robbery victims. When a person jumps on another person and takes her wallet, that's robbery even though the aggressor has used no more force than is necessary to accomplish the act. Yet, to prove sexual assault, the law demands additional force beyond what's needed to accomplish a nonconsensual sex act, MacKinnon complained.[12] The additional force altered the question from whether a woman wanted to have sex (a subjective inquiry) into the objective question of how much coercion was used to overcome her will. The way courts interpreted force requirements enabled male access to women's bodies.

Similarly, in consent to search cases, the Supreme Court decided to focus on the amount of coercion or force used by police instead of asking whether police conducted a search against the person's will. Five years after *Terry* v. *Ohio* was decided, the Supreme Court delineated the consent exception in *Schneckloth* v. *Bustamonte*.[13] The officer in *Schneckloth* pulled a car over in a traffic stop after midnight, called for backup, and ordered everyone out of the car. After Joe Alcala, a passenger, explained that he borrowed the car from his brother, the officer asked if he could search the car and was told to "go ahead." When the officer then asked whether the trunk opened, Mr. Alcala helpfully opened the trunk with his key. Police found three stolen checks in the trunk and charged Robert Bustamonte, a front seat passenger, with possessing them. The trial judge refused to suppress the evidence because Mr. Alcala "voluntarily consented" to the search, and the Supreme Court agreed. It didn't matter that the police lacked probable cause for the search. It didn't matter that Mr. Alcala was detained at the time he gave the go-ahead. It didn't matter to the Court that the police officer never told the civilian he could refuse consent.

What mattered to the Supreme Court was that it "was all very congenial at this time."[14] Prior to the "consent," the Court noted, "no one was threatened with arrest." Congenial is a good word to describe tea with a favorite aunt, but it hardly describes an encounter with police officers on the edge of a dark highway who want to look through your possessions as you wonder if you will drive away in your own car or in the back of a cruiser.

What the Court described as "congenial" turned on the officer's phrasing and tone of voice. Had the police officer threatened arrest or pointed his gun at the civilian while asking if he had the keys, the cooperation would be involuntary. Or, if police "ordered" the civilian to hand over his keys, courts would acknowledge that his cooperation was "no more than acquiescence to a claim of lawful authority."[15] This is semantics. Everyone knows police have the power to arrest us; we don't have to be told. The Supreme Court's *Schneckloth* decision created a roadmap for police to search people without cause. Now police could simply turn their orders into requests. Instead of telling people to turn out their pockets during a stop, police might rephrase the order: "Do you mind turning out your pockets so I can see if you have drugs or weapons on you?" Or police can simply attest to that phrasing.

I interpret *Schneckloth*'s focus on congeniality as creating a de facto force requirement. Unless consent was "the product of duress or coercion, express or implied," the Court explained, judges should not suppress evidence. When law enforcement don't use actual force or threat of force, the Court will presume consent from mere cooperation. In reality, powerful people, including police officers, often accomplish their goals without threats or violence. By analogy, a teacher who asks his student for sex might not openly threaten a bad grade, but that doesn't make the threat disappear. In *Schneckloth*, by refusing to recognize that the threat of arrest exists even where police officers act "congenially," the Court overlooks gaping power differentials between civilians and police officers.

Just as feminists argued that whatever force it takes to pressure a woman to have sex against her will should suffice (to prove rape), so the consent to search doctrine should not assume consent unless civilians prove police coercion beyond their monopoly on state violence and power to arrest. In a sense, everyone has some ability to choose, even a person with a gun pointed at them. Even now, we allow men to cajole, badger, trick, and pressure women into "consent" for sex. But why import that into the Fourth Amendment? Looking at the police officers' methods of persuasion misses the point. The consent to search doctrine should not ask whether police used reasonable methods to coerce consent. Instead, the question of consent should remain with the Sylvia Mendenhalls and Gerome Thompsons of this nation: Did they actually want to give up their rights?

THE RESISTANCE REQUIREMENT

Resistance is an important concept in the laws of sexual assault. You didn't run away or scratch him? That means you probably wanted it. If you really did not want sex, the reasoning goes, you would resist the other's advances. People who resist rape place themselves in danger of retaliation. That's why judges demanded that women show bruises or other injuries to prove resistance. Bruises helped to prove that a woman resisted a man's advances to the point where he retaliated, using physical force to hurt her. Although resistance was never specifically an element of the offense of rape, courts used a woman's resistance to measure the quantity of force used against her.

Essentially, resistance formed an extra element to establish nonconsent within traditional rape law. If a woman didn't resist, the government could only establish rape by proving that the aggressor drew a weapon or uttered threats.

Although the Court never explicitly says that people must fight off police officers who try to take advantage of them, there's an unspoken resistance requirement akin to traditional rape law. Remember that Justice Potter Stewart rejects Sylvia Mendenhall's argument that "she did in fact *resist* the search" when she told the police officer that "she had a plane to catch?" The *Mendenhall* dissenters wrote that the Court was wrong to conclude that she voluntarily consented "based on the absence of evidence that Ms. Mendenhall *resisted* her detention."[16] The justices knew that Sylvia Mendenhall didn't want to take off her clothes, but she failed to resist in a way that a majority of justices were willing to recognize. In this way, the Supreme Court created a Fourth Amendment resistance requirement for consent searches.

In rape law the force and resistance requirements enabled privileged men to seek sex aggressively, since most victims were not able to meet this high bar of proving nonconsent. Similarly, consent to search rules privilege police access to people like Sylvia Mendenhall or our client Gerome Thompson. Rather than ask what Sylvia Mendenhall or Gerome Thompson wanted, the Supreme Court frames their cooperation with authority as consent.

Why should Ms. Mendenhall, Mr. Thompson, and my law student Lawrence even have to say "no"? Most of us submit to airport patdowns because they are mandatory if we want to board our flight. Common sense informs us that unless it's mandatory, civilians won't want officers feeling the contours of their body or looking inside their undergarments. Consent makes sense when separating out wanted sexual trysts from assaults, but not within search and seizure rules. After all, lots of people want to have sex, but who wants officers lacking constitutional justification to search their property or bodies? No one. Anyone would say "get a warrant" if they believed the police wouldn't retaliate.

Requiring civilians to say "no" to a police officer puts the burden on the victim rather than the aggressor. If the Constitution forbids officers from searching because they lack a good reason (other than supposed consent), they shouldn't search. Consent should no longer excuse unwanted aggression.

It's often the complete capitulation to authority that produces the congenial effect. If a victim of a police stop argues or resists in any way, the atmosphere will not be congenial. Just as the resistance and force requirements mutually reinforce each other within traditional rape cases to support findings of consent, so do resistance and coercion work together within current consent to search rules to find searches are consensual.

"That some men rape provides a sufficient threat to keep all woman in a constant state of intimidation," Susan Brownmiller explained. Similarly, Andrea Dworkin wrote: "By the time we are women, fear is as familiar to us air; it is our element."[7] Catharine MacKinnon noted that it is hard to resist a seducer without risking behaving in an unladylike manner. "Women are socialized to passive receptivity" and to "perceive no alternative to acquiescence."[8] A similar problem befalls men, women, and youth when police seek consent. That some officers use brutality provides a sufficient threat to keep all civilians in some neighborhoods in a constant state of fear. Civilians must try to resist every request without annoying officers. Exercising one's constitutional right to say no to searches where police lack probable cause can be as dangerous as exercising one's freedom to walk away from the police. Of course, the Supreme Court does not really want civilians to resist the police. The ideal search subject would graciously consent to anything the officer wants, thereby vanquishing any Fourth Amendment checks on police power.

One reason I teach teenagers to memorize the phrase "With all due respect, Officer, I never consent to searches" is because cases like *Mendenhall* and *Schneckloth* turn on semantics. There's both the phrasing of the request to search by the officer to distinguish it from an order to search (the force requirement) and the phrasing of the civilian's response (the resistance requirement).

There's a game I played as a child where I stood in a row with three or four other kids facing an older child, a leader. We all hoped to get close enough to tag the leader while she was not looking. The kids took turns. When it was my friend Daniel's turn, he asked, "May I take one giant step forward?" The leader would usually reply "yes." Nevertheless, Daniel must respond, "Mother, may I?" If Daniel took a step without the words "Mother, may I," he must return to the starting line.

This game reminds me of the Supreme Court rulings on consent that place great emphasis on how officers phrase their requests and on how civilians register their resistance. Police can advance to the finish line and score drugs from clients legally if they follow the script in the Supreme Court's consent game. Civilians need to fine-tune their hearing to distinguish requests from orders. Civilians also need to follow a script because of their one-down position vis-à-vis the officer. If the civilian forgets the magic words (which are "must I?"), their punishment is more severe than in the child's game. Use the wrong language and you forfeit your constitutional rights.

Sylvia Mendenhall's protest was indirect. Linguistics equate this type of speech with "women's language," namely speech patterns that indicate a lack of confidence. Feminist researchers have pointed out how power imbalance infiltrates language. "Women's language developed as a way of surviving," adopting a "female register" to "soften the presumptiveness of a direct statement" when communicating with those with more power. In contrast, "men's language . . . is meant to be direct, clear, succinct, as would be expected of those who need not fear giving offense."[19] The "greater the imbalance of power in the communicative relationship, the more likely the powerless speaker is to use features associated with the female register."[20] Courts are more likely to fail to recognize resistance from speech that is stereotypically "women's language."

Interrogation presents a tremendous power imbalance between officer and civilian. While women and girls may be at a particular disadvantage, all civilians face the "female language problem" when they are questioned by an authority figure with a badge. As law professor Janet Ainsworth pointed out, the power asymmetry between officer and civilian creates the milieu for indirect or "female" modes of communication. Then the Supreme Court exploits the power asymmetry between interrogator and civilian by refusing to recognize that a person has exercised her rights because she stayed quiet or used other "female" methods of communication.

On the other hand, the Supreme Court justices may not be responding to Ms. Mendenhall's speech patterns at all, but to her status as a woman or criminal defendant. After examining three decades of oral arguments, political scientists at the University of Alabama found that, overall, the justices interrupt female advocates sooner than male lawyers and give them less time to speak.[21] Female staffers during the Obama presidency found that other aides ignored their comments or coopted them, so they strategized. "When a woman made a key point, other women would repeat it, giving credit to its author. This forced the men in the room to recognize the contribution – and denied them the chance to claim the idea as their own."[22] This "amplification" worked, showing it's not the how but the who. This perspective also fits well with how most of the Supreme Court justices hear Sylvia Mendenhall's protest; the Court claims that it's how she speaks that's ambiguous, but, in reality, they ignore her because of who she is, namely someone guilty of smuggling drugs.

"BAD" WOMEN AND "GUILTY" SUSPECTS

Early in our country's founding, sexual assault described a crime against a husband or parent rather than the actual victim, because sexual violence damages a man's property. Even as the law evolved to imagine that the person assaulted was the victim, black women, whether enslaved or free, and women with "bad reputations" were treated differently than chaste white women. As Professor MacKinnon phrased it, "bad girls" are "unrapable" because juries will presume they consented.[23] That makes certain women (the "bad girls") fair game for men in the mood for a frolic. Even today, sex workers often face an uphill battle in convincing juries that they have the right to withhold consent.

All rape victims were presumed to be guilty until they proved otherwise, theorized law professor Anne Coughlin to explain the origins of the resistance requirement. Sex out of wedlock was illegal, so those who alleged rape themselves became suspects. Although out-of-wedlock sex was illegal for both men and women, the law treated women as more blameworthy; they were the more guilty party unless they convinced judges that they fully resisted. This explains why traditional rape law required all rape victims to show they resisted to the utmost, and also prove that the aggressor used force or threatened to use force. Consent was intentionally compli-cated so that women presumed to be "guilty" of sexual intercourse would not succeed in their claims.[24]

Thanks to the double standards of gender and race, white men who were suspected of fornication (sex outside wedlock) did not receive the same hostile treatment as their female sexual partners. They could still be viewed as innocent. "The law of rape divides the world of women into spheres of consent according to how much say we are legally presumed to have over sexual access to us by various categories of men."[25] When courts decide whether what happened "counts as a violation," explains Dorothy Roberts, the answer turns on hierarchies "based on race and class, as well as gender."[26]

We can also trace the deficits in Fourth Amendment consent rules to a similar fear of benefiting the guilty. People who bring motions to suppress are viewed as "guilty" in the eyes of many Supreme Court justices. That's logical, I suppose, because everyone who brings a motion to suppress has been charged with a crime and now asks the court to disregard evidence that will help the government prove their guilt. Under consent to search rules, the Court privileges police power over people like Sylvia Mendenhall or our client Gerome Thompson. Sylvia Menden-hall sought to keep the jury from learning about the drugs that she was smuggling.

Robert Bustamonte tried to keep out bad checks that the police found. Gerome Thompson had heroin in his pocket.

In contrast to the guilty civilians, the Supreme Court often views police officers as making innocent mistakes when they violate constitutional limits.[27] That's because the majority of justices on the Supreme Court view the mission to hunt down wrongdoers as more important than obeying constitutional limits. Except when behavior is egregious, most Court opinions characterize officers who violate the Constitution as good-faith actors. Even the DOJ reports that illuminated rampant disregard for the Constitution failed to move the conservative majority on the Supreme Court to see Fourth Amendment violations as a serious problem. In their view, police are less guilty than the individuals they arrest because they violate the law in order to keep society safe.

Let's not forget that the consent rules grant police free access to innocent people as well as guilty ones. But the innocent victims such as my student Lawrence don't come to court moving to exclude drugs found on them during an unconstitutional search. The innocent have no drugs to suppress.

The Supreme Court opinions don't explicitly say that guilty people are incapable of withholding consent, but they come close.

RIDDLE: What's the opposite of a subjective definition of consent?
ANSWER: The "reasonable innocent person" test.

Here's the Court's dilemma: someone like Sylvia Mendenhall would never consent unless police made her believe that resistance was useless. As another writer phrased it: "How much of an idiot – how stupid, moronic, imbecilic – would a person carrying a gram of crack cocaine stashed in her underwear, for example, have to be, to really consent – 'freely and voluntarily' – to being searched by a police officer?"[28] If the Court acknowledged that people would never voluntarily consent to a search where they had hidden drugs, that would undercut the whole purpose of the consent doctrine, which is to provide police an easy avenue to justify seizing evidence from the guilty. To prevent virtually all criminal defendants from defeating the government's claim of consent, the Court created a "reasonable innocent person" test in the context of consent stops. The Court now asks whether this imaginary person would feel free to decline an officer's requests.[29]

This mythical innocent person, the Supreme Court fleshed out in a later case, would be motivated by a desire to help the police protect safety and would therefore freely and voluntarily give up any right to privacy he or she possesses. I'm not kidding. Here's Supreme Court Justice Sandra Day O'Connor explaining why every bus passenger submitted to Tallahassee Police Department investigators who boarded the bus and sought "cooperation" to search everyone's bags: Bus "passengers answer officers' questions and otherwise cooperate not because of coercion but because the passengers know that their participation enhances their own safety and the safety of those around them."[30]

Under the innocent person standard, judges should not ask whether someone like our client, who has drugs in his pocket, would consent without coercion, because obviously Mr. Thompson would only consent if he felt he must. Instead, judges are directed to ask whether an imaginary innocent person in Mr. Thompson's position would consent. This goes beyond what I call the force and resistance requirements that the Court implicitly built into the reasonable person standard of consent. Already, the force and resistance requirements turn a subjective question of what a person wanted into an objective question for both rape law and Fourth Amendment consent. Instead of "what did he want?," the question becomes "how much coercion did the police apply, and did he resist as much as we expect a man to resist who truly did not want to be searched"? That's like a rape case where the judge says that the rape victim did not resist, did not say 'no' – when the alleged wrong-doer was standing over her with a holstered gun with his partner just a few feet away – so we can only infer that she, in fact, consented." Feminists have long opposed that type of reasoning.

The imaginary "reasonable innocent person" test is even worse than the Court's former "reasonable person" test because the archetype excludes the very people whose consent is at issue.[31] It creates a fictitious person who is motivated to help a police officer punish the guilty – in other words, this reasonable person would want to punish himself. This is the opposite of a subjective test that values the autonomy of the individual. The subjective experiences of guilty men and women are of no value to the law.

Imagine the outcry today if a judge illegally imported the "reasonable innocent person" test from search law into rape law, and ruled: "The alleged rape victim did not want to have sexual contact, but this Court concludes that she consented as a matter of law because a 'reasonable woman' would have wanted to engage in sex with this man."

I contend that a similar outcry should be heard today when people learn that courts apply this test to consent searches.

THE "CONGENIALITY" TEST DRAMATIZED

Back at Howard law school, Brad prepared for a hearing on his motion to suppress. My law student was correct that the case law appeared to doom his chances of winning his motion to suppress, even though Gerome Thompson was only submitting to authority, not freely choosing his fate. The free to leave doctrine favored the government. The officer who stopped our client never used the word "stop" or "halt" or other words that courts recognize as an "order." The officers did not scream or touch our client to prevent him from walking away; instead they stood in front of him and his friend, and started asking questions. According to the case law, it was our client's own fault for stopping to answer the officer's questions.

For the search, our facts were worse than that of the *Mendenhall* case. Unlike Sylvia Mendenhall, Gerome Thompson put his hands behind his head for a frisk or search without protest, not even a mild protest about being late to meet a friend. Unlike Sylvia, who was in a small office with four officers, our client was on the street, where police coercion is less of a problem according to Supreme Court pronouncements. Unlike Sylvia, who appears to have no criminal record, our client had been stopped numerous times, so judges are more likely to imagine he knew his rights. Sure, Brad might convince the trial judge that Mr. Thompson thought he had no choice. However, Sylvia Mendenhall clearly thought she had no choice and it appears that the authorities would have searched her whether she demurred or not. Things turned out well for Mr. Thompson in the end, but that was an anomaly. Mr. Thompson should have lost, given that the Supreme Court decided Sylvia Mendenhall consented as a matter of law.

Brad and I planned to use social science literature to show that, in reality, even stops that appear congenial on the surface feel coercive to the men and women who are stopped. Brad sought to convince a judge that the request to frisk would sound like a demand to a reasonable civilian in Gerome Thompson's place. This was vital because the officer claimed he "asked" to search our client rather than "ordering" him to submit. And the officer never threatened to arrest him if he didn't consent. Despite the case law that grafted force and resistance requirements onto consent to search cases, we would try to convince a judge that Mr. Thompson was just submitting to authority when he said yes.

Reality check: If a police officer asked me "did I mind" giving him my license during a stop, I would view the request as polite, but still an "order," a congenially phrased order. I would not think I had the right to refuse. As it turns out, most people hear requests as orders when they come from a person of authority. Employees do not distinguish between a boss informing them "don't be late again" or using the softer approach: "can you try not to be late again?"[32]

Days before the hearing on Brad's motion, I decided to stage a live demonstration of the social science hypothesis that Brad was about to argue in court.

> I asked Brad if he would like to redo the cross-examination of the officer and give it to me later that day. His face fell; he looked devastated. Feigning surprise, I asked: "Did you interpret my request as an order?" and explained that I was just demonstrating a point he made in his brief that people hear requests as orders when they come from someone in a position of power. "Now that my heart stopped pounding," my law student replied, "I would have to agree that your experiment worked."

I wish judges would agree to undergo similar experiments, but they would have to be in situations where they had significantly less power than another human being.

Trials and hearings have a life of their own and one never quite knows how things will come out. Fortunately for Mr. Thompson, the officer remembered very little about the encounter other than the four lines written in the police report. He did not even recognize the Google map of the location where the men were stopped. But he did remember that the encounter was congenial.

During the motion to suppress in Brad's case, the prosecutor questioned the officer using what have become stock phrases within DC motion hearings:

Prosecutor: When you asked Mr. Thompson if he had drugs, how far away were you?
PO: An arm's distance away.
Prosecutor: Did you pull your gun?
PO: No. I kept it holstered.
Prosecutor: Describe the tone of voice you used when you spoke to Mr. Thompson.
PO: Real conversational, just like I am talking to you today.

The purpose of this interchange was to show the officer was not unduly coercive in obtaining Mr. Thompson's cooperation. Litanies of this sort have become common when the prosecution seeks to demonstrate a consensual encounter or consensual search. This attention to mostly irrelevant detail gives these hearings what Justice David Souter called "an air of unreality," and reminds the trial judge that the case law is almost uniformly against any defendant who argues that he was only acquiescing to authority, not voluntarily consenting.[33]

Brad's cross-examination brought out conflicting accounts of why the officer searched his client. On direct examination, the police officer testified that he had asked Mr. Thomson whether he would agree to a search and our client had said "okay." Oddly, during cross-examination, the officer testified that our client told him he had drugs on him before the officer asked for consent. This would give an officer probable cause to search and the officer wouldn't need consent. Then there was another bit of testimony that probably influenced the judge's perception of the encounter. During cross-examination, the officer agreed that before he searched Mr. Thompson, he told him to interlock his fingers behind his head and stand with his feet a couple of feet apart. This position hardly conforms to the notion of a consensual search.

We lost the "free to leave" argument. Apparently, a reasonable person in Mr. Thompson's position would feel at liberty to ignore the police and continue on his way. Since officers did not completely block the sidewalk, the judge ruled, our client could have walked around them as they stood directly in front of him and his friend to ask questions. By deciding the stop was merely a consensual encounter where police need no justification, the judge followed the law laid down by the Supreme Court.

Next, the judge ruled on the search. Had the judge concluded that our client consented to a search, the police would need no justification for either the stop or search. Mr. Thompson would lose his motion and face a trial he was bound to lose. Alternatively, had the judge concluded that our client told the officer he carried drugs, that would have provided the probable cause necessary for a search. Instead, the judge ruled that the government did not meet its burden of proof to justify the search. The judge explained that because the officer offered conflicting testimony about why the search was conducted, it appeared that the officer could not remember why he had searched Mr. Thompson. Therefore, the government proved neither avenue to the court's satisfaction.

Mr. Thompson walked out of court a free man. He just got lucky. Consent law is stacked against people like him.

BLAMING THE VICTIM

Historically, most rape victims were blamed for what happened to them. Women were blamed for wearing the wrong clothing, walking in the wrong place and for not fighting back against aggressors. Arguably, the blame game still survives. Blaming the victim helps perpetuate a system that advantages the powerful. As Professor Estrich explained, rape law blamed the victim by changing the question from what the woman wanted (a subjective question) to an objective test that measured the quantity of force used against her and the quantity of her resistance. "Because the will of a reasonable woman by definition would not have been overcome, a particular woman's submission can only mean that she is sub-par as women go."[34]

The Fourth Amendment effectively does the same thing, first blaming civilians for attracting the attention of police and then blaming them for submitting to police.

Why were you in that neighborhood at that time? Why were you wearing that outfit? That's what rape victims are often asked, suggesting they are responsible for the unwanted attention. Similarly, to justify Terry stops, the law blames civilians for walking in a "high-crime neighborhood" even when that's where they live. Young men wearing hoodies and baggie pants – what NYPD check off as "Wearing Clothes Commonly Used in Commission of Crime" – invite the unwanted police attention for how they dress.[35] For transgender stops, women are blamed for wearing high heels that police connect to prostitution. If the stop is flimsy, it doesn't matter, because civilians can also be blamed for cooperating.

Why didn't you run away? Why didn't you fight back? Unfortunately, even today, too many sexual assault survivors are asked these accusatory questions. Just as rape victims have been told they "asked for it" by not running or fighting back, stop-and-frisk victims are often told they asked for it by submissively extending their arms to be searched. They are told it is their fault that the police touched their thighs or looked in their pockets. They are told that they should have resisted the police incursion, even if resistance risked triggering further charges or unpleasant responses from the police. One might say that the law punished Sylvia Mendenhall for giving in too easily. The Court intentionally sets up consent law to ensure broad police access to suspects and then blames those suspects when they allow access to their bodies and property.

In Mr. Thompson's case, the law forced us to ask our client why he didn't walk away and why he submitted to the police. Had Brad lost his motion, the judge would essentially be telling our client that it was his fault for not walking away and for letting the officer search him. The law would be telling our client: "you wouldn't be serving time in a cage if you had resisted; you brought this fate onto yourself; you have only yourself to blame."

PRETENDING THAT CONSENT BESTOWS DIGNITY

The Supreme Court likes to pretend that consent fosters self-determination. As Justice Anthony Kennedy once phrased it when sanctioning a patdown where police lacked reasonable suspicion: "In a society based on law, the concept of agreement and consent should be given a weight and dignity of its own."[36] This is a fig leaf.

The Supreme Court did not fashion the consent exception with the aim of self-determination, but its opposite. In 1973, the Court was more forthright when it justified a broad consent exception because requiring probable cause for all searches would lead to the loss of good evidence. A consent search "may be the only means of obtaining important and reliable evidence."[37] In other words, that pesky Fourth Amendment that limits police power gets in the way of prosecuting criminals. Without a broad exception to the Fourth Amendment's requirement that police possess probable cause before they conduct a search, some criminals will inevitably walk free; some drugs will remain in pockets.

None of the Supreme Court justices could truly believe that Sylvia Mendenhall wanted to be searched or even that she had a choice to stay or leave. What's really going on in the *Mendenhall* case is that most of the Supreme Court justices do not want to suppress the drugs found during the search where police lacked probable cause. That's why the Court pretends that there is nothing coercive about three male police officers taking a woman to an isolated room and telling her they want her to wait for a female agent to conduct a strip search.

Since the *Mendenhall* case was decided in 1980, the antipathy by conservative Supreme Court justices has grown to the point where the Court is likely to overturn the "exclusionary rule" (the rule that evidence seized in violation of constitutional rights should not be used to convict a person). Without this rule, the prosecutors and courts become complicit in illegal police behavior, like parents who sends their sons into the illegal drug trade so they can pay their rent. When courts introduce tainted evidence into criminal cases, they benefit from ill-gotten gains. Aside from morality, it's a historical fact that the exclusionary rule changed police behavior, curbing the worst abuses as soon as the courts began to enforce it. For example, when the Court applied the exclusionary rule to the states in 1961, departments suddenly trained officers how to apply for search warrants and police stopped breaking into people's homes without them.[38] When the guilty go free, it helps the innocent too.

The Court shouldn't pretend it protected Sylvia Mendenhall's autonomy and self-determination when it allowed the government to prosecute her with the evidence seized from her bra. To support the war on drugs, the Court hides the power imbalance between civilian and officer, and uses that camouflage to increase the power imbalance. Thanks to this Supreme Court decision, police can sometimes conduct strip searches without any proof of wrongdoing. And the Court does this by blaming the victim. After all, she's the one who "voluntarily" took off her clothes.

In thwarting Ms. Mendenhall's true will, the consent doctrine mirrors feminist critiques about common law rape. In *Against Our Will: Men, Women and Rape*, bestselling feminist author Susan Brownmiller envisioned rape as "a female's right to her bodily integrity."[39] In 1975, this idea was radical.

CONSENTING TO SEX WITH POLICE OFFICERS

Consent to search explicitly morphed into consent for sex when two plain-clothed NYPD officers pulled over a car for a traffic violation in 2017, hoping to find evidence of drug violations. The driver was an 18-year-old white woman with a presence on social media, where she blogs under the alias Anna Chambers.[40] The encounter began with police activity that courts often excuse under Fourth Amendment consent rules. The detectives, Edward Martins and Richard Hall, asked the driver to raise her shirt to prove that "she was simply adjusting her nipple piercing" rather hiding drugs, which she did, saying "See, I'm not hiding anything." They searched her car, where they found marijuana in a cup holder, and searched her bag, where they found pills without a prescription. Police then arrested Ms. Chambers, placing her in their van. Had police stopped there, they might have successfully argued consent and it would not have made the national news. Instead, detectives sought to barter their advantage into sexual favors.

According to the young woman's lawyer, the detectives told Ms. Chambers: "This is what you're going to do for us, and we'll let you go."[41] In the van, as requested, Ms. Chambers performed oral sex on both detectives and then Detective Martins had intercourse with her. The detectives then released her without charges. Ms. Chambers reported the assaults and went to the hospital, where staff gathered DNA from her that matched the detectives, and they were later slapped with a fifty-count indictment. Naturally, the accused detectives claimed that they were innocent because the young woman consented to sex.

The public was outraged. Editorials lamented the "nauseating" consent defense. "Claiming to have received consent … betrays a policing culture that refuses to recognize its own outsized power over those it alleges to protect and serve," wrote one columnist. It's "not the absurdity of a teenage girl wanting to leave her friends behind just to go have sex with two police officers," wrote another, "but the fact that a suspect in custody can't have consensual sex."[42] Quite rightly, pundits condemned the officers for raising consent when the young woman was not free to leave. In fact, Ms. Chambers said she was handcuffed at the time she allegedly consented. Politicians recognized the systemic nature of the problem and fixed it legislatively. Governor Andrew Cuomo called the consent defense an "egregious loophole" that had to be closed.[43] The state changed the penal code in 2018 so that "a person under arrest, detention or otherwise in the actual custody of law enforcement" has no capacity to consent to sex. With the new law, New York joined fourteen other states where police can't raise a consent defense when the alleged conduct occurs on duty.[44]

I once offended a liberal law professor by comparing nonconsensual policing to nonconsensual sex, but Anna Chambers provides an opportunity for me to double down. Let's start with understanding of why it's wrong to suggest that Ms. Chambers has the power to withhold consent for sex. Most importantly, police have all the power in this position. Ms. Chambers knows that if she doesn't do what the officers ask, she will be charged with a crime. The power to arrest alone creates an insurmountable power imbalance. Additionally, Ms. Chambers would naturally be aware that police can inflict physical harm, such as tightening her handcuffs; they even carry guns. The power imbalance is so great that the law should presume coercion. Any consent she gives must be viewed as mere submission to authority.

Of course, that same power imbalance came into play the moment detectives started to question Ms. Chambers and her friends as they sat in her car. Police had all the power in that situation, including the power to arrest and the power to allow Ms. Chambers to go on her way. In Ms. Chambers's case, Detectives Martins and Hall promised to drop all charges against her if she cooperated in the sex acts, and the detectives stood by their agreement, even handing her back the "controlled substance" that they seized.[45] Police often tell suspects that things will go better for them if they cooperate, but my clients, at least, still end up facing charges.

Thus, any cooperation or consent Ms. Chambers provided to police in their hunt for drugs must also be viewed as submission to authority. She pulled up her shirt for the same reason Sylvia Mendenhall did, because she was afraid of the consequences of saying no.[46] The power imbalance is so great that the law should also assume that police officers overbore her will when they searched without probable cause.

Today, consent can no longer serve to excuse certain improper police conduct in New York, namely improper sexual conduct. Unfortunately, in all fifty states, consent still serves to excuse other conduct, namely conduct that would otherwise violate the Constitution.

Now to address my law professor friend's objection that consent for sex is different. Detectives Martins and Hall went outside of their job description when they started seeking sexual gratification. In contrast, when police looked for drugs under her shirt or in her bag, they did what we pay them to do. While this distinction is intuitively appealing, it won't hold up under scrutiny. Consent doctrine is systemically wrong, and we lose track of this when we point the finger at bad actors. By distinguishing between good officers who search without probable cause and bad officers who engage in sex, my friend follows the pattern where courts view police officers as innocent when they violate the Constitution, and view as guilty the victims of improper searches when police find drugs and other evidence of criminal activity. But Ms. Chambers was no less guilty than our client Gerome Thompson, and no less guilty than the thief in *Schneckloth* v. *Bustamonte*. In fact, this notion of wrongdoing echoes rape narratives that view only certain women as credible. Lawyers for the charged detectives lost no time harnessing such narratives against Anna Chambers by pointing to "provocative photos" on her social media page as proof, as well as the drugs found on her person to discredit her.[47]

Even from a victim's point of view, my friend assumes that a woman is much more harmed by nonconsensual sex than a nonconsensual search. However, this assumption does not reflect the reality of many people's lives. "Jail inevitably interrupts the ability to take HIV medications on a regular basis," Human Rights Watch pointed out, and really any civilian who needs ongoing treatment or medication for any ailment might fear arrest more than sexual coercion.[48] For some people, the search that lands them in prison feels even more antithetical to their autonomy and self-interest. Several men I've represented expected to be raped repeatedly during their years in prison. We understand why sex workers agree to sex with an officer to avoid arrest. The law should treat any consent to search that damages a woman or man's long-term liberty – and may also involve various kinds of unwanted touching – as involuntary and against their will.

In short, it shouldn't matter legally whether Ms. Chambers said "yes" to sex in a "congenial" atmosphere or whether Ms. Chambers resisted. Similarly, it shouldn't matter legally whether the atmosphere was congenial when Ms. Chambers consented to raise her shirt or allowed police to search her bag. The law should close both "egregious" consent loopholes. The law should not burden the civilian with resisting the sexual or investigative advances of officers who possess all the power in these situations. Even people who think Ms. Chambers should be able to say yes to sex in the back of a police cruiser will see that women's autonomy lands differently when thinking about consent to search. At the very least, there should be a presumption that complying with police requests is nonconsensual and judges should never find consent when a search is clearly against someone's interest, such as when they've hidden contraband on their person and now agree to a search.

This chapter has shown that feminist critiques of consent for sex should be applied to consent to search. Under common law, courts defined consent within rape law to make it easier for men, especially privileged men, to have access to women's bodies. Similarly, the Supreme Court created a consent to search exception that makes it easier for police to gain access to civilian bodies and possessions.

Civilians are expected to resist the police when officers seek to search their bodies or possessions unless officers employ an unusual amount of force and can't describe the atmosphere as "congenial." The way consent works, civilians lose their constitutional rights by cooperating rather than resisting, and then the law blames them for their weakness.

Some states now recognize that it is wrong to allow police to claim consent when they have sex with someone in their custody. It's time to recognize that the consent doctrine within Fourth Amendment law is also a cruel loophole that must be closed.

4

Punishing Disrespect: No Free Speech Allowed Here

Police are very big on respect – when it comes to how people treat them. When it comes to how they treat others, well, not so much. There's a double standard, one that unfortunately remains deeply ingrained in the culture of law enforcement.

Professionals, especially law professors and judges, put too much stock in controlling police behavior through legal rules. Change the law and *voilà*: stop-and-frisk will cease to create a pattern of control and humiliation. Sociologists, however, tell us that police culture trumps legal rules. Or as Vanita Gupta phrased it when she headed the Civil Rights Division at the Department of Justice, "culture eats policy for lunch every time."[1] Assessing the culture will help us unpack the many ways that stop-and-frisk harms our communities. Those on the losing end of stop-and-frisk experience the triumph of engrained police culture over established black letter law. Nowhere is that more apparent than in police attempts to coerce respect.

"CONTEMPT OF COP" TICKETS AND "ATTITUDE ARRESTS"

It's so quiet, it's hard to believe that I am walking into the same DC Superior Court where, on weekdays, my clinical law students at Howard University School of Law represent clients charged with misdemeanor offenses. A few teenagers slouch on benches in the hallways, catching up on sleep, but there are no lawyers and no court officers. Soon there will be twenty to thirty teens checking in with staff, and three or four Howard law students setting up in a courtroom. It's a typical Saturday morning in Youth Court. We keep our *Know Your Rights* training interactive, but my law students perform the first skit, so the actors try to bring enough energy to the scene to wake up the teenagers.

For our first skit today, law students play teenagers who are walking down the street after leaving a party; my law student Mosi cracks us up with her perfect portrayal of the "funny" teenager.

A law student playing a police officer steps imperiously in front of the two "teens" (careful to keep this a "consensual" contact) and barks, "Where are you heading?"

Confident and close to six feet tall, "teen" Mosi appears to enjoy being on stage. She points at the officer and tells him off, starting with, "I know my rights and you're just messing with me."

Her finger is wagging, her head is rolling, her loud voice gaining volume: "I know you didn't see me do anything wrong. You cops are all the same. You gonna plant some evidence? Is that how you do it? That's how you all do it. You're messing with the wrong person." Mosi's increasingly outrageous comments start all of us laughing.

At the end of this *Know Your Rights* skit, the officer arrests Mosi for "disturbing the peace," even though she wasn't guilty of that or any crime. Actually, Mosi's arrest was for "contempt of cop." In the trial courts of Worcester, Massachusetts, we called this an "attitude arrest." Mosi nicknamed it "Know Your Place 101." These are all ways of talking about the same thing – that police officers punish perceived disrespect. My law students write on the board:

- Rule #1: Always be respectful to police.

Teaching young people to say "yes, sir," or "no, officer," in a deferential tone does not sound like teaching a right. In fact, it teaches them how to surrender a right. Paradoxically, while seeking to empower young people, the first lesson at *Know Your Rights* trainings teaches kids to relinquish their fundamental right to free speech.

We don't teach free speech rights to youth because law enforcement officers do not honor these rights on the streets. This is another example of "paper rights"; that is, rights that only exist on the pages of Supreme Court opinions. This lesson that trains youth to give up their free speech rights sadly hints at a core cause of why modern policing is a daily stomp on the Constitution. I'm aware of the irony in selecting "don't dis the police" as Rule #1. Here we are not teaching constitutional law, but its opposite. Even more uncomfortable, the lesson is loaded with racial tensions.

"Why should I respect them if they don't respect me?" asked a talkative kid during a Youth Court training one Saturday. He was sitting in the jury box in Courtroom 111 in the Superior Court of the District of Columbia, swiveling slightly in his chair to see if any of the other teenage "jurors" would back him up. Police had recently arrested this young man for truancy. That's why he was sitting in Youth Court. I loved his question. Indeed, why should this young man show respect when the officer was disrespecting him? Why should he give up his dignity just to make some police officer feel better? Was teaching young people of color to show respect to the men and women in blue perpetuating the modern-day version of "yes, master?" This was the question many of our Youth Court teenagers were thinking about.

Giving voice to the issue handed my students a chance to drive home the point of Rule #1 and explain why we stressed respect and obedience (despite the Supreme Court language to the contrary). As Mosi said that day at Youth Court,

> Out on the street the police officer always wins. He's got the badge; he's got the gun; he's got the power of arrest. Our goal is for you to survive this encounter. We don't want you to get arrested. We don't want you to be searched. We want you to leave as soon as it is safely possible. Live to make a complaint later.

"Live to become a law student like Mosi," I thought to myself. That was a subliminal message of Youth Court. Maybe they would enter my law school classroom in six years or so or at least start to see the benefit of attending college. Mosi's answer also foretold a later lesson on how to file complaints against police who abuse them, and why it was important to know when your rights were violated so you could file a complaint with independent watchdogs.

"Police really do punish you for giving them attitude," Mosi told the Youth Court teenagers, telling them the story of her encounter with a police officer in the Adams Morgan section of DC Seeing a traffic jam ahead of her, and no cars driving the opposite direction, she had "busted a U in the middle of the street, as most sane drivers would have." But she was pulled over. These teenagers don't drive yet, but they all understood the concept of "driving while black."

> When the officer pulled me over, at first I followed the rule book. I freshened my lip gloss, check my mascara (getting eyelashes ready to bat), and cleared my throat to put on my deepest southern Mississippi accent. I also made a mental note to say "sir'"at the end of each answer that I gave to him.

But she got restless as she waited and unleashed her true anger. This was a recent encounter, Mosi's voice sometimes crackled with frustration even as she tried to hold back her emotions.

> I got out of my car and walked to the rear of my car where he was standing and informed him that he was holding me for an unreasonable amount of time, and if I was not in custody he should either ticket me or let me go. . . He took out his black book of police codes and found everything in his power that he could cite me for, which took an additional 30 minutes . . . returned to my car with $745 worth of traffic citations . . . I knew I'd received these tickets not because of my U-turn, but because of my attitude. I tell you this because I don't want it to happen to you.

Mosi was punished for speaking up for herself, for speaking truth to power. My law student's story captures what so many of my students tell me, that even small indignities are highly upsetting and there is an unspoken racial dynamic within many of these unwanted interactions. Mosi's story implicates gender along with race. Mosi recognizes this, for she consciously performed femininity to avoid a ticket before abandoning the effort in the face of the officer's disrespect. While this attitude ticket may seem minor, even microaggressions can sting. Researchers tell us that people who face repeated microaggressions suffer stress reactions that often mirror the response to one severe incident.[2]

The law gives the officer the power to ticket, but does it allow him to punish her for questioning his authority? Once again, we turn to the law, trying to understand why the Bill of Rights can't prevent these ritual humiliations.

COERCING RESPECT IS PART OF THE JOB

While the *Know Your Rights* skit struck a humorous chord in the encounter between an officer and a disrespectful civilian, Sandra Bland's arrest in 2015 was far from a laughing matter. Sandra Bland, a 28-year-old college graduate and Black Lives Matter supporter, had just moved to Texas to work as a student outreach coordinator at her alma mater, Prairie View University.[3] What began as a commonplace "driving while black" traffic stop escalated into an arrest for assaulting the trooper. Sandra Bland died three days later; she was found hanging in her jail cell. The video of her arrest exposes ugly truths about the cost of police retaliation for disrespect.

The same day that Sandra Bland drives from Illinois to Texas to start her new job, a Texas state trooper, Brian Encinia, pulls her over for changing lanes without a signal when she moves over to get out of the way of his cruiser.[4] Sandra Bland isn't disrespectful at first, just honest. After the Trooper spends several minutes running her license, she asks, "When're you going to let me go?" The Trooper replies, "I don't know, you seem really irritated," and she responds, "I am . . . I feel like it's crap what I'm getting a ticket for." The confrontation continues to escalate. When the young black professional refuses to put out a cigarette when asked, the Trooper retaliates by ordering her out of the car and Ms. Bland refuses to do so. "I'm not under arrest – you don't have the right to take me out of my car," she says. He responds, "You are under arrest!" and threatens to use a taser, screaming, "I will light you up! Get out! Now!" He arrests her for contempt of cop (the actual charge was "assault on a public servant"). "For a failure to signal?" she says. "You're doing all of this for a failure to signal?" As the Trooper takes Bland into custody outside of the camera lens, viewers can hear Sandra Bland being forced to the ground and hear her tell the officer that it hurts her wrist when he yanks her around. "You about to break my wrist" and "You just slammed me, knocking my head into the ground. I got epilepsy, you motherf*****," Ms. Bland shouts, still off-camera.

The Texas trooper brazenly used his "contempt of cop" arrest for what we in the teaching profession call "a teachable moment"; that is, to teach Ms. Bland to respect police in the future. Slapping down a warning ticket he had written on the hood of her car, the Texas trooper explains to Ms. Bland that he initially planned to give her the warning and let her drive away. The trooper explains that he changed his mind because of her behavior. Sandra Bland's real crime: refusing to be nice, insinuating that the "crap" traffic offense was driving while black, and questioning his authority. As ugly as his behavior was, Trooper Encinia honestly believed he was doing his job by arresting Sandra Bland because of her bad attitude. Trooper Encinia had no need to hide his motive for the arrest – teaching her a lesson – because punishing disrespect has long been part of a patrol officer's unwritten job description.

Sandra Bland's teachable moment offers the country a different lesson. On paper, the Constitution gave Ms. Bland the right to tell the trooper that she was irritated because the stop was "crap," an abuse of authority, and racist. On paper, the Constitution gave Ms. Bland the right to question the trooper's power to make her put out her cigarette.

But the badge also gave the trooper some rights, including the right to order Ms. Bland out of the car without justification and then to arrest Ms. Bland for refusing. In fact, the badge gave the trooper the power to arrest Ms. Bland merely for changing lanes without signaling, separate and apart from whether she failed to obey an order. Even the charge of resisting arrest that the troopers sets up, was legally defensible. "When you pull away from me, you're resisting arrest," we hear Trooper Encinia saying off-camera, a true statement of law although the physical violence she complains about – being forced to the ground, yanked about and hurting her wrists – appears gratuitous, an unlawful dose of domination and oppression.[5] I'm not saying that contempt of cop arrests pass constitutional muster. On the contrary, the next section will explore how retaliatory arrests violate free speech and how the courts ignore the illegality. Of course, the whole encounter from stop to arrest was gratuitous and counterproductive, if one views the mission of law enforcement as protecting the peace and keeping communities safe.

Watching the tape of Sandra Bland's arrest, I witness the failure of *Know Your Rights* trainings. Here's a woman who tried to empower herself by learning her rights and who tried to exercise them. While Ms. Bland was mostly correct about the rules, she didn't realize that she had to obey orders like "step out of the car" upon pain of arrest. Her death increases my fear about teaching non-lawyers their rights: people never remember everything from a class, and, unlike an exam, real-life mistakes can be fatal. Her apparent suicide reminds us of how one typical police encounter can destroy a person when built upon a lifetime of other forms of discrimination based on race and gender.[6] Most urgently, Ms. Bland's death points to the hopelessness of every man, woman, and child who believes that constitutional rights will protect them during police encounters, until one police officer steeped in the culture of coercing respect destroys that faith. An officer's need to dominate can overpower all else in these encounters. As Sandra Bland's treatment illustrates, when race and/or gender augment an officer's need to control the situation, the result is toxic.

FREE SPEECH GUARANTEE

According to long-settled law, police violate free speech rights when they punish disrespect. The First Amendment within the Bill of Rights guarantees that the government will not punish us for what we say or for how we express ourselves. In 1987, the Supreme Court warned us of the centrality of free speech as a limit on police power: "The freedom of individuals verbally to oppose or challenge police action without thereby risking arrest is one of the principal characteristics by which we distinguish a free nation from a police state."[7]

Until recently, the Court continued to treat free speech as one of the most important guarantees against unfettered police power. In 2006, the Court explained that "the First Amendment prohibits government officials from subjecting an individual to retaliatory actions for speaking out."[8] Under common law, "policemen are not exempt from criticism any more than Cabinet Ministers."[9]

Free speech protects more than political speech or artistic expression. Americans have a right to use language that others find rude and boorish without fear of arrest. Back in 1971, the Supreme Court protected a young man's right to wear a jacket saying "F*** the Draft," even though the lower court concluded that the words had "a tendency to provoke others to acts of violence." Free expression should protect men's ability to wear pants that sag below their underwear line on public streets or to wear skirts, bending gender norms. Only "speech that is likely to provoke an immediate, violent response" can be prosecuted as "fighting words," a narrow exception to our Constitution's broad promise.

For one civilian to call another civilian a "goddamn motherf*****" to his face in a hostile manner can be criminally prosecuted as fighting words, the Supreme Court ruled, but Justice Lewis F. Powell suggested that the result would be different if the accused had directed those words to a police officer. As the Justice saw it, "a properly trained officer may reasonably be expected to 'exercise a higher degree of restraint' than the average citizen, and thus be less likely to respond belligerently to 'fighting words.'"[10] Of course, civilians won't know whether the officer confronting them has been "properly trained." Still, I love Justice Powell's vision of a police force trained to de-escalate rather than arrest when faced with a civilian cursing him out in a threatening manner. Alas, that's not the current state of most US police forces and no Supreme Court justices currently on the bench take the position that police should tolerate fighting words.

On the books, the law protects us. Police are expected to withstand yelled obscenities and taunts (other than fighting words) so that people will not feel "chilled" when they wish to express dissatisfaction with the police. Prosecutors are not supposed to charge for verbally "disturbing the police." Certainly, there is no legally recognized exception to free speech rights for merely disrespecting a police officer – not on paper. Officers violate the First Amendment when they arrest people because they dislike their attitude.

IGNORING RETALIATORY ARRESTS – FOURTH AMENDMENT STYLE

Generally, police officers don't admit that they are arresting someone because the person was rude. Instead, police find another reason – a pretext. That's what the trooper who arrested Sandra Bland did. Although Trooper Encinia told Ms. Bland he was arresting her instead of giving her a warning because of her attitude, the Texas state trooper officially used "assault on a public servant" as his official reason. If Ms. Bland hadn't died in custody, and the incident hadn't been video-taped, pretext would have protected Trooper Encinia. The Supreme Court directs trial judges to ignore the retaliation lurking behind pretext arrests during motions to suppress evidence, and in civil lawsuits alleging Fourth Amendment violations.

Ever since *Whren v. United States*, police officers are free (under the Fourth Amendment) to make retaliatory arrests as long as there's probable cause to arrest the person for some felony, misdemeanor, or traffic offense.[11] So officers may arrest someone for trespassing or for changing lanes without signaling and the Fourth Amendment won't let you prove that the arrest was really retaliation for exercising the fundamental First Amendment freedom to "verbally oppose or challenge police action … one of the principal characteristics by which we distinguish a free nation from a police state."[12] This is true for other bad motives, such as racial or gender harassment.[13]

Imagine if the trooper who cuffed Sandra Bland had baldly declared, "I don't like it when black women talk back." In that case her arrest would plainly run afoul of the equal protection clause (Fourteenth Amendment) and the free speech clause (First Amendment) that forbids punishment for speaking out, but, nevertheless, the retaliatory arrest would still survive a Fourth Amendment challenge. In reality, Ms. Bland's traffic offense, and failure to exit the car when ordered, provide all a court would need to uphold the arrest under the Fourth Amendment. In this way, the Supreme Court's interpretation of our constitutional rights won't protect us. The badge and gun gave the trooper the power to punish Sandra Bland and any other civilian who dared to question his authority.

In sum, there's a contradiction. The Fourth Amendment prohibits prosecutors from introducing evidence against you in court that's tainted by illegal arrests (such as arrests based on the right to silence, free speech, racist, or LGBTQ profiling) and that's still good law, except that the Supreme Court encourages police to flout the law by refusing to entertain this issue when police can later show "probable cause" for any offense, large or small. Probable cause also wipes away police sins when people file civil rights claims under the Fourth Amendment.

IGNORING RETALIATORY ARRESTS — THE FIRST AMENDMENT CATCHES UP

In 2019, the Supreme Court muddied the free speech guarantee in a case called *Nieves v. Bartlett*.[14] The events took place at a campsite during "Arctic Man," an annual multi-day winter race in Alaska. A white 45-year-old man who had drunk at least a couple of beers, Russell Bartlett, was visiting with his friends inside their RV when he felt a tap on his right shoulder. State Trooper Luis Nieves was beside him, asking to talk. Refusing to engage, Mr. Bartlett responded, "What for?" The police were investigating underage drinking. Later that same evening, when Trooper Bryce Weight, a second officer, approached the son of a friend to question him about drinking, Mr. Bartlett intervened, saying "You can't question a minor without a guardian present." (The Constitution doesn't require a guardian be present when police question minors, although local rules might.) Captured on film, Mr. Bartlett never touches the officer, although he speaks loudly and stands close to him. The second officer pushes Mr. Bartlett on the chest and Trooper Nieves then quickly intervenes, arresting Mr. Bartlett for disorderly conduct and resisting arrest. Mr. Bartlett flunked "Know Your Place 101." The Trooper's parting words appear to prove retaliation for Mr. Bartlett's attitude, for he tells the handcuffed man, "Bet you wish you would have talked to me now."

In this context, "what for?" was both free speech (signifying that he doesn't like police) and an exercise of the right to silence (for the words also signify "leave me alone"). The Supreme Court treats *Nieves* as a free speech case, ignoring the question whether the officers violated Mr. Nieves's right to silence (discussed in Chapter 5). Although the Court affirmed that police violate the First Amendment when they punish people for disrespectful speech, it threw out Bartlett's lawsuit and made it harder to bring free speech retaliatory arrest claims when police can show another possible valid reason for the arrest.

Nieves v. *Bartlett* announced a new rule for free speech retaliatory arrest claims when there's probable cause to make an arrest. Before claims like Mr. Bartlett's can get to a jury, the lawyers must present "objective evidence" to a judge that officers "typically exercise their discretion not to" arrest in such situations. Strangely, judges may no longer take into account police statements, such as "bet you wish you would have talked to me now," when deciding whether the case can go to a jury (because that might discourage police officers from speaking their minds). Because the Court eliminated the officer's smoking gun statement from consideration, Mr. Bartlett won't be allowed to present his free speech claim to a jury. Applying the new standard to Mr. Bartlett's arrest, the Supreme Court found probable cause for disorderly conduct and then assumed that police would exercise their discretion to arrest in such situations.

Significant to Youth Court participants, Mr. Bartlett lost his civil rights lawsuit because, in the Court's words, "a reasonable officer in Sergeant Nieves's position could have concluded that Bartlett stood close to Trooper Weight and spoke loudly in order to challenge him, provoking Trooper Weight to push him back." While the Court views these facts as open and shut probable cause for disorderly conduct, the Youth Court participants could have told us that what really went down is this: when Officer Nieves saw his fellow officer push Bartlett, he automatically responded with an arrest for some "cover your rear-end" charge like disorderly conduct or resisting arrest to help his fellow officer fend off future accusations of excessive force. Courts should ask members of heavily policed communities how officers typically exercise their discretion. Or read the Twenty-First Century Policing Report commissioned by former President Barack Obama, which lamented how law enforcement "is seen as an occupying force coming in from outside to impose control on the community."[15] In this age of mass incarceration and YouTube clips filled with unconstitutional police behavior, isn't it absurd that our rights now depend on whether police routinely arrest for certain kinds of behavior? Even if police "typically exercise their discretion" to arrest people who "verbally oppose or challenge police action," this hardly should excuse the behavior. That's like a parent saying, it's wrong to hit your sister, but, because other kids do this to their sisters, go right ahead.

The majority opinion in *Nieves* applauds "contempt of cop" arrests by explicitly allowing police to retaliate against uncooperative *Terry* victims despite free speech protections. Putting aside Mr. Bartlett's earlier lack of cooperation, he's arrested because he tries to prevent an officer from violating a minor's constitutional rights. Yet the only mention that Mr. Bartlett's "challenge" might be protected speech is this passage: "protected speech is often a 'wholly legitimate consideration' for officers when deciding whether to make an arrest" because "the content and manner of a suspect's speech may convey vital information – for example, if he is 'ready to cooperate' or rather 'present[s] a continuing threat.'"

Riddle: What's the difference between (a) exercising one's constitutional rights not to cooperate in Terry stops, and (b) deserving arrest because one is not "ready to cooperate?"

Answer: One concept eviscerates the other. When police can arrest you because you are not ready to cooperate, there's no longer a right not to cooperate. When police can lawfully arrest for protected speech, it's not "protected."

One of my Howard students served as a police officer before going to law school. This is the same third-year law student who told the class it would be irresponsible to tell Youth Court teens that they are free to leave. Once, during a *Know Your Rights* training, he explained how his department described the three charges that are most likely to be used against civilians with bad attitudes. "They called them the holy trinity," he said: disturbing the peace, disorderly conduct, and refusing to obey a police order. Those statutes are broad enough to give an officer cover for contempt of cop arrests. Cover does not mean that the arrests are legitimate or even that they pass the constitutional smell test.

Chief Justice John Roberts appears to support contempt of cop arrests, both in his opinion and during the oral argument in *Nieves* when he stated: "The first time you get an in-your-face interaction with one of these people, you want to get them, you know, cuffed and out of the way if it's something within the range of disturbing or disorderly."[16]

While the Chief Justice's remarks (and the decision he authored) left hope for journalists unfairly targeted for jaywalking, this sentiment eliminates the First

Amendment coverage for most "contempt of cop" arrests. When police retaliate for speech they find insufficiently deferential, they typically turn to one-size-fits-all misdemeanors such as the "holy trinity." The Chief Justice's view encourages aggressive policing that ignores new evidence which shows that de-escalation techniques can keep officers just as safe, while avoiding the collateral consequences of arrest.[17]

Worse still, most police departments don't even teach First Amendment law.[18] The absence of appropriate training leaves officers lacking key information about when contempt of cop arrests are illegal. They are not taught about citizens' rights to engage in "bothersome behaviors" protected by the First Amendment: freedom of speech and association. These behaviors include talking back and standing on street corners. On the other hand, officers are well versed in coercing respect, a hallowed virtue in police culture.

That's why we don't teach free speech during *Know Your Rights* trainings. When it comes to police encounters, our free speech rights are only paper rights. In practice, police can lawfully arrest you for exercising your right to rebuff an officer's request because, in their judgment, you are uncooperative and a threat to police continuing an investigation. Even if your case goes all the way to the Supreme Court, some justices might view your unnecessary retaliatory arrest as good police work – protected speech that deserves no protection. And we do not want to risk our students going against the unwritten rule that officers must "enforce" respect.

MASCULINITY THEORY ON COERCING RESPECT

Masculinity theory uses feminist analysis to investigate male behavior. Some tenets of the theories on masculinity include the idea that there are "hierarchical relationships among men and … those relationships affect *both* men *and* women."[19] Because our society places the highest value on one form of masculinity – financially successful white-collar heterosexual white men (a category that includes some transgender men) – the culture creates constant pressure on other men to prove their masculinity in other ways. This includes police officers and others who work in blue-collar jobs. Another tenet: performance of masculinity intersects with race, class and gender. When it comes to policing, masculinity scholars offer unique insights into why police culture demands respect and requires officers to punish people for standing up for themselves or criticizing police.

"Police work is gendered male."[20] This works on a systemic level and describes how police train and promote masculine ideas such as competition, aggression, control, and the capacity for violence. Often this theory also helps decipher individual behavior, such as the officer who punished Mosi for demanding that he let her go. Like any hypermasculine culture, policing is bound to attract officers who willingly enforce the cultural norms, and the system protects officers who use excessive force and "accomplish masculinity" in racist, sexist, homophobic, and other unconstitutional ways.

Sexual harassment of female officers is one manifestation of the masculine policing culture. Notoriously, women who join the force must put up with verbal harassment and even physical violence, messages that they are not wanted, that policing should remain an all-male club.[21] While only certain individual officers (one might call them "bad apples") insult or assault their fellow officers, it takes a culture to permit such bad behavior to thrive. When we see harassment that's widespread throughout departments, it proves that those at the top, and many rank-and-file members, share the ideal of keeping policing gendered. An expert on partner abuse, Leigh Goodmark, writes that nationwide, officers commit domestic violence at home at greater rates than the general population, a sign of toxic masculinity within our police departments.[22]

Although individual officers may seek to prove their masculinity, this section primarily addresses the systemic problem, namely a policing culture that rewards certain behaviors, a culture rooted in masculine pride. It's the culture that rewards power and aggression, and demands deference to the badge.

Before there was masculinity theory, sociologists recognized the central role of culture in explaining police behavior and misbehavior. Sociologist William Westley explained in his pioneer work, *Violence and the Police: A Sociological Study of Law, Custom and Morality*, that the "attempt to coerce respect from the public" is deeply entrenched within American policing culture. The need to coerce respect stems from an "us against them" mentality, a sense that police officers occupy communities as outsiders.[23]

Command presence lies at the heart of the tension between civilian rights and police dominance. Departments encourage officers to display an aggressive demeanor known as "command presence" when they interact with members of the public. Command presence means demonstrating control over every situation. By definition, this describes aggressive policing that meets opposition with force, rather than engaging in negotiation or de-escalation. It explains why the belligerent "Arctic Man" was arrested for standing too close and speaking loudly as he contested the officer's right to talk to his friend's son. To control each situation means asserting command presence and immediately stamping out opposition.

Police may find, on occasion, they need to use command presence, but other tactics would work just as efficiently in many situations without treading on constitutional rights. Yet police are trained to believe that any challenge to their authority creates danger. This idea links with masculine power and pride. Police view disrespect for their authority as a transgression that should be punished even if a citizen has engaged in no rule-breaking. Perceived disrespect can lead to increased use of force as well as improper arrests.[24] A culture that coerces respect can lead police to violence.

Angela Harris uses the term "hypermasculinity" to describe the policing profession because of its hierarchal structure and emphasis on physical strength and violence. Police officers perform their masculinity by protecting nice neighborhoods and disciplining the "others," the criminals, the "community of savages."[25] As the theory points out, police across the country use language like "the brotherhood" to create bonds, similar to the way that fraternities or gangs inculcate loyalty among their members. Like gangs, police are "sovereign protectors of turf, defenders of the innocent, and possessors of a monopoly on violence and moral authority." Punishing disrespect is also endemic in gang codes. Journalist Ta-Nehisi Coates's describes how, as a law-abiding teenager, he viewed the Baltimore police as one more rival gang during his school days.[26] Coates explained that within the black community, there was "no real moral difference from the crews and the gangs" and the police. "The police were another force to be negotiated."

"Who's the Man?" That's my favorite name for a law review article ever.[27] Masculinities expert Frank Rudy Cooper explains that when one man asks another "Who's the man?" when shooting hoops, the person with the most baskets comes out on top. The taunt represents a challenge, a "masculinity contest." Professor Cooper interprets stop-and-frisk through the lens of masculinities theory and posits that some police officers instigate Terry stops as a "masculinity contest." The officer has not observed criminal behavior, but instead engages in a stop to prove his masculinity, sometimes acting alone and sometimes in concert with one or more fellow officers. This model explains why some officers intentionally escalate encounters. Unlike basketball, where talent prevails, the badge guarantees that officers will win these duels. Additionally, using the masculinity theory lens helps account for disproportionate excessive force against people of color.

Take Richard walking home at night in Chapter 1. My student was on his way home from work at a restaurant when police stopped, frisked and beat him. Why did the officers stop Richard in the first place? Why did they react violently when he called out racial profiling? In selecting targets, police officers select "contrast figures," explains Frank Rudy Cooper – those lower on the hierarchy, "most notably women, gays and racial minorities." Ann McGinley argues that masculinity pressures require men to compete with each other and that explains why men are more often the target of bullying by police. Stopping Richard gave the officers an opportunity to prove their dominance. In targeting Richard for abuse, "the assault simultaneously enhanced the masculinity of the officers involved by demonstrating that their manhood was superior to that of the suspect, and also demeaned the masculinity of" the person assaulted. Assaulting a black man also serves as a message to other black males "that the police department is superior to them."[28]

Whose streets? Our streets! Whose streets? Our streets!

This chant was heard on the streets of Ferguson and in many anti-violence protests since. But this time, it was St. Louis police officers during street protests in 2017 following the acquittal of a fellow officer on first degree murder in the death of Anthony Lamar Smith. The chant is reminiscent of the control theory of policing where NYPD supervisors taught their units to prove they owned the streets. As the ACLU pointed out, "in a certain sense, the police are right: In many cities, the streets are theirs."[29] The officers' appropriation of the chant also fits with what Professor Cooper calls "cop macho," where "a challenge to their respect is a challenge to their manhood."

One aspect of toxic masculinity is that it needs to be proved again and again by those who are invested in proving their worth. When an officer uses stop-and-frisk to create a rigged contest, the win can create a short-lived high so the officer might cast about again for another ego boost.

One might read the confrontation between Trooper Encinia and Sandra Bland as a masculinity contest. The video tape shows Trooper Encinia goading Sandra Bland to do something so that he can escalate the confrontation and come out on top. In keeping with Professor Cooper's theory, the trooper must save face when Ms. Bland has the audacity to honestly to tell him that she feels "it's crap" to ticket her for a turn signal rather than batting her eyelashes, as my law student recommends. Certainly her race and gender fit within the "contrast figure" categories that Professor Cooper describes as being likely targets for officers seeking to prove dominance.[30] Stanford University researchers analyzed police body camera videos from the Oakland Police Department and found that officers speak significantly less respectfully to black than to white community members in everyday traffic stops.[31] These findings fit with masculinity theory.

Stop-and-frisk serves as a perfect vehicle for masculinity contests because officers select whoever they wish to target. Officers control the whole encounter from whether to stop, whether to frisk, what questions to ask, and how long to hold a person. Finally, the statute books provide officers with misdemeanors that are easily deployed to punish disrespect.

Masculine culture passes down generation to generation within the policing profession, helping to define what it means to be a good officer. Because policing culture echoes masculine values, it is deeply entrenched and difficult to change.[32] As sociologists see it, culture is stronger than laws. Because coercing respect is deeply embedded in police culture, the Supreme Court pronouncements on free speech do not trickle down into the police academy or onto the beat. In fact, as the next example will show, officers might see unconstitutional "contempt of cop" arrests as part of the job description.

WOLF-WHISTLES AND SMILING PRETTY

Comedian and television producer Tina Fey explored what it means to be female in America. In her memoir, Ms. Fey asked young women when they first felt like a woman.

"I was babysitting my younger cousins when a guy drove by and yelled 'nice ass,'" one woman responded. "Almost everyone first realized they were becoming a grown woman when some dude did something nasty to them," Ms. Fey found. She wondered about these men who yell at strangers: "Are they a patrol sent out to let girls know they've crossed into puberty?"[33]

Although this was written with humor, Tina Fey's point is well taken. Wolf-whistles teach girls at a young age that they are not completely equal to their brothers. Notice that Fey uses the word "patrol." Street harassment is a form of microaggression, teaching girls that men control the streets. Rebecca Solnit calls this "an initiation rite, a reminder that even after you cease to be a frequent target you're vulnerable."[34]

While Tina Fey writes about girls learning what it means to be women, UCLA Law Professor Devon Carbado describes learning to be a black male in America. Professor Carbado had recently immigrated to the United States from Great Britain as a young man. "Pursuant to . . . the law on the street for black people, they forced us against the side of the patrol car. Spread-eagled, they frisked and searched us." This was how "I became a black American," Carbado writes.

Trystan Cotten had to learn what it meant to be an African American man in his forties, because that's when he transitioned from female to male.

Other African American and Latino Americans grew up as boys and were taught to deal with that at an earlier age. I had to learn from my black and brown brothers about how to stay alive in my new body and retain some dignity while being demeaned by the cops.[35]

The messages police send by their treatment of black civilians resonates deeply across cities, communities, and states. I overheard one of my students say about then-candidate Obama that he may have been the editor-in-chief at *Harvard Law Review*, but he'll still be black to the police officer who pulls him over. In other venues, I've heard similar statements from Jews about people who don't consider themselves Jewish "but to Hitler they're Jews." For many of my black students, policing appears to define their condition as second-class citizens.

My black students have learned to modify their behavior when interacting with police. This is performance, a survival skill to make the officer feel unthreatened. A male colleague of mine at the law school changes the radio station to his classical music preset on his car when police pull him over, thereby countering stereotypes about black men as violent thugs. He hopes that this will offset officers' unconscious bias that equates black men with dangerous criminals, making him safer and shortening the ordeal.

That might sound extreme, but consider this: in the wake of the Ferguson protests, a District of Columbia police officer visited a law school class at Howard and explained to them "your job is to make the officers feel safe." He told this class of mostly black students that it was their job to counter the unconscious bias and stereotypes of others. His admonition upset several of the students, but I suppose he thought he was being honest. Unreasonable fear by police toward black men and youth create the conditions for dangerous encounters. Since the police have not fixed the problem among themselves, the burden shifts to victims of bias to prove that they are not dangerous.

For Mosi, the performance was transparently gendered: mascara and lip gloss. Singer-songwriter Ani DiFranco, a white feminist folk musician, sang about being pulled over by police throughout the United States: "And every state line / There's a new set of laws ... but the same rule always applies. Smile pretty [and watch your back]."[36] Given the hypermasculine culture of the policing profession, it makes sense that male officers might soften when women put on the feminine costume to make police feel safe.

Columbia University assistant professor Enrichetta Ravina filed a sexual harassment lawsuit that went to trial in 2018. She testified about "a pattern of sexual commentary, unwanted touching and stalled work" by an established professor who controlled the data she needed for her research. Professor Ravina described how Geert Bekaert told her that "if you were nicer to [me], your papers would move faster."[37] The senior Columbia business professor "demanded that Ms. Ravina provide him with compliments, warning her of a fragile ego in need of positive feedback." Like police officers who coerce respect, the senior professor "sabotaged her work" when she rejected his advances. The jury delivered a verdict in favor of Ms. Ravina.

Professor Ravina's ordeal is instructive and points to more similarities between Terry stops and workplace harassment:

1. Officers who have "fragile egos" use their substantial power to send a message to civilians that they failed "to be nice" and therefore deserve to be punished.
2. What counts as "nice" depends on a person's status, with different treatment for those who are female, people of color, LGBTQ or an intersection of multiple "outsider" identities.
3. Victims must decide how "nice" to be, and whether the toll on one's self-esteem is worth the price.
4. Sexual harassment, like police retaliation, depends upon the culture of the workplace.

While only one individual subjected Professor Ravina to a pattern of relatively low frequency indignities, in other workplaces victims may suffer a pattern of harassment by several individuals. That's similar to the policing situation where multiple encounters with a variety of officers cause a sense of continuous harassment.

Mosi blamed herself for failing to follow the script, for not being "nicer" as the Columbia professor phrased it. In this way, even mild retaliation creates psychological damage – in Mosi's case, she felt stress and not only because the expense ate up her textbook allowance. Yet, what Mosi and my other law students pass on to Youth Court participants might also create psychological damage. Inadvertently, girls might think we recommend playing up their sex appeal, not the message I would want to send. Protect yourself from retaliation, but at what cost?

By now, I hope readers will agree that every Terry stop counts as harassment. The only question is whether this harassment counts as sexual harassment, or racial harassment, or both. One minute you are walking down the street; the next minute you find yourself face-to-face with officers questioning you, or feeling your body up and down for weapons. This attention is unwanted and yet, because of the power differential, this is something you must endure. There is no choice here.

Unwanted attention need not be motivated by sexual desire to count as sexual harassment. Sexual harassment is generally defined as hostile behavior (in a workplace) targeting a person because of that person's gender or sex. Similarly, racial harassment involves hostile actions based on the race of the victim. To understand Sandra Bland's treatment means recognizing that she is both black and female. It's both sexual harassment and racial harassment if an officer consciously or unconsciously views black women as subservient and treats them differently than they would a black man or white woman. The same reasoning applies when police select black men because of their dual status as black and male. In other words, you don't have to be female or LGBTQ to be sexually harassed by a male cop.

Frank Rudy Cooper and Ann McGinley's description of police stops as "masculinity contests" suggests that all Terry stops (based on mere suspicion rather than probable cause) are a form of sexual harassment. They may be racial harassment as well, but it's the gendered culture of policing that creates command presence and elevates the importance of dominance. And it's hegemonic masculinity (meaning dominant masculine norms) that inform an officer's selection of whom to stop, whom to frisk, and whom to punish. It's a gendered culture that encourages police to escalate conflict and punish verbal resistance.

When police selected Richard (my law student whose stop was described in Chapter 1), this might exemplify both racial and sexual harassment. It's racial harassment if he was selected and abused based on his race, and there are several ways to reach the conclusion that Richard's stop was also a form of sexual harassment. First, if Richard's treatment was based on his intersectional identity, the stop counts as sexual harassment. This seems entirely likely, for the sexual assault of women often unfolds differently (as Chapter 6 will show). Second, if police selected Richard as a "contrast figure," because of the police department's masculine norms, that also renders the stop a form of gender discrimination. Third, if Richard's treatment grew out of a hypermasculine police culture that rewards aggression and violence, that counts too. Masculinity theory helps us move beyond analogy. Stop-and-frisks are not merely similar to sexual harassment, they are sexual harassment.

WHEN THE PRESIDENT CALLS AN ARREST "STUPID"

Many retaliatory arrests violate both free speech and Fourth Amendment guarantees. One of the most famous "holy trinity" arrests occurred in Cambridge,

Massachusetts, in 2009. Renowned Harvard professor and television personality Henry Louis Gates, whom the *New York Times* describes as "a prolific scholar of African American history and one of the nation's leading black intellectuals," was arrested on the front porch of his home for disorderly conduct.[38] It began when the 58-year-old professor had difficulty opening his front door with his key, asked the cab driver who drove him home to assist, and a neighbor called 911. By the time Sergeant James Crowley arrived to investigate, Professor Gates was safely inside. Sergeant Crowley quickly realized that Professor Gates was in his own home, probably even before the officer entered Mr. Gates's home, uninvited and without a warrant. Nevertheless, the badge requires that he retaliate for Professor Gates's "very uncooperative" attitude, even if it meant entering his home without consent.

Sergeant Crowley wrote in his report:

> I asked if he would step out onto the porch and speak with me. He replied, "no, I will not." He then demanded to know who I was. I told him that I was "Sgt. Crowley from the Cambridge Police" and that I was "investigating a report of a break-in progress" at the residence. While I was making this statement, Gates opened the front door and exclaimed "why, because I'm a black man in America?" I then asked Gates if there was anyone else in the residence. While yelling, he told me that it was none of my business and accused me of being a racist police officer.[39]

The officer set up a pretext, or excuse for an illegal retaliatory arrest. Even if he did not recognize the name Henry Louis Gates, the officer would have looked at his Harvard identification and known he's an innocent homeowner rather than a burglary suspect. Still, Sergeant Crowley decided that the affluent homeowner must be punished for his attitude and connived a way to arrest the professor for contempt of cop. There's a "public" element to the disorderly conduct statute, so Sergeant Crowley set up the professor by luring him out of his home and telling him that he would like speak to him outside. Outside, Professor Gates continued to berate the Sergeant who then slapped handcuffs on the Harvard professor, arresting him for "contempt of cop" dressed up as "disorderly conduct."

Many media reports discussed the racial angle of the arrest and the public debate that swirled around race. Lost in the news coverage lay a key problem to many holy trinity arrests: Sergeant Crowley lacked probable cause, so the arrest violated the Fourth Amendment. And that's in addition to infringing on First Amendment free speech.

Even though Sergeant Crowley could place a checkmark next to the "public" element needed for a disorderly arrest, the eleven-year veteran of the Cambridge police department surely knew the conduct didn't come close to meeting the other statutory elements. "The interpretation of the term 'disorderly' . . . has had a 'tortured history,'" the Massachusetts Supreme Judicial Court explained, "driven principally by the difficulties of defining the offense in a way that avoids infringement of free speech rights."[40] Rather than throw out the statute altogether, the Massachusetts highest court narrowed it down so it only applied to "violent or tumultuous behavior" with "tumultuous" defined as "characterized as involving riotous commotion and excessively unreasonable noise."[41] To quote one case, "loud protestations" directed toward the police do *not* violate this statute even when accompanied by "flailing arms . . . a physical manifestation of [a man's] agitation."[42]

Stupid is one thing, unconstitutional another. Attitude arrests are worse than stupid because they stomp on the government's basic promise to respect our right to express ourselves freely. Professor Gates's insults were speech, not violence. To describe his accusations as "riotous" would be the stuff of late-night comedy. Nor could the officer claim he met a third element, that the professor purposefully or recklessly created a risk of "public annoyance or alarm," given that the professor only walked out onto his porch because he fell for Sergeant Crowley's invitation to continue the conversation outside. In fact, the arrest was precisely what the Massachusetts courts repeatedly tried to avoid by narrowing the statute, to protect free speech and free expression. Sergeant Crowley purposefully overstretched the misdemeanor offense because he didn't care that a prosecutor would refuse to charge the crime. The arrest itself was punishment.[43]

Arrests are themselves an exercise of state violence, even for those who don't die in custody, as Sandra Bland or Freddie Gray did. The sergeant broke the law to make the point that calling an officer a racist is an arrestable offense. Like Sandra Bland's arrest six years later, the arrest of Professor Gates was intended to teach a lesson about respecting the badge. Unlike Sandra Bland's arrest, there was no traffic offense or refusal to obey an order to serve as cover for the unconstitutional punishment. Because the arrest was transparently unconstitutional, when the police unions defended Sergeant Crowley's action, they were actually defending the idea that police power should exceed constitutional constraints. And based on public support for Sergeant Crowley's illegal arrest of the distinguished professor, police are doing exactly what much of the public wants them to do.[44]

It's problematic when pundits focus solely on the racial aspect of Gatesgate, as the arrest was dubbed, missing a chance to highlight our vanishing constitutional rights. When President Obama weighed in to call the arrest "stupid," the country became polarized, with almost half defending the officer and reacting negatively to President Obama's rather mild observation that "separate and apart from this incident . . . there is a long history in this country of African-Americans and Latinos being stopped by law enforcement disproportionately." In polls taken shortly after the event, the country was divided about Professor Gates's arrest, with many viewing the officer as blameless.[45] The split mirrored the general divide over racial politics. By focusing on race rather than the Constitution, most white Americans failed to notice how Sergeant Crowley's behavior undermined their own fundamental rights. In an absurd ending to Gatesgate, Sergeant Crowley was invited to a beer summit with the president and Professor Gates, as if both officer and civilian were equally at fault. While the beer summit was a politically astute move, it unfortunately equated

Professor Gates's exercise of his constitutional freedom to verbally "oppose or challenge police action without thereby risking arrest" with the officer's illegal abuse of power. Would the polls change if people realized that the arrest was unconstitutional? Perhaps not, for it's as if many white Americans don't think we need or will ever need a Constitution to protect us from police overreach.

Ironically, the Sergeant even taught diversity training. Police who make these unconstitutional arrests may be proverbial "good cops" who don't use the arrest to shore up weak egos, but still view their job as commanding respect for the badge. Even men who are individually secure in their manhood are trained and ingrained within a hypermasculine institution where respect and servility are more important than the law. The illegal arrest of Henry Louis Gates nets an important takeaway: all the fine words from courts will not protect a civilian's free speech rights on the street. When it comes to coercing respect, police culture is stronger than law.

The semester following Gatesgate, I created a short assignment in my seminar where I asked students whether masculinity theory helped explain the events, and whether race played any role in the infamous arrest. Some of their answers surprised me. Professor Gates did not behave the way most black men do when they are confronted by police, a few students pointed out. Black men are socialized to be compliant and deferential to police, my students told me. Every student agreed with law professor Devon Carbado that black men have learned to survive police encounters by acting subservient. According to Professor Carbado, black Americans learn the "racial conventions of black and white police encounters, the so-called rules of the game" that include: "Don't move. Don't turn around. Don't give some rookie an excuse to shoot you."[46] In the United States, black men might feel anger, but generally they would not show their anger to a police officer. Blacks and Hispanics consent to police searches and patdowns in greater numbers than whites in order "to make the officers racially comfortable."

Professor Gates did not follow Carbado's description of "conscious black obedience." He refused to be named a suspect or a criminal. That was his crime. As the Gates affair demonstrates, no person, no matter how famous or affluent, can exercise his constitutional right to insult a police officer without retribution. At least no black person.

THE POWER TO NAME PEOPLE AS CRIMINALS

Even white middle-class adults are not immune from contempt of cop responses. In 2014, in an upper middle-class suburb of Washington DC, police came to the door of the residence where Danielle and Alexander Meitiv lived with their two children, ages 10 and 6. A bystander had alerted the police that the children were not chaperoned as they walked home on city streets. The police had transported the children in their cruiser, and when the police asked to enter the home to look around, Mr. Meitiv bluntly rebuffed them. Mr. Meitiv, who works as a chemist told the police they needed a warrant to enter his home.

Angry at the rebuff, the officers called for backup and four police cruisers pulled up to the home. The Meitivs explained to the police that they allowed their children to walk together to the nearby city playground without an adult. However, the next time the police were notified that the children were walking alone, officers held the children captive in their cruiser for over an hour and then for another four hours at the police station without notifying the frantic parents.[47] While the media has focused on what the Meitivs call "free-range" parenting, there is another story here too, a story of extrajudicial punishment for lack of deference. While their unappreciative manner may have rubbed the officer the wrong way, the couple's primary offense was their refusal to consent to a search of their home.

If the arrest of Professor Henry Louis Gates proved that privilege will not always protect one from retaliatory abuse, the Meitivs' ordeal confirms that being middle class, Jewish, and white will not bestow immunity for perceived disrespect.

Recall also that Russell Bartlett, the "Arctic Man" racer who ended up in the back of a cruiser for disorderly conduct in the *Nieves* case, was a white man. Earlier, we looked at his arrest from the standpoint of an officer's legal authority to use the arrest to punish protected verbal dissent. It's also useful to investigate how the Supreme Court outsources the power to name someone a criminal, relinquishing this authority to police officers. Although Mr. Bartlett does not break any laws, and his only weapons are his voice and his presence as he stands between an officer and his friend's child during a supposedly consensual contact, the Supreme Court embraces the police label. By arresting the man, police declare "this man represents a threat; this man is a criminal."[48] And the *Nieves* Court says to the police, "we trust you." Through the power of naming, anyone arrested by police becomes "the other," even a white man with the financial means to take a ski holiday.

I'm not suggesting that white people are at equal risk of discipline and punishment as people of color. Not at all. As we know from researchers at the Plain View Project, hundreds of officers across multiple cities posted vile racist comments to each other.[49] The Project uncovered Facebook accounts from approximately 3,000 active and retired officers, and found that 20 percent of active duty officers posted offensive material. The numbers doubled for retired officers. That's in addition to implicit biases that sociologists discover in those who strive to rid themselves of racism. Even without the Facebook trove, the statistics tell the story.[50] Masculinity theorists explain the centrality of categorizations of race and gender within police encounters. At risk of stating the obvious, what counts as "uncooperative" rests as much on race, class, gender, and gender nonconformity as it does on how close a person stands to an officer, or the volume of his speech. When the Court approved the arrest of the white Alaskan ski racer, it sent a message that police can continue to use their power to coerce respect and punish anyone who fails to answer their questions.

While the Supreme Court presumes universality, the practice is never so. What "retaliatory arrest" means will change based on race, class, gender, immigration status, and age. Feminism demands that we acknowledge the particularity with which rulings burden individuals. If you are transgender, police will perform an intrusive gender check strip search in assigning you to a cell. If you are poor, you may not make bail and you will lose your job. If you are black, an arrest hurts your chances of getting a job more than if you were white. Then consider what happens to young children when their parents are arrested for disorderly conduct. In addition to the problem of abandonment, this can create lasting psychological harm for both parent and child.

By surrendering the authority to police to label a white man as threatening, the Supreme Court limits white privilege and simultaneously grants police officers additional power to racially profile. Police will read the decision as giving them lawful permission to treat black men and women as inherently dangerous, LGBTQ civilians as deviant, and demand complete subservience from anyone they might later call threatening, even pregnant women.

Judith Butler, a feminist philosopher, argues that the power to discipline and punish is not law, but its opposite. In the policing context, we literally see discipline and punishment replacing law, supplanting the Bill of Rights (our legal inheritance). For police, "their decision, the power they wield to 'deem' someone dangerous, and constitute them effectively as such, is a sovereign power" and how they use this power "does not signify an exceptional circumstance, but rather, ... the exceptional becomes established as a naturalized norm."[51] While Judith Butler writes about the prison in Guantanamo, her analysis translates to stop-and-frisk: by granting police the power to name people as dangerous or deviant, the Court destroys law. It is a linguistic *coup d'état*.

Although punishing speech violates the Constitution, the law can't help us when we find ourselves tapped on the shoulder or visited at home by police, as the arctic racer, Henry Louis Gates, and the Meitivs found out. Because people know that police punish disrespect, whether real or imagined, stop-and-frisk has become an exercise in subservience. There's no easy fix. Coercing respect lies at the heart of police culture, how police understand their role, and their relationship to the communities they serve.

Free speech is not the only casualty of a police culture that views coercing respect as core to its mission. In fact, the culture of coercion underpins all the aggressive policing stories told throughout this book. The culture of coercion helps explain why Freddie Gray received a "rough ride" and Walter Scott suffered a bullet in his back. Running away from the police disrespects the badge even more than talking back, for it denies officers the power to detain them at all. As one Youth Court participant asked during a *Know Your Rights* training, "What if the police think I'm a smart-ass if I ask *am I free to leave* (and retaliate by hurting or arresting me)?" Great question, for we teach teenagers to ask "am I free to leave" and tell police "I don't consent to searches," but if that makes an officer view them as uncooperative or lacking respect for the badge, it renders every right meaningless. Police officers might view any exercise of any right as disrespectful. That includes the right to pull out one's phone and record the exchange.

The culture of coercion underscores the central argument in this book that consent stops, consent searches and "voluntary" interrogations are neither voluntary nor consensual. By punishing perceived disrespect, police officers make it risky to exercise any rights.

5

Beyond Miranda's Reach: How Stop-and-Frisk Undermines the Right to Silence

Watch enough police procedurals on television and you probably know the Miranda warnings by heart:

- You have the right to remain silent.
- Everything you say can (and will) be used against you in a court of law.
- You have a right to a lawyer.
- If you cannot afford a lawyer, one will be appointed for you.

By and large, Americans feel protected by Miranda rights, unaware that these rights provide scant protection in police stations and even less on the streets. During a Terry stop or car stop, police don't need to recite these warnings, but that shouldn't mean our rights evaporate; it should mean that we learn them elsewhere, such as in *Know Your Rights* trainings. Nevertheless, "you have a right to remain silent" no longer remains the proud Fifth Amendment right that the Miranda Court annunciated in 1968.

As the Supreme Court works to undermine Miranda's clear articulation of the right to resist interrogation, it leaves a rubble of contradictions and unanswered questions. By now you know it's extremely difficult to exercise your rights during Terry stops. Asserting the right to silence in the face of police questioning might be the most difficult of all. More disturbing still, we may have lost even the pretense of a right to silence outside of interrogation rooms. What does the law say now? Is there still a right to silence during stops and frisks? If so, is it possible to exercise silence in a manner that the courts will respect?

I argued in Chapter 1 that *Terry* v. *Ohio* was built on a false assumption, a fatal flaw as it were. The Supreme Court justified stop-and-frisk in *Terry* v. *Ohio* as an exception to the probable cause requirement because police needed to be able to ask questions that could lead to arrest and prosecution, making these stops a legitimate method of fighting crime. However, in order for judges to admit statements into a trial, they must be "voluntary" rather than coerced. In other words, we have to be able to stay silent. *Terry* v. *Ohio*'s justification fails if readers agree with me that we don't have a choice to talk or not talk during Terry stops, that resistance is often punished, and that cooperation signifies submission to authority rather than voluntary consent.

This chapter builds on my premise that fear of retaliation makes a lie of *Terry*'s promise that people have a right to refuse to answer questions during stop-and-frisk. Starting with a Youth Court lesson, I explore the consequences of the Supreme Court allowing police to mislead and deceive us during questioning. Next, I turn to what's left legally of our right to silence during Terry stops, a right grounded in the First, Fourth, and Fifth Amendments to the US Constitution. Finally, the chapter will consider some feminist perspectives on big and little legal lies.

THE LIES OFFICERS TELL

On the streets, police officers blow past any potential right to silence to turn stops into arrests. For a decade, New York City police stopped black teenagers (mostly) and asked them if they had marijuana. Many admitted to having a joint or two, hoping to get off easy. Carrying marijuana is actually not even a crime in New York, unless it's out in the open, so police would then ask to see it; when the teens showed their joints, that's when they were arrested. No wonder marijuana was the number one crime uncovered during New York City's full-throttle implementation of stop-and-frisk.[1] DC police also turned stop-and-frisk into opportunities to make marijuana arrests. As a result, black teenagers in the district were more than eight times more likely to be arrested for marijuana than their white counterparts, even though the percentage of marijuana users is the same in both populations.[2] Some of the DC youth who admitted carrying marijuana cigarettes ended up in Youth Court.

Training Youth Court participants gave my students and I a chance to reach these young people before the police stopped them again, but what lesson could we teach them about silence that wouldn't be too complicated to remember later?

In my *Know Your Rights* trainings with black youth, we keep it simple. We focus on post-arrest silence where the rules are easier to explain, and even so, young people are easily confused. My law students role-play police officers who "arrest" two trainees for possession of marijuana found in one of their bags. Jeff, a tall law student who serenely imitates the "whoop, whoop" of the DC police siren at the beginning of this skit, plays one of the officers. Jeff and another police officer arrest two Youth Court volunteers and place them in separate cells. At Youth Court, the cells are just the defense table and the prosecution table, but the kids still look unhappy to be separated from the others. They look small, hunched over the tables.

"Sit down. I'll be back," Officer Jeff tells one of the arrestees, directing him to his cell.

Coming back with a Miranda form, Officer Jeff drones through the litany of rights and then, hovering above the hapless teenager, Jeff slaps down a pen and the

Miranda form, points to a line, and says, "Understand? Sign here." The kid, wanting to finish this skit and join the free teenagers, signs. This young man has just waived his Miranda rights. Candy from a baby.

Next comes the lie.

"Looky here" exclaims Officer Jeff, pulling pretend marijuana from the bag he seized during the arrest. "Your friend in the other cell told us this was your bag. And look what I found! A blunt (marijuana cigarette). Oh man, you're in trouble man."

"That's not mine," the kid responds.

"That's not what I heard," chuckles Officer Jeff. "That's not what your friend in the other cell tells me. He says you quickly handed him the bag when you saw the cop car."

This skit teaches two lessons which are written on the poster board propped up in the well of the courtroom (that is, the place where the lawyers pace around during their arguments to the jury in *Law and Order*):

- Always say "I want a lawyer."
- Police are allowed to *lie* to you.

Although "I want a lawyer" is the easiest part of the whole training, some participants are baffled when they learn that they won't actually get a lawyer, not until they are brought to court (up to forty-eight hours later), even if they follow our script. Why should I ask for a lawyer when they won't ever give me one? "Lawyer" is the safe word, my students explain. Say "I want a lawyer" because these are the court-approved magic words that require police to stop harassing you into giving up your right to silence. When they hear "lawyer," police must cease questioning.[3]

The Youth Court teenagers like learning how to take the Miranda form and write "I want a lawyer" across it, but the companion lesson confuses them.

"Remember when I said your friend told me it was your bag?" asks Jeff. "That's a lie. Police can lie to get you to talk."

"So the cop will just say I waived my rights no matter what I do," says one teenager. Others nod.

"And you just told us to stay and ask 'am I free to leave' and not to run, but the cop will just say I ran no matter what I do or don't do," chimes in another.

"The cops will just lie and say I had the blunt on me," the first kid says, processing this new lesson aloud.

The teens now think everything we taught them up to this point was futile. All along they suspected that constitutional guarantees were just rich lawyer words, and this proves they were right and we are just wasting their time. My law students look for me to take over here.

The police are only allowed to lie sometimes, I explain. They can lie to get you talk, but they cannot lie in their police reports. They *cannot* falsely write that they found the blunt on you. And police *cannot* lie in court.

Now the teenagers look at me skeptically. If they were not so polite, they would say "Yeah, what planet are you from?" One middle school student challenged me directly: "Are you telling me that police don't lie in court?"

No, nobody intended to tell him that. Wherever this young man learned such cynicism, his information about the law as lived was accurate.

In my first week as a public defender, I shadowed a tall senior colleague who took me under his wing and helped me get my bearings. Walking down the Worcester courthouse corridor together one morning, Ted pointed to a Worcester police detective sitting on the bench outside a courtroom. "Remember that cop," Ted advised me. "He's honest. Not easy to cross-examine because he's smart and he'll evade and try not to answer, but he won't commit perjury." The weight of this moment has stuck with me: if it was rare to find one cop who *wouldn't* lie on the stand, I grasped what awaited me in most courtrooms. As any criminal defense lawyer learns quickly, police commonly lie to evade the consequences of searching without probable cause or skipping Miranda warnings to get confessions. During motions to suppress, police pretend that their stops and arrests conform to the Constitution's commands. This type of lying "is so common and so accepted in some jurisdictions ... that the police themselves have come up with a name for it: 'testilying.'"[4] Later, I would remember Ted's remark every time a police officer would find a way to fill in weaknesses in the government's case, such as when an officer – not mentioned in any police report – miraculously saw my client walking quickly away from the crime scene during the important gap between the time of the robbery and the time police showed up at my client's home to arrest him because he lived nearby and had a prior conviction for a similar crime.

So nobody wanted to tell the Youth Court participant that police don't lie in court. My focus in *Know Your Rights* trainings is on sanctioned trickery, how the Supreme Court permits police to lie during stops and interrogations. Civilians need to know that they can't trust what police tell them during questioning. That doesn't signify that we should ignore illegal perjury. Everyone needs to know the difference so they can file a complaint when police break the law by fabricating facts or evidence. Police can conceivably face criminal charges for falsifying police reports. Although it's rare, in 2018 Chicago prosecuted three police officers for falsifying the facts leading up to a fourth officer's fatal shooting of 17-year-old Laquan McDonald.[5] To truly know our rights, we must distinguish routine police trickery (lawful) from courtroom police perjury (unlawful).

It's not just teenagers who can't distinguish good lies (such as lying to suspects) from bad lies (such as falsifying police reports). It's a slippery slope for those who wear the uniform. Courts justify lying to suspects to draw confessions because lies might draw out the truth. This sends the message that the ends justify the means. But officers can easily justify "testilying" by that same logic.

This is an "Emperor Has No Clothes" teaching moment. The young man's question shines a spotlight on embarrassing behavior that society tries to keep hidden because most criminal convictions rest on the premise that police officers testify truthfully. He revealed a fault line between *law on the books* and *law in practice*. If the law forbids police perjury but officers do so regularly and with impunity, what does it mean to say that police are not allowed to lie in court or in their reports? Arguably, that becomes yet another falsehood.

His question exposes the many ramifications of the Supreme Court's decision to sanction police deceit. As we tell the Youth Court participants:

> Police will tell you that "you'll do better when you talk to us" when in fact the opposite is true. Police will pretend they know things that they don't know or pretend they are investigating one crime when in fact they are investigating another; officers can pretend that you are not a suspect when you are their prime suspect. Those who think they can make smart decisions based on false information are dupes.

By sanctioning this behavior, the Court gives police even more power than the uniform and badge already bestow. Both legal and illegal lies destabilize the listener and make it almost impossible for teenagers to withstand the pressure to answer questions at the police station and on the street.

Deceitful techniques heighten the likelihood of false confessions. False confessions are common, especially among youth.[6] The documentary *Making a Murderer* shows the taped confession of a 16-year-old white teen, Brendan Dassey, who waived his Miranda rights and admitted he was involved in a horrendous rape and murder, even though the physical evidence demonstrated that his confession must be false. Miranda warnings didn't prevent the 16-year-old's confession. Watching the tape of Mr. Dassey's interrogation, it looks as if the teenager eventually succumbs to false memories as he adopts the officers' version of events.[7]

According to a University of Michigan Law School study, in the first fourteen years following the advent of DNA science, 42 percent of all exonerated juveniles falsely confessed or made damaging admissions leading to their wrongful convictions. The percentage of false confessions was even higher for those aged 12 to 15: the study showed that 69 percent of those exonerated youngsters made false confessions.[8]

In the stop-and-frisk context, police lies combine with a muddy doctrine on pretrial silence to make navigation treacherous for civilians. The Youth Court teens would be easy prey to those who wanted to manipulate them into confessing. During Terry stops, police are under no obligation to recite Miranda before asking incriminating questions, not unless officers put civilians in handcuffs or place them in police cruisers or unholster their guns during questioning.

But the answer is not to require Miranda warnings during Terry stops. With or without Miranda warnings, most juveniles don't have the wherewithal to withstand the pressure. Teenagers need lawyers, not Miranda cards.

Fortunately, a 19-year-old client of Howard's Criminal Justice Clinic had a lawyer when he needed her most.

One February day when I was in the basement cafeteria in the DC courthouse on a break, a law student named Brittany came flying over to my table. "My client just texted me," she said, holding her cell phone tight. "He says the police have him down at the police station and are asking him questions about burglaries, and what should he do?" Our client had texted surreptitiously, cell phone in lap, while the officer talked.

I was certain the police allowed our client to keep his phone so that they could later claim the whole meeting was a consensual exercise – not "custody" – so Miranda didn't apply. Because this law student volunteered a couple of times in Youth Court, she had a good idea of what to say, but since I was there to help, she sought advice. I answered: "Tell your client to say he won't talk without a lawyer and ask 'am I free to leave?'"

I heard the results before I left court that afternoon. When our client repeated my student's advice verbatim, the officer looked furious and demanded, "Did you just text your lawyer?" When our client nodded yes, the officer said, "Okay, you can leave but we are taking your coat 'for evidence.'"

Our client stood outside in below-freezing temperatures for thirty minutes without a coat, waiting for a friend with a car to pick him up. The coat was not really evidence, so our client was able to pick it up the next day. Taking the coat was payback for exercising his right to silence.

Neither Miranda nor our *Know Your Rights* training would have helped our client withstand the pressure. He needed to dial his "lifeline" – to borrow a phrase from *Who Wants to Be a Millionaire* – where people could dial an expert or friend and confer for thirty seconds about how to answer a question. Our client was one of the lucky few to have a lawyer, a lawyer who quickly responds to texts.

VANISHING FIFTH AMENDMENT PROTECTIONS: WHEN WHAT YOU DON'T SAY CAN BE USED AGAINST YOU

"You have a right to remain silent." That's how in 1968, in *Miranda* v. *Arizona*, the Supreme Court translated the Fifth Amendment's command that the government shall not force people to incriminate themselves.

Three different constitutional amendments support our right not to respond to police interrogation. The right to silence derives primarily from the Fifth Amendment privilege against self-incrimination. *Terry* v. *Ohio* was decided under the Fourth Amendment (when it answered the question of how much justification police needed to detain Mr. Terry). *Terry* incorporated the right to silence into the Fourth Amendment when it created a legal structure where police may stop and ask questions based on reasonable suspicion, but people don't have to answer. This is what I call *Terry*'s promise – the promise that during a stop-and-frisk, "the person stopped is not obliged to answer, answers may not be compelled, and refusal to answer furnishes no basis for an arrest."[9] There's also a First Amendment right against compelled speech that should prevent police from arresting us for refusing to answer their questions.

Despite these assurances, the right to silence is almost nonexistent during Terry stops. The following sections will show how courts find loopholes around all three guarantees, starting here with the Fifth Amendment's failure to protect us during Terry stops.

For history buffs, the Fifth Amendment right against self-incrimination was inspired by England's infamous Star Chamber during the time of King Henry VIII and Queen Elizabeth I, where the accused faced a "cruel trilemma."[10] Facing hostile questioning, the hapless English gentleman had three options, but all pointed toward ruin: (1) he could confess to a crime and be punished; (2) he could be punished for refusing to answer; or (3) he could be punished for perjury if the answers he gave were untrue. In response to this hated Star Chamber, the Fifth Amendment guarantees that police solve crimes without compelling individuals to confess. "In sum," the Fifth Amendment "privilege is only fulfilled when the person is guaranteed the right 'to remain silent unless he chooses to speak in the unfettered exercise of his own will,'" the Supreme Court declared in 1966.[11] Given this history, if the law were still a legitimate protector of rights, a person's silence could never be used against them in a criminal trial. Fast forward to 2013 and the Supreme Court backpedals.

In 2013, the Supreme Court reviewed the murder conviction of Genovevo Salinas. Texas police recovered shotgun shell casings from the scene of a double murder and investigated Mr. Salinas because he had been at a party at the victims' home the night before they were slain. Police officers then came to Salinas's home, took his gun for ballistic testing and drove him to the police station. No Miranda warnings were given before the interrogation and the trial judge concluded that none were needed. That's because Mr. Salinas had "voluntarily" accompanied the police to the station for questioning, or so the judge concluded (a sham consensual encounter). Still, Mr. Salinas bravely chose silence when police asked him if the shotgun his father had given him would match the shells recovered at the scene of the murder. At trial, the prosecutor argued that silence proves guilt, telling the jury:

> He wouldn't answer the question ... An innocent person is going to say: "What are you talking about? I didn't do that. I wasn't there." He didn't respond that way. He didn't say: "No, it's not going to match up. It's my shotgun. It's been in our house. What are you talking about?" [But the defendant Salinas] wouldn't answer that question.[12]

This is the "silence proves guilt" argument. This belongs in a country where "anything you say *or don't say* will be used against you." That's the opposite of "you have a right to silence."[13]

Tellingly, Mr. Salinas lost his appeal. When police don't recite Miranda warnings, Justice Samuel Alito explained, staying silent isn't good enough. Mr. Salinas lost because he did not utter some magic words like "I invoke my Fifth Amendment right to silence."

If police ask you questions during a stop or "consent" stop, your silence can now be used against you in a court of law.

This is the situation for Youth Court teenagers because police don't give Miranda warnings during Terry stops. For a person to properly exercise the right to silence before warnings, she "must, counterintuitively, speak—and must do so with sufficient precision."[14]

Here's some examples of what does not count as invoking the right to silence:

1. "I just don't think that I should say anything." (This did not preserve the civilian's rights and could be used against them at trial because it was "not a clear request to remain silent");
2. "Okay, if you're implying that I've done it, I wish to not say any more. I'd like to be done with this.'Cause that's just ridiculous. I wish I'd ... don't wish to answer any more questions." (This did not preserve the civilian's rights. Apparently, it's "ambiguous because conditioned on officer's implication that suspect committed specific assault").
3. "I'm not going to talk about nothin'." (This did not preserve the civilian's rights because the court understood it "as much a taunt –even a provocation – as an invocation of the right to remain silent").[15]

"How can an individual who is not a lawyer know which particular words" – such as "I hereby invoke my Fifth Amendment right to silence" – "are legally magic?"[16] Who speaks with sufficient precision to exercise the right against self-incrimination in a manner that a judge was bound to respect after *Salinas*? Not the participants I met in Youth Court. Many can't remember to ask the law student role-playing a police officer "Am I free to leave," even though we practically turn these five words into a chant.

I don't teach the Youth Court participants to utter a magic Fifth Amendment incantation about "exercising the Fifth" during Terry stops. It's not just that they will forget the proper phrasing, although they will. And it's not just that answering questions makes it less likely the teenagers will be kept longer or fall victim to retaliatory arrest, although that's true too. Most importantly, the magic words only come in handy months later if they are charged with a crime and face trial. Generally, stop-and-frisk victims are suspected of low-level offenses like jaywalking or drug possession. Knowing the magic words won't help teenagers in Youth Court because they will never face trial, and the Fifth Amendment won't even help innocent Terry stop victims sue the police for arresting them in retaliation for exercising their right not to answer police questions. So the Fifth Amendment is useless when it comes to protecting our right to silence during stop-and-frisk.

VANISHING FOURTH AMENDMENT PROTECTIONS: THE "STATE YOUR NAME" EXCEPTION

That still leaves the question of whether the Fourth Amendment permits police to arrest us in retaliation for refusing to answer their questions. Never, said the Court fifty or so years ago in *Terry v. Ohio*. Sometimes, said the Court fifteen or so years ago in *Hiibel v. Sixth Judicial District Court*. *Hiibel* allows police to arrest a person for refusing to identify himself during a *Terry* stop when two conditions are met: (1) the officers have reasonable suspicion that the individual just committed a crime, and (2) the state law requires people to turn over identification.[17]

By making an exception for identification checks, the Supreme Court altered *Terry v. Ohio*'s promise so it now reads:

> Of course, the person stopped is not obliged to answer [except if the officer asks for your name] . . . answers may not be compelled [unless a state statute compels you to answer the officer's question about your identity, and] . . . refusal to answer furnishes no basis for an arrest [but you can be arrested for failing to give your name if the officer had reasonable suspicion to stop you in the first place].

As the *Hiibel* dissenters bemoaned, the Supreme Court overturned law that was settled "for nearly a generation."[18]

Here are the basic rules for police demanding identification:

1. Drivers need to hand over their licenses but, so far, the Supreme Court has not adopted this requirement for nondrivers. Still, many officers demand that people physically hand over physical IDs to make sure the person is giving their true name.
2. Civilians must state their name when police ask, facing arrest for giving a false name or refusing to give a name.
   - Technically this *Terry* exception applies only when the officer has reasonable suspicion that you are committing or have committed a crime, and then only in states that spell this out. (So when the officer asks for your name, ask whether you are free to leave. If the answer is no, then you must give your real name.)
   - No harm in googling if there's a law in your state that requires you to identify yourself, but don't expect the officer to realize he can't compel you to disclose a name without a statute in place. Even law students get that one wrong on the exam. (Where there's no law on the books, aggressive officers can retaliate by arresting you for something else like "disorderly conduct." See Chapter 4.)
   - When police tell you to hand over a piece of identification, that turns a "consent" stop into a Terry stop because you are not free to leave while the officer has your identification. If the officer requests a

physical ID, you can say "I always follow orders – please tell me, is this an order?" (If you are driving a car, it's always an order.)

Identification checks are a huge concern to the transgender community. When police see that a person's name or sex does not match what's on her license "an officer's request for identification can quickly escalate to verbal abuse, physical violence and arrest."[19] As Senior Staff Attorney Gabriel Arkles wrote for the ACLU website in 2019, Linda Dominguez, a 43-year-old Spanish-speaking transgender woman, was on her way home one night when she got off a bus in the Bronx and cut across a park after it was closed. Although police initially arrested her for trespassing, they ultimately charged her with "false personation" when she provided her previous legal first name instead of her new name.[20] Even though she had legally changed her name to Linda, she thought she was required to give her original masculine name. Her lawsuit claims that police taunted her, placed her in pink handcuffs, and left her cuffed overnight.

Andrea Richie wrote about how police profiled two transgender women in a town outside of Chicago. Bianca Feliciano, 17 years old and Latinx, walking with a black friend, was stopped although officers had no reason to suspect the women of committing a crime. Police threatened Ms. Feliciano with "fraud charges" for misrepresenting her sex when her identification listed her as female but the officers perceived her to be male.[21]

Identification checks also cause particular anxiety for immigrant groups. Arizona Sheriff Joe Arpaio infamously flouted the Constitution in creating a policy of ID checks simply based on Mexican appearance. While the Supreme Court down-played the importance of identification checks as compared to other forms of compelled speech, history is not on the Court's side. During apartheid in South Africa, police would arrest any nonwhites who failed to carry a pass. And during slavery in the United States, slaves carried passes to prove they were allowed to walk outside their masters' plantations.

In theory, the Supreme Court still left you a Fourth Amendment right not to answer questions other than identification and the right not to give your name during "consent" stops. If you did a poll today, I wager you would discover that most police officers believe (incorrectly) that they have a right to demand identification whenever they want and arrest people who don't hand it over. When Michelle Cooks told the officer that she didn't have to give him her name, she was correct. But challenging the officer helped trigger an illegal retaliatory arrest (discussed in Chapters 2 and 4). Michelle Cooks's illegal retaliatory arrest for initially refusing to give her name and then walking away also reveals that police sometimes use unnecessary violence during arrests when they don't get their way. If an officer feels entitled to tackle a woman as visibly pregnant as Ms. Cooks in a school parking lot for not cooperating, then we must use abundant caution in *Know Your Rights* trainings. We don't tell Youth Court teens to withhold their names, even though it may be their legal right. "Just ask 'am I free to leave?,'" we tell them, hoping that even that magic question won't infuriate the officer.

That's two strikes against the guarantee that we need not respond to officers' questions. In addition to losing our Fifth Amendment right in the context of stop-and-frisk, we no longer have a viable Fourth Amendment right to silence, either, thanks to the Court's *Hiibel* decision that bolsters a police culture where illegal retaliation thrives, and where the refusal to answer questions will likely be interpreted as a form of disobedience or disrespect. That should still leave the ban against police officers compelling us to answer their questions under threat of arrest. That violates the First Amendment ban against compelled speech, doesn't it?

VANISHING FIRST AMENDMENT PROTECTIONS AGAINST COMPELLED SPEECH: THE BOOT ON THE NECK

Vicki Koch stood up for her rights.[22] One day in 2005, an officer came to her home, in Del City, Oklahoma, without a warrant to inquire about the whereabouts of an elderly woman who used to live there. Ms. Koch, a middle-aged white woman, was outside on her porch at the time. Instead of answering his questions, she told the officer to talk to her lawyer and to get off her property. That sounds like Ms. Koch knew her rights and uttered the magic words. But when Ms. Koch turned to leave, the officer arrested the homeowner, forcing her to the ground and injuring her wrists with tight handcuffs.

The charge: obstructing a public officer by refusing to answer his questions. In other words, the officer didn't pretend that he was arresting Ms. Koch for anything else except exercising her right to silence. There was no probable cause for any other crime. If the courts upheld the arrest, this would spell out the end of the right to silence – not just as a practical matter, but as a legal doctrine. If her arrest was lawful, this would mean that people are compelled to respond when officers ask them questions.

In several respects, the arrest of Vicki Koch is reminiscent of Michelle Cooks's retaliatory arrest for initially refusing to give her name and then walking away (discussed in Chapter 2). Legally, Ms. Cooks had an absolute right not to give her name and not answer questions. Similarly, Ms. Koch was under no legal obligation to answer the officer's questions, although the courts didn't see it that way.

Ms. Koch and Ms. Cooks's lawsuits met with different results. While Ms. Cooks successfully settled her civil rights suit with the city of Barstow,[23] Del City fought Vicki Koch's complaint and a federal judge dismissed it. A higher court affirmed the dismissal. The Supreme Court never entertained Ms. Koch's appeal, so the circuit decision still stands.

Ms. Koch's lawyer argued that the officer violated her First, Fourth and Fifth Amendments rights by arresting her for refusing to answer his questions.[24] Vicki Koch lost on every count.

Ms. Koch argued that under the Fifth Amendment, the officer violated her right against self-incrimination by arresting her for "obstructing a public officer" by refusing to answer his questions – and she lost. Indeed, the Fifth Amendment only prevents a prosecutor from claiming at trial that a person's silence suggests guilt because an innocent person would have talked to the police (although the *Salinas* decision discussed above carved huge exceptions into that protection). The Fifth Amendment does not stop police from punishing us for silence.

Ms. Koch lost her Fourth Amendment argument that *Terry* v. *Ohio* gives people the right to refuse to answer questions. How did the appeals court get around the Supreme Court's language in *Terry* about how the person detained was "not obliged to answer" and how "refusal to answer furnishes no basis for an arrest"? Oh, that was just "dicta," said the appeals court, so it's not binding on future courts. Dicta is language that explains a court's thinking but does not create duties or rights. After all, the appeals court reasoned, if *Terry*'s promise had teeth, police could not arrest people for failing to identify themselves as the *Hiibel* case allows.

That still leaves the First Amendment. For her First Amendment claim, Vicki Koch's lawsuit argued that forcing a person to answer police questions is a type of "compelled speech." Therefore, the officer violated her First Amendment rights when he arrested her for refusing to answer his questions. Vicki Koch didn't have to prove pretext, for the officer admitted that he arrested her for refusing to talk. The officer stretched the misdemeanor "obstructing a public officer" to mean "she won't talk to me."

"The right of freedom of thought protected by the First Amendment against state action includes both the right to speak freely and the right to refrain from speaking at all," the Supreme Court explained in 1977.[25] But Vicki Koch lost her chance to prove her First Amendment argument before a jury. The court rejected Ms. Koch's compelled speech claim because the right only extends to "ideological or political speech," while the officer demanded answers of a non ideological sort.[26] Therefore, her retaliatory arrest did not violate the First Amendment. Essentially, the Tenth Circuit found Ms. Koch's silence unworthy of constitutional protection.

Six years later, another appeals court followed suit in *Alexander v. City of Round Rock*, where an officer pulled over a car in a hotel parking lot and questioned the driver about what he was doing there.[27] When Lionel Alexander gave the officer his license and informed Officer Garza "that he would not answer any of the officer's questions," the officer called for backup, pulled the passenger out of the car, and pinned him face down on the ground. Pressing his boot or knee against the man's neck, the officer asked, "Are you ready to talk to me now?" The complaint explained how there were at least three officers on top of his torso, neck, and head and that they "mashed" his face "into the concrete." Because the passenger still refused to talk, the officer arrested him for "resisting a search." A judge threw out Mr. Alexander's lawsuit, but the appeals court reinstated the Fourth Amendment claims of unlawful arrest and excessive force. Nevertheless, the appeals court refused to allow Mr. Alexander to proceed with his compelled speech claim. As with Vicki Koch's arrest, the officer here conceded that Mr. Alexander's arrest was based upon the driver's refusal to answer, so there was no complicated issue of pretextual arrest. Even though the officer essentially admitted to compelling the man to talk, the Fifth Circuit Court of Appeals ruled that this was not a situation that the First Amendment clearly protects. The officer was not compelling "a particular political or ideological message," so it did not count as First Amendment "compelled speech."

Both courts rejected First Amendment protections when police compelled people to "voluntarily" answer their questions and arrests were based purely on people's failure to talk. A suspect's silence isn't worthy of such protection.

A FEMINIST PERSPECTIVE ON BIG AND LITTLE LIES

We should be wary of court decisions that pretend to be viewpoint neutral while they reject First Amendment protections because the government is not compelling the type of speech that the Constitution was designed to protect.

Vicki Koch and Lionel Alexander literally lost their compelled speech claims because the courts viewed their predicament as a private matter rather than matters of ideological or political importance. These courts are wrong. Not talking to police expresses an ideological position. It often means "police are bullies" or "I don't cooperate with the enemy." The police represent the government and there's nothing more political than people's view of the government.

Also, it's hypocritical for courts to claim that only "ideological or political speech" merits protection. Paying union dues on a job amounts to compelled speech, the Supreme Court ruled in 2018, even when unions assure their members that the money won't be spent on political candidates or political efforts. Even when the money just goes to help the union negotiate better salaries and working conditions for the litigant and his fellow employees, mandatory dues still count as compelled speech.[28] Compelled speech is also starting to make inroads into the equal protection arena for commercial speech. Lawyers for a baker argued to the US Supreme Court – and Justice Clarence Thomas agreed – that Colorado engaged in compelled speech by fining a baker for refusing to make a cake for a party celebrating a gay wedding.[29]

Workers who refused to pay union dues never risked arrest or prosecution before the Court decision, and Colorado bakers only face fines when they discriminate. In contrast, during stop-and-frisk, people face arrest and violence when police compel answers. Thus the "compelled" part of "compelled speech" is more meritorious in Terry stops and traffic stops than for union dues. As for the importance of the speech or silence, once upon a time the Supreme Court lauded the rights of citizens to express dissent (as recounted in the last chapter). When Lionel Alexander handed over his license but refused to tell police what he was doing, it's equivalent to answering that "it's none of your business." Mr. Alexander's silence expresses dissatisfaction with government authority as surely as Sandra Bland telling an officer that "it's crap what I am getting a ticket for." Compelled speech and free speech (silence and talk) are twin protections within the First Amendment to the US Constitution; both protect autonomy, free thought, and dissent.

Feminists know what happens in the abortion context when the government decides that only certain viewpoints are worthy of First Amendment protection. Some states force doctors to read scripts about adoption to women seeking abortions, or tell them about sham side effects, such as "increased risk of suicide ideation and suicide." These laws require doctors to telegraph "a denigrating message about abortion" and force "the provider and the woman to participate in enacting a narrative of motherhood and fetal personhood that the state has imposed upon them."[30] Planned Parenthood argued that these scripts violated the doctors' First Amendment protections against compelled speech. Because these anti-abortion statutes literally force doctors to speak in ways that undermine many of their core beliefs, one would expect these anti-abortion laws to be struck down. Instead, the Supreme Court upheld the statutes.[31]

Compare the forced anti-abortion advice case with how conservative Supreme Court justices respond when statutes require the anti-abortion side to speak. In 2018, the Court looked at laws that regulated so-called crisis clinics.[32] These "fake" women's health centers "prey on women at a vulnerable moment in their lives by pushing medically inaccurate information" and use deceptive tactics to run out the clock on abortions, explains NARAL Pro-Choice America.[33] The Supreme Court struck down a California law that required counselors who held themselves out as medical service providers to tell their pregnant clients about free abortion providers in the vicinity. Feminists called this "honest information [for] pregnant women" to correct the lies.[34] The Court called it "compelled speech."

The dueling decisions in the access-to-abortion context illustrate that First Amendment protections against compelled speech apply only when a majority of justices consider the viewpoint to be worthy. Even if compelled speech must be of a political or ideological nature to merit protection, both healthcare cases involve personal, individual decisions that connect to a larger issue; namely, the constitutional right to control one's body. Justice Stephen Breyer hit the nail on the head when he asked rhetorically in his dissent: If a state can require a doctor to inform a woman seeking an abortion about adoption services, then "why should it not be able to require a medical counselor to tell a woman seeking prenatal care or other reproductive health care about . . . *abortion services?*"[35]

Returning to our Terry stop cases, the courts should answer this: If it's compelled speech to require a "crisis clinic" to inform a pregnant woman about her options, then why is it not compelled speech when a police officer puts a boot on a person's neck and then arrests them for not answering a question?

The two abortion cases offer a window into how falsehoods allow courts to shift the power balance away from pregnant women and onto the government. I explore these here with an eye toward policing, where a range of lies help shift the power away from victims of Terry stops who wish to resist interrogation. There are several layers of lies at work in the access-to-abortion decisions.

- state-sanctioned lies
- "for her own good"
- pretending our constitutional rights are still intact.

First, forcing doctors to tell patients information that the doctors consider to be false are state-sanctioned lies. These scripts are private in the sense that they are told to women one by one in private, but they are also public, for it's the government that mandates the doctors' speech.[36] Second, "for her own good" is a phrase that should scare us, for it's often heard as feminists battle for fair treatment by the medical establishment. Courts often pretend that statutes compelling doctors to scare women away from terminating pregnancy serve to protect women's health. When the Supreme Court approves of laws compelling doctors to inform patients of misleading scripts, this is done to "help" women choose. Regulations that close clinics are done, supposedly, to support women's health. Waiting periods were allegedly enacted "for her own good," as if women are the weaker sex and can't make decisions without strict oversight. Third, there's an overarching lie when courts give lip service to a woman's constitutional right to choose while rendering decisions that literally force providers to shut their doors.

These layers of deception all pair with decisions in the context of stop-and-frisk.

State-sanctioned lies: Just as doctors in some states must tell patients falsehoods, the Supreme Court empowers police to lie to civilians during Terry stops and other interrogation situations. This authority to deceive props up the power of police to discipline and punish, for it makes it likely that whoever police select as the suspect will soon become a "confessed" criminal defendant, someone who will plead guilty. Then there's testilying – how, in practice, police supplement lawful lies with unlawful ones, further fueling the power imbalance. Giving these representatives of the government the sole power to lie, while simultaneously empowering police and prosecutors to punish civilians for telling lies, adds to the power that police already possess by virtue of their monopoly on state violence.

"For her own good": In the abortion context, courts pretend that compelled speech and other anti-abortion measures serve to protect women's health. In the context of policing, the Supreme Court sometimes pretends that it helps civilians when it gives them an opportunity to consent and thereby give up the right to be free from unwanted searches. Remember when Justice Kennedy wrote that "the concept of agreement and consent should be given a weight and dignity of its own" to justify upholding a conviction where police lacked reasonable suspicion?[37] That's "for her own good" language. In other words, the justices bestow "dignity" on civilians by sending them to prison if they accidentally waive their rights, even when police don't tell them they have a right to say no. It's the paternal state swooping in to tell the subjects of policing, probably envisioned as less educated souls, why the state is punishing them in a way that one day they will "appreciate."

Pretending our constitutional rights are still intact: In the abortion context, some courts give lip service to a woman's constitutional right to choose while gutting healthcare protections. In policing cases, the Court pretends that people retain their fundamental right to silence even as its decisions make it impossible to assert. Maybe the federal court that decided Vicki Koch's appeal was right in concluding that the Supreme Court abolished the right to silence. After all, the Supreme Court allows officers to arrest people for refusing to give their name. And the Court pretends that a reasonable officer won't understand "I just don't think that I should say anything" as exercising the right to silence. After all, the Supreme Court allows police to make retaliatory arrests as long as they point to a pretextual reason.

Riddle: Is there a right to silence if courts allow retaliatory arrests?
ANSWER: No.

This gets to the overarching lie within *Terry* v. *Ohio*. You may remember that Chapter 1 recounted how stop-and-frisk was built on the false premise that people can refuse to answer questions and withhold consent and, in some situations, even walk away when the police are asking them questions. Given the state of the law now, it's sheer pretense to claim that civilians still possess a right to silence and that their answers are not compelled.

WHAT'S LEFT OF YOUR RIGHT TO SILENCE DURING TERRY STOPS

If I had a dollar for every client who told me I would easily win his case because police did not give him Miranda warnings ... One of the most common misconceptions about Miranda is that police must give you Miranda rights as soon as they stop you. Here are Miranda's current limits during Terry stops:

- Unless police point a gun in your face or handcuff you, don't expect to hear your Miranda rights. Your detention won't be called "custody-like" even though you are certainly not free to leave, and the deprivation of your liberty certainly feels significant to you.[38]
- But if police arrest you and then fail to read warnings before questioning, prosecutors might have a problem later if they try to introduce your non-Mirandized answers into trial against you. That's when your defense attorney will move to suppress the statements as Fifth Amendment violations.

Here's a summary of the basic law that governs police questioning during Terry stops. The lists below lay out what happens if civilians talk or don't talk. (For the issue of identification checks, see the rules for police demanding identification on p. 108.)

Imagine you have been stopped by police. Reviewing your two options during a stop: you can either talk or not talk.

Here's what happens *if you talk* to the police during a Terry stop:

1. Everything you say can be used against you.
2. You waive your right to silence simply by talking.
3. Police can use your words as a basis to arrest you.
4. Prosecutors can use your words to put you behind bars.

If you are later charged with a crime, you will regret talking to the police since your own words might form the basis for which you are convicted. On the other hand, not talking is probably worse.

Here's what can happen *if you don't talk* when the police question you:

1. The officer may detain you longer and continue to question, and it may lead to a frisk. No constitutional violation here.
2. Perhaps the officer will arrest you for no other reason than that he views your silence as "disobeying an order" or a similarly elastic law. Although that arrest violates the spirit of *Terry*, some jurisdictions consider this to be constitutional or at least unsettled law.[39]
3. The officer might arrest you for an offense that otherwise would have netted you only a warning. (Similar to Sandra Bland's retaliatory arrest for speaking her mind, discussed in Chapter 4.) Although retaliatory arrests violate the First Amendment, if police find drugs or other contraband as a result of the arrest, that evidence can be admitted against you thanks to the case of *Whren* v. *United States*.[40] And thanks to *Nieves* v. *Bartlett*, your civil rights lawsuit will be thrown out unless you can show that officers "typically exercise their discretion not to" arrest for those offenses. (This is difficult to do because it may require access to substantial data that may be hard to obtain.)
4. The officer might arrest you because he considers your silence incriminating. If a reasonable officer starts with reasonable suspicion, adds guilty silence and now he's got probable cause, the arrest might pass constitutional muster. (Yes, this contradicts the Supreme Court's original pronouncement that in Terry stops, "refusal to answer furnishes no basis for an arrest." However, the Court recently suggested in *Nieves* that police may arrest in situations where refusal to answer suggests noncooperation.[41])
5. There's a danger that the officer will physically punish you for your noncooperation (perhaps adjusting the handcuffs so they cut off

circulation or an unnecessary and intrusive frisk or even a rough ride in the back of police transport). These would be illegal, but fairly common.

6. Even if you are silent and you end up on trial, the government will use your silence against you. A prosecutor might argue that if you were innocent you would have responded to the officer's question. (This is legal after the Supreme Court ruled in *Salinas* that pre-arrest silence can be used to convict a person unless she "invoked" the right to silence using unambiguous language.)

Miranda-type warnings can't cure the stop-and-frisk problem because a Terry stop warning would sound like this:

- You *must* speak to the officer.
- If you don't, you might be arrested for obstruction (although the Supreme Court has not yet ruled on this).
- However, if you remain silent, your silence can be used against you in court.
- You must tell the truth, even though your statements will be used in court to prosecute you.
- If you lie, you may be prosecuted for obstructing an investigation.

As in the hated English Star Chamber, victims of Terry stops face a similar trilemma. A civilian's response to police questions during Terry stops include no opt-out clause: (1) she can confess to a crime and be punished; (2) she can be punished for refusing to answer (principally by retaliatory arrests, but if she's prosecuted, her silence may now be used as proof of guilt); or (3) she can be punished for providing false information if she provides wrong or misleading answers.[42] That's the Terry trilemma.

THE BIGGER THE LIE, THE HARDER IT IS TO SEE

Delving into *Terry* v. *Ohio*'s original vision of how stop-and-frisk solves crime, Chapter 1 laid out how the Supreme Court imagined that statements would be voluntary, and prosecutors could therefore fairly use these statements to convict. Similarly, the Court thought prosecutors could fairly use evidence found during consent searches at trial for the Court imagined that people would trust police not to penalize them for saying no. Instead, consent is a sham (including consent stops, consent searches ,and consenting to waive one's right to silence). This realization undermines *Terry* v. *Ohio*'s justification for stop-and-frisk. Lawless harassment and fishing expeditions for warrants, drugs, or other contraband are all that remain, all blatantly illegal purposes. Once we reject consent as a fictional construct, a cruel lie that blames the victim for officers' excess use of power, then *Terry* v. *Ohio* must fall too.

The Supreme Court should admit that there is no such thing as "voluntary" consent or "voluntary" answers during police interrogation. And as soon as the Court admits that, *Terry's* crime-fighting justification implodes, for, as I have shown in this book, consent and Terry stops are solidly intertwined.

The bigger the lie, the harder it is to see. Author Margaret Atwood created a dystopian world in *The Handmaid's Tale*, where the rulers disguise ritual rape as a monthly religious ceremony. After it was turned into a television show, the producers realized that viewers became acclimated to the ruler's worldview and no longer noticed the violence within the ceremony.[43] Perhaps that's why people can't see that *Terry* v. *Ohio* was built on a lie. The notion of voluntary answers to *Terry* questions is so pervasive that lawyers and judges don't see that it's false. I didn't see it as a practicing lawyer. Instead, I took *Terry* as a given and just tried to fit my facts into the prevailing law. The idea that suspects choose whether to engage with a police officer's interrogation formed the core of *Terry's* architecture, integral to how stop-and-frisk is perceived, and justified, and therefore invisible.

Judges are routinely asked to determine whether police had sufficient suspicion for a stop or whether the person was in custody for the purposes of Miranda. They are never asked to keep out statements from trial because *Terry* v. *Ohio* is a legal edifice that hides compelled speech. And if lawyers did raise the issue, trial judges would respond that this was beyond their pay grade. It's up to the Supreme Court to decide. Until then, judges must simply fit the facts into the existing structure set by *Terry* and *Hiibel* and *Whren*.

Supreme Court opinions employ language in a way that helps disguise the theft of rights. The cases after *Terry* often appropriate language in a way that distorts its meaning. When the Court uses the word "voluntary" to describe an action that we would ordinarily understand as involuntary and the word "consent" to describe an action that we would ordinarily understand as nonconsensual, this renaming makes the theft of rights invisible. Lower courts must conform to the twisted meanings that nullify rights.

Under the current legal framework, courts look at Terry stops from the standpoint of what officers knew, the difficult job they do, and the importance of the evidence seized. While these are legitimate considerations, it's also important to consider the civilians' perspective that the Supreme Court has generally ignored. Even if the issue were squarely before them, the majority of Supreme Court justices are unlikely to recognize how our Youth Court participants are trapped in a "trilemma" that compels them to answer the officer or risk retaliation.

Most people do not realize how stop-and-frisk policing shrinks the Bill of Rights. The loss of fundamental protections guaranteed by the founders of this country is one of the destructive and hidden consequences of current stop-and-frisk practices. The Court appears impervious to the suffering caused by the rules that burden civilians with a lose–lose situation, perhaps because most justices don't look at their rules from the point of view of the people that have to live in the structure they built. The justices are like architects who build a finely balanced structure but forgot that people need plumbing in their kitchens. They forget people need to live inside.

If influential white people saw their neighbors stopped, questioned, and punished for insubordination it wouldn't take fifty years to change the system. Race and inequalities provide further explanation for why *Terry*'s lie stays invisible and why the Supreme Court won't revisit *Terry*'s unscrupulous usurpation of fundamental freedoms.

So the Youth Court participants hit the nail on the head when they suggested that the rights we teach them are one big lie. *Terry* was built on the lie that civilians have a choice to talk or remain silent during Terry stops. Instead, individuals are trapped in a legal warp where there is no way out except to tell the police what they want to hear. This analysis is fatal to *Terry*'s justification as a crime-fighting tool, implicating the very reason for its existence.

This book calls for abolishing stop-and-frisk because its original concept of allowing officers to pose questions which people need not answer does not describe reality, and it should no longer be used unconstitutionally, to control poor communities, or constitutionally, as a pretextual method to search for drugs, or as a pretext to run warrant checks. If we think of the Supreme Court balancing the public's need for stop-and-frisk on less than probable cause against the harms created, then Part I of this book has mostly focused on how *Terry* v. *Ohio* got "the need" wrong, while Part II will focus more on the harms of Terry stops and how to reclaim our constitutional rights.

PART II

The Fallout

6

The Frisk: "Injuries to Manhood" and to Womanhood

One Saturday morning, my students and I were in Youth Court to teach a new group of teenagers their constitutional rights. I stood on the side of the jury box listening to my law students present. Not far from me, in the jury box in a DC Superior Court courtroom, sat a slender 16-year-old dressed in the ubiquitous District of Columbia uniform of tee shirt, jeans, and sneakers. This young man kept his phone in his pocket and leaned forward in the jury box chair, listening intently. When the law students took a moment to switch scenes, the teenager beckoned me over to ask me a question. The last time he was searched, said the sixteen year old, "it felt like rape."

When people think about sexual assault, they think of police arresting the perpetrator, but what do you do when a frisk feels like a rape? The Youth Court participant above felt violated and wanted to know whether there was something he could do about that. This was not an easy question to answer, and it motivated me to write this book.

Even when police officers follow proper procedures, the frisk may feel like sexual harassment or rape to the person touched. I am not talking about a strip search at the station house after a person has been arrested, but the initial "patdown" that officers often perform during Terry stops. Some frisks are unconstitutional or turn into rapes, as I discuss later in this chapter, but here I'm talking about officers doing just what we train them to do. The academy teaches officers to frisk thoroughly and include the groin.

"GROIN AND BUTTOCKS BEAR SPECIAL MENTION"

Law professor Seth Stoughton spent five years as a police officer in Tallahassee, Florida. When he worked as a police officer, Professor Stoughton frisked methodically, in this way:

> I would start at either the front or rear center of the suspect's midsection and run my fingers along and beneath their belt, then frisk their waistband, front and back pockets, groin, and buttocks. The groin and buttocks bear special mention, as it had been drilled into me in training that criminals knew and took advantage of the fact that officers were naturally uncomfortable searching these areas. The potential for avoiding discovery made those areas particularly attractive as hiding spots, which in turn made it particularly important for me to search there. To do so, I would make the same motions as I've just described, reaching around over the front of the thighs and doing the same from the back, running my hand along clothing between suspects' legs starting on one side and making my way across. Inevitably, this involved contact (through gloves and clothing) with suspects' buttocks and genitalia, but that contact was essential for an effective frisk.[1]

For Officer Stoughton, frisks were routine. But, as he readily admits, the adults and youth who felt his fingers on their buttocks and genitalia would experience the touching quite differently.

To help me prepare for a talk about the sexual nature of frisks, my research assistant forwarded a link to a YouTube video of a male-on-male Terry stop where the civilian asks the officer why he's "fingering my ass."[2] The video shows a well-groomed black man in his twenties, wearing a pink shirt and white pants, stopped on a tree-lined sidewalk.

> Initially, the anonymous civilian on the YouTube film complies fully, raising his arms above his head and spreading his legs apart, as the officer commands. But as the officer feels around his groin, the young man jumps. "I am a man, brother," he tells the officer. He jumps again, even after the officer handcuffs him before resuming the search. "Stop fingering me!" he exclaims. "Why [are you] fingering my ass?"

The frisk here looks precisely as Professor Stoughton describes, routine for the officers who are simply intent on getting the job done. But for the civilian on the receiving end, it is an indignity. Worse, the frisks taught in the academy create sexual harm. That's what the exclamation "I am a man, brother" meant in the video. Men can feel sexually violated by male officers. This man felt violated.

The video depicts four other officers in the frame. The primary frisker has his body against the civilian and he reaches around the man's body as he searches. At least three other officers have frontal views. As Paul Butler tells it: "Often other cops participate, either as voyeurs, or by doing another guy at the same time."[3] He's right; I've witnessed groups of young men facing a wall in certain neighborhoods in DC. As I drive by, police officers stand side by side feeling buttocks and legs. Here, one officer stands a few feet away, watching, silent, inscrutable behind his dark sunglasses. No one can tell if the surplus officers derive sexual pleasure from watching the degradation or find it an unpleasant duty. But if I was frisked like that, I wouldn't want them to look.

Watching the frisk on YouTube, I am struck by the absurdity of the exercise. All the officers aim to do, supposedly under *Terry*, is ask the man a few questions to "dispel their suspicions" before they let him walk away. During the frisk, police handcuff him, presumably because he jumps when they touch him and they want to be thorough. Even if the police did not handcuff the man, it's hard to imagine how the suspect could reach into the region of his groin to pull out some small weapon without alerting the officer who is permitted to hold his arms while he asks him questions. One of the first scholars to point out the sexual nature of frisks, Paul Butler, wrote: "The police 'cop' a feel. To 'assume the position' is to make oneself submissive – one turns and offers his backside to another person."[4]

Frisks are only legal when an officer has a legitimate concern that the person is "armed and dangerous." This means that the officer believes the person conceals a weapon that poses a potential threat during the minutes it takes for the officer to ask him questions, questions that will help the officer confirm or dispel his valid concerns that the person is committing a crime. But come on, the video shows four police officers serving as backups to the frisker. It's fantastic to think the civilian kept a gun or knife between his butt cheeks and, after first complying with the officer's command to put his hands over his head, will stick his hands down his underwear and whip out the weapon in front of five officers armed with guns. Nevertheless, a judge could easily deem this frisk lawful under the *Terry* regime. While you and I may wonder if the officers enjoyed the spectacle and humiliation, the Supreme Court orders judges not to think about officers' motives in conducting stop-and-frisks. As long as the officer later points to reasons why the civilian might have posed a threat to him (such as "high-crime neighborhood," acting nervous, suspected of carrying drugs, and so on) many judges won't second-guess a frisk.

As the video illustrates, frisks can be demeaning, even when they are done by the book. What the teenager at Youth Court experienced as "like a rape" might have been an intentional humiliation, a standard by-the-book frisk, or a combination of the two.

THE DRUG WAR ENCOURAGES SEMI-LAWFUL PATDOWNS
OF GENITALIA

The drug war provides a pass to police who explore groins and buttocks where weapons are unlikely to be stored and impossible to access. While courts claim that frisks are only allowed to protect police from potentially dangerous criminals, really it's not weapons police hope to find in a buttock crack, but crack itself. That is, crack cocaine. Technically, the Constitution forbids police from using frisks as an excuse to shake some clothing and see if drugs fall out, but courts condone it all the time. Remember that police can always claim to be afraid.

When experts crunched the numbers in New York City's decade of extensive stop-and-frisks, they found that fully half of all Terry stops included frisks.[5] Meanwhile, police found weapons in less than 2 percent of the stops, but police persisted in frisking nevertheless. So police are not frisking primarily to discover weapons. It's about drugs, humiliation, or both.

The practice is so common that I once found (and bought) a postcard at a Greenwich Village corner store that shows four men and a dog against the side of a building. Everyone lines up for the frisk, while a police officer pats down one of the men. Even the dog has his paws up on the building "assuming the position."

That's what happened to Howard law student Gabriel, whom I describe in the Introduction. When the undercover officer pulled out the elastic band of Gabriel's skimpy gym shorts, he hoped that drugs would fall out. Gabriel's stop-and-frisk is an example of an unconstitutional search (because there was no reason to believe he carried a weapon and no reason to believe he was committing a crime). And yet, from the way Gabriel described the officer's manner, the man did not personally enjoy humiliating my future law student. Compared to the search Richard suffered, where one of the abusive officers dug his hand into his rectum, Gabriel was treated well. To the officer, this was a job. To Gabriel, the frisk went beyond the racial indignity of the accusation that he looked like a criminal; there was a sexual component to this indignity. But trainings direct police to run "fingers along and beneath their belt."[6]

Police academies design the frisk lessons to maximize the chance of discovering drugs.[7] Instructors teach police how to recognize drugs during a patdown so they may claim in court that "merely running my hands along the exterior of the suspect's lower body, I felt a bulge consistent with the way that crack is packaged." The prosecutor then argues with a straight face that during the patdown for weapons, the officer happened to feel a bulge underneath the clothing that he was trained to recognize as a bag of drugs; this allowed the officer to look inside the clothing to confirm that the bulge was in fact contraband. Testimony like this is so common that the Court turned it into a doctrine called "plain feel." From the Supreme Court down to the officer on the beat, everyone knows that the frisk is a game where officers must pretend to be afraid for their safety. Civilian groins have become one more casualty in the drug war.

FRISKING THE OPPOSITE SEX

Frisking across gender is a logical extension of the stated purpose of the Terry frisk; namely, police need to frisk in order to disarm a potentially dangerous foe. Waiting for backup on the street for a frisk would belie that danger. Although some police departments require male officers to wait for a female officer to arrive to patdown female civilians, this was not true where I practiced. Since most police departments have more male officers, cross-gender frisks usually entail female civilians frisked by male officers. Although courts pretend that there is nothing sexual about frisks, one Maryland officer admitted his discomfort when it came to frisking female students.

One Sunday, my law students and I went into a church in Maryland to conduct a Know Your Rights training for teenagers. The church also invited a police officer from a neighboring jurisdiction to address the youth. The talkative black officer in his forties provided a starkly different perspective than we had. Focusing on the importance of behaving well, the seasoned patrol officer explained to the teenagers how he had to "subdue kids" who became unruly. He was looking at tables of boys aged 12 to 15. (He would tackle them if they mouthed off to him during an encounter.)

Then, approaching a round table where most of the girls sat, he cautioned them differently: "Now when ladies don't behave, I just taser them," he explained.

Please remember that the patrol officer was a good man who volunteered his time to come to a church basement on his day off because he cared about the community. This officer acknowledged the sexual dynamic inherent in patdowns. Zapping "ladies" with tasers was a favor, he believed, precisely because he was more discomforted by the sexual contact than with using bolts of electricity. But he only admitted to the sexual dynamic inherent on male-on-female frisks. He ignored the sexual dynamic in male-on-male contacts.

#HIMTOO

While Eric Garner is best remembered for his final words "I can't breathe," he could be the poster child for why *Terry* v. *Ohio* was a mistake from its inception. On July 17, 2015, officers tackled the 43-year-old black New Yorker, holding him down first in a chokehold and then compressing his chest as Mr. Garner's friend recorded the deadly encounter in a video that went viral.[8] The tragedy of what happened to Mr. Garner drew so much attention and outrage that demonstrations were held across the country in which people carried signs that read "I can't breathe." Scholars properly point to his needless death to criticize the chokehold and excessive force. They correctly use his death to indict broken windows policing, a theory closely aligned with stop-and-frisk.[9] But Eric Garner's death is a tale of so much else that's wrong with Terry stops and Terry frisks.

After Mr. Garner was killed, the NYC police department claimed that he was resisting arrest.[10] This claim troubled me, because the video does not show him committing any crime, and my research uncovered no evidence that would give officers probable cause to arrest. The lawyer who represented the family in their claim against the police department, Jonathan C. Moore, verified that the police lacked an arrest warrant and probable cause.[11] "It was a bad *Terry* stop," Attorney Moore explained. Not only did the police lack probable cause for arrest, but they did not even possess reasonable suspicion for a Class A or Class B misdemeanor.[12]

Assuming the officers wished to arrest Mr. Garner for untaxed cigarettes, they must see him sell them, or they must witness loose cigarettes in his possession.[13] This was a classic stop-and-frisk conundrum. If Mr. Garner had cooperated, the police would have called this a consensual encounter, a mere "contact," camouflaging their unlawful detention as the civilian's choice. Under *Terry*, Mr. Garner was free to tell the police to leave him alone and he was free to leave. As the *Terry* Court stated: "Absent special circumstances, the person approached may not be detained or frisked but may refuse to cooperate and go on his way."[14]

As Attorney Moore put it, "he was walking away, just as he is supposed to be able to do." "He had an absolute right to do all of that."

Because police knew from past arrests that Mr. Garner sometimes earned money selling loose cigarettes, they wanted to search Mr. Garner's pockets. To search Mr. Garner's pockets under *Terry* v. *Ohio*, police needed probable cause to believe that their suspect possessed contraband, or they needed his consent to search. But Mr. Garner did not consent to a search. He told police "I'm minding my business, officer ... Please just leave me alone."

Personal history may have played a role in Mr. Garner's failure to consent. Seven years earlier, he filed a civil rights lawsuit against another police officer for performing a strip search on him in public during a pedestrian stop. In the complaint, Mr. Garner alleged under oath that police stopped him on the street, patted him down against a cruiser, handcuffed him, and, while he remained handcuffed, the officer performed a "cavity search on me by ... digging his fingers in my rectum in the middle of the street." In the box asking for injuries, Mr. Garner wrote "the injuries I received was to my manhood ..."[15]

Fast forward to Mr. Garner's fatal encounter. Caught on video, Eric Garner uttered another chilling phrase before his infamous last three words, "I can't breathe." As the police surrounded him, moments before they would tackle and strangle him, he pleaded with them not to touch him.[16] In the context of his earlier experience at the hands of the police, Mr. Garner's final plea for dignity and liberty gathers new meaning.

> Every time you see me, you want to mess with me. I'm tired of it. It stops today. Why would you...? Everyone standing here will tell you I didn't do nothing. I did not sell nothing. Because every time you see me, you want to harass me. You want to stop me [garbled] Selling cigarettes. I'm minding my business, officer, I'm minding my business. Please just leave me alone. I told you the last time, please just leave me alone. Please, please, don't touch me. Do not touch me.[17]

When Mr. Garner refused their touch, the investigatory stop morphed into an arrest. The NYPD called it "resisting arrest." But his crime was actually "refusing to consent." Eric Garner's death illustrates what can happen under *Terry* when a man tries to hold onto his dignity and rights.[18]

The chokehold that ended Mr. Garner's life must be recognized as his punishment for refusing to give the police what they wanted. It's become a symbol of police abuse by all sides. "It's a good day for a chokehold," a Phoenix police officer posted on Facebook. It was among hundreds of retired and active officer postings in

2019 that applauded violence, scoffed at due process, displayed bias or used dehumanizing language.[19]

Who can blame Mr. Garner for not consenting to a frisk or full-blown search? Who can blame Mr. Garner for wishing not to be touched? Even airport frisks can be especially upsetting for people with a history of sexual assault.[20] In Mr. Garner's case, the history was close to home because the prior sexual abuse was at the hands of an officer. In fact, the prior strip search also began as a simple Terry stop.[21]

Mr. Garner's public strip search was unconstitutional even if the police were searching for drugs rather than satisfying a prurient interest.[22] Assuming that it happened the way Mr. Garner remembered, the frisk was also sexually abusive, for it served to humiliate and dominate. These are motivations akin to the forms of abuse showcased in the #MeToo movement.

"Women often experience [strip and cavity] searches as rape and sexual assault, regardless of legal justification," explains Andrea Ritchie. "In other words, they constitute 'state-sanctioned sexual assault,' rendering sexual violence an inherent part of policing." In addition, police perpetrate sexual assault against women of color, including transgender women, through a range of behaviors starting with strip searches on the street looking for drugs; "extortion of sexual services from women engaged in the sex trades; or rape or sexual assault using the power of the badge."[23]

We are more likely to recognize sexual assault when the officer is male and the civilian is a woman or a girl. If Eric Garner had been a woman, he would be called a sexual assault victim. Eric Garner was a big black man, someone the police or general public may perceive as scary instead of vulnerable. Owing to implicit bias and stereotypes, people do not think of big black men when they think of victims of sexual abuse, but they are not immune.

Let's add a "#HimToo" for Eric Garner. #HimToo for my law student Richard. And #HimToo for the 16-year-old Youth Court participant who was brave enough to name his pain. We have come a long way from thinking about police sexual misconduct as a situation where females consent to an officer's overtures. Indeed, we cannot discuss police violence against women without talking about sexual violence. It is because we now talk about abuse against women that we can also finally talk about abuse against men in a more open and honest way.

STATISTICS ON SEXUAL MISCONDUCT

Sexual abuse is the second most common civilian complaint lodged against police officers in the United States. The Cato Institute announced this surprising statistic in 2010 when they compiled and analyzed existing data from multiple sources.[24] Others have followed the Institute's lead, attempting to quantify the number of allegations that resulted in arrest or discipline. An *Associated Press* study concluded that in a six-year period, approximately one thousand officers lost their badges for sexual misconduct.[25] Reporters included serious criminal conduct, namely rape, sodomy and other sexual assault as well as less serious misconduct such as "consensual" intercourse with citizens while on duty. The *Buffalo News* compiled its own database in 2015 and summarized its findings in this provocative sub-headline: "Every five days, a police officer in America is caught engaging in sexual abuse or misconduct. Others are never caught."[26]

Even the International Association of Police Chiefs recognized sexual misconduct as a national problem. The Department of Justice underwrote an executive guide created by the Association that set out policy recommendations for eliminating sexual misconduct in police forces.[27] Explaining the high incidence of sexual misconduct, the executive guide opined that the job itself inadvertently creates opportunities; namely, police have power and authority over others; officers work independently; and officers engage with vulnerable populations.[28]

Most abuse stays hidden, in part because the conduct is shielded from discovery. Researchers complained back in 1995 that there are huge obstacles to finding data on police sexual misconduct, noting that "it is almost impossible to obtain information without a court order."[29] There is still no national database and no national reporting requirements for sexual misconduct by police, not even for reports of on-duty rape. Even more problematic, the existing data only illuminates situations where the police were charged with crimes or discharged from the force.

Sexual abuse is vastly underreported in general, and even less likely to be reported to authorities when the perpetrators are police. Nevertheless, there is enough evidence for the Cato Institute to conclude that "sexual assault rates are significantly higher for police when compared to the general population."[30]

Researchers agree that police who are arrested for sex crimes represent only the tip of the iceberg.[31] Philip Stinson, a Criminal Justice professor at Bowling Green State University, is one of the primary researchers quantifying and analyzing data on police misconduct. When Professor Stinson gathered data on officers who were arrested or charged for sexual violence, he found 548 cases across the country in a three-year period.[32] But almost all of the cases involved male police officers abusing women or girls. Crunching the numbers, Stinson notes that the "simple odds of an officer's arrest for a sex-related crime versus some other type of police crime decrease by 97 percent if the victim is male."[33]

There's every reason to suspect that police sexual abuse against men is more widespread than the data suggest. First, men and boys are just as vulnerable to uniformed officials as are women and girls.[34] Second, Professor Stinson's data captured only those incidents that prosecutors considered egregious enough to arrest or charge the accused officers.[35] Third, men and boys face the same or greater barriers to reporting sexual abuse as do women and girls. Even when there's a safe method for lodging complaints, stigma and shame often dissuade reporting. Valorie Vojdik studied several masculine institutions, including the US military, and showed how members assert this collective masculine identity through repeated sexual violence against men as well as women. Because male victims arguably face even greater shame and stigma, this helps to render male-on-male abuse largely invisible.[36]

The high rate of officers who are prone to commit sexual offenses either off duty or on duty creates a problem of legitimacy for the daily use of frisks. Statistically, there's a high likelihood that some patrol officers are prone to intentional sexual misconduct.[37] When male police chiefs in the St. Louis metropolitan area answered questions about the prevalence of sexual misconduct among their staff, on average the chiefs suspected 20 percent of their staff. In their opinion, one out of five officers committed at least low-level acts of sexual misconduct while on duty, such as pulling over cars to fish for dates, as well as more serious offenses.[38] These are the same officers who initiate Terry stops and conduct frisks.

WHERE TO DRAW THE LINE ON A BODY BETWEEN POLICING AND HARASSMENT

Criminologists recognize a continuum of police sexual violence ranging from humiliation to rape. If we charted frisks on a continuum of legitimacy, on one end would be the frisk where an officer is simply confirming if a bulge in the waistband of a person's pants might be a gun. On the other end of the continuum are frisks that turn into sexual assaults or rape. In the middle of the continuum, we find frisks that are unconstitutional in scope or frisks performed with voyeuristic intent or a desire to humiliate.

It is telling that lawyers and judges cannot always discern when a frisk crosses the line from ordinary policing over to sexual assault. One film that had the courage to look at this situation was *Crash*, the winner of the 2004 Oscar for Best Picture. The film brings strangers "crashing" together in Los Angeles through a series of seemingly disconnected scenes, including the most powerful scene in the movie: a racist white police officer conducts a traffic stop and then decides to humiliate the driver and passenger. Terrence Howard plays the driver, a black man coming home at night with his lighter-skinned wife, played by Thandie Newton. The couple appear well off, drive a nice S.U.V. and are wearing cocktail attire. In the car, Thandie is pleasuring her husband and they are laughing. The primary officer, a patently white racist played by Matt Dillon, observes this behavior from his police car. Although the driver's behavior certainly violates a regulation or two, the audience realizes that the stop represents a racist officer's power play against a couple he mistakenly sees as interracial. The scene is filled with tension that escalates when the Thandie Newton character refuses to submit to the racist officer. During the traffic stop, when a second officer conducts a patdown of the male driver and finds no weapons, the racist officer orders the passenger (Thandie Newton) out of the car.

Inebriated and angry, the affluent passenger tells the officer to get his hands off of her as he starts to take her out of the car. The racist white officer in *Crash* then begins to touch Thandie Newton's character as she stands with her hands on the hood of the van dressed in a shimmering dress and heels. It starts as a patdown that travels down Ms. Newton's sides and legs, but eventually the officer's hands move up under her dress. Viewers understand that the officer uses his hand to penetrate her. What starts as a frisk in *Crash* turns into a sexual assault, yet it is difficult to pinpoint where the frisk ends and the sexual violation starts.

Fact follows fiction, for San Diego paid out over $550,000 dollars for a frisk of a woman that lasted twenty minutes.[39] She called the "patdown" sexual assault. When other women also stepped forward to accuse Officer Christopher Hays of sexual misconduct, he pleaded guilty to groping and illegally detaining four women and he served a year in jail. In both fact and fiction, what starts as a frisk can turn into a touch that's recognized as sexual assault.

Should we draw a line on Thandie Newton's character's body and say that the sexual violation started at a particular point on her leg? I think not, for while the definition of a criminal sexual assault requires the touching of specific body parts, sexual humiliation comes in many forms and is recognized within sexual harassment law. Clearly, Ms. Newton had nothing to hide under her cocktail dress. The officer employs frisk as a tool to humiliate her and her husband. In the film, the whole frisk reads like a sexual assault. The officer forcefully communicates a prurient pleasure in touching her well before his hands take a detour underneath her skirt.

Race, gender, violence, and sex are intertwined beyond the film. The *Crash* passenger resists and dares to show legitimate anger. Like Sandra Bland's situation, the officer in *Crash*, upon meeting resistance from the passenger, escalates the punishment and humiliation. The explicitly sexual invasion must also be understood as part of the overall plan to dominate and control.

While rape is most often a crime aimed at women by men, the gendered aspect is more complicated in *Crash* because the officer intends to humiliate the husband as much as his wife. The officer expects her husband to watch the violation and then meekly thank the officer for letting them drive away with only a warning. As the film recognizes, sexual harassment is not just about men harassing women and can be part of the dynamic when male police officers confront male civilians.

Crash may be fiction, but the problem is real. NBC4 reported on a lawsuit against two male police officers for intentionally tasering a man's genitals.

Daniel Johnson was a light-skinned black man from Los Angeles who had graduated from UC Berkeley. The twenty-six year old had no criminal record, and he comes across as smart and reasonable in the television interview. Los Angeles Deputies stopped Daniel's father because he had thrown a cigarette butt on the ground and Daniel intervened, hoping to talk the officer out of the $1,000 ticket. Instead, the officers became violent. After one deputy grabbed him and forced him to the ground, the other officer fired his Taser at point-blank range. The officer tasered Daniel ten times until he could "smell [his own] flesh burning." This was not a misfire, Johnson explained: "He was right above me as he Tased me, so there's no mistake that he was trying to Tase me in my genitalia."

Daniel's mother told the press that the officer was "looking directly at me every time he pulls that trigger." She screamed every time until finally "I realize this guy is doing this because I am reacting." Just as the police officer in *Crash* sent a message that the husband was impotent to prevent the assault, the LA officer sent a similar message to Daniel's mother.

Tasering Daniel Johnson was as flagrantly sexual as the rape in *Crash*. When feminists talk about rape being a crime of violence, they mean that sexual assaults are about power more than attraction. Sexual abuse represents a particular flavor of domination. This domination is not merely a male-on-female phenomenon.

There were no repercussions to the officer who perversely aimed his taser gun at Daniel. In fact, the Los Angeles County Sheriff's department called him "the best deputy in the department."[40] While the tasering of Mr. Johnson wasn't categorized as a sexually invasive act or even as an unconstitutional use of force, some court cases have acknowledged the sexual nature of certain search procedures.

THE GRAY AREA BETWEEN UNREASONABLE SEARCHES AND SEXUAL ASSAULT

Drawing the line between sexual humiliation and protective frisks can be complicated. Wherever that line might lie, one male police officer from Dumfries, Virginia, obviously crossed onto the humiliation side when he searched Lisa Amaechi.[41]

Officers visited Lisa Amaechi's home twice. First, Dumfries police officer Stephen Hargrave responded to a noise complaint against her children for playing their music too loud and Ms. Amaechi then called the police to complain about the officer's behavior. In retaliation for her complaint, the officer took out an arrest warrant against Lisa Amaechi three days later for allowing her children to violate the town's noise ordinance. Two other officers then made a second visit to her home at 9 p.m., this time to arrest her on the misdemeanor warrant. Lisa Amaechi had nothing on under her robe as one of the officers, Matthew West, led her toward the police car and then searched her on a public street. According to her complaint, Officer West allowed the robe to fall open "stood in front of Amaechi, squeezed her hips, and inside her opened dress, 'swiped' one ungloved hand, palm up, across her bare vagina, at which time the tip of his finger slightly penetrated Amaechi's genitals. Amaechi jumped back, still in handcuffs," and the officer "proceeded to put his hand 'up into [her] butt cheeks,' kneading them."

Taking advantage of these blurred lines between sexual humiliation and searches for weapons and contraband, lawyers for the police officer claimed their client was not on notice that the Constitution prohibited "slight penetration" of a woman's genitalia during a search. As in the film *Crash*, Ms. Amaechi's "dress was thin and was almost completely open, making any weapons immediately apparent," negating any security justification for the search. Officer West tried to exploit the "search incident to arrest" rule that allows police to conduct a full search for weapons and contraband without proof that the arrested person actually poses a danger. Police officers often block lawsuits by arguing that qualified immunity shields them, and Officer West tried this tactic, arguing the law was not settled since no previous case forbade "the 'swiping' and 'slight' penetration of an arrestee's genitalia pursuant to a search incident to an arrest." It can't be "clearly unreasonable," West's lawyers argued, if the issue never came up before. Fortunately, the federal court found such a "sexually invasive search" in these circumstances would clearly violate the Fourth Amendment right to be free from unreasonable searches. Unlike *Crash*, the Fourth Circuit never describes this behavior as rape. Because the issue concerned Fourth Amendment law, the abuse was reduced to a legal discourse about the scope of what's reasonable within the officer's right to search for weapons or contraband. Lisa Amaechi's ordeal will not be found within the sexual assault statistics.

Thirteen years later, the same federal appellate court went a little further in describing the harm when it reviewed a lawsuit against a Manassas, Virginia, police officer who left no stone unturned when investigating a sexting complaint. In 2014, Officer David Abbott obtained a search warrant authorizing police to seize 17-year-old Trey Sims in order to photograph his naked body, including his erect penis, for identification purposes. Police wanted to compare the new photo with photographs that police had already seized from the cell phones belonging to the teenager and his girlfriend. Officer Abbott instructed Trey "to use his hand to manipulate his penis in different ways" to obtain an erection. Although this took place in a private space, the order was given by an armed officer while two other armed officers watched. The lower court threw out the lawsuit because qualified immunity shields only intentional or reckless bad acts by police officers, but the Fourth Circuit disagreed and ruled in favor of Trey Sims.

Thankfully, although this was a male-on-male search, the federal appeals court recognized the manipulation of a boy's penis to be a "sexually invasive search" and demanded that officers take into account the potential psychological damage of these actions upon a child. Reversing the lower court judge, the Fourth Circuit explained that "both the outrageous scope of the sexually intrusive search and the intimidating manner in which the search was conducted weigh strongly against any finding that the search was reasonable." Nevertheless, the court stopped short of viewing the behavior as criminal. Presuming that the officer was motivated by law enforcement rather than sexual gratification, the court refused to allow Trey to prove he was the victim of child pornography. "Even though we previously explained that the search as alleged was unjustified and unlawful, this conclusion does not transform the purported purpose of the search into one involving lascivious intent."[42]

Both decisions favored victims of unwanted sexual touching, and found that the conduct, if true, violated the Constitution. Still, the decisions categorize the conduct as falling within the gray area between unreasonable searches and sexual assault. I would classify the conduct as sexual violations when an officer "slightly penetrated" a woman in retaliation for her lodging a complaint against him and when another officer ordered the teenager to manipulate his penis to compare it to a photo on his girlfriend's phone. While the court named the sexual nature of the police conduct in both instances, it also grappled with the fact that the Fourth Amendment allows sexual intrusions, such as strip searches, in certain instances. Thus, the offending conduct was labeled as unreasonable rather than as a criminal violation. Even as it disallowed the manipulation of a boy's privates, the court stopped short of allowing a jury to find lascivious intent. In both cases, the court assumed that officers were motivated by law enforcement goals. Perhaps the court fears opening the floodgates, since police often touch men, women, and children in ways that society calls sexual assault when performed by non-police.

One sexualized frisk that made the news occurred on a cold January day in Philadelphia in 2014. It was unusual because the police officer was a woman.

> Darrin Manning was sixteen years old and a straight-A student with no history of arrests. He also played on his school's basketball team, and that day the team was off to a match within Philadelphia. Because of the cold, Darrin Manning and his teammates emerged from the subway wearing matching scarves that the police later claimed they mistook for ski masks. All the players, including Darrin, were black. Two police officers watching the black teenagers emerge from the subway began chasing the group, perhaps because of a smart-aleck remark from one of the ball players. Darrin Manning ran at first and then stopped, thinking that his innocence would protect him. It did not.
>
> A female police officer caught up to him and frisked him. As Darrin described it, after an initial frisk, the officer patted him down a second time and this time "I felt her reach, and she grabbed my butt." When she got to his testicles, "she grabbed and squeezed again and pulled down." The officer charged the sixteen year old with resisting arrest and several other offenses.[43]

After negative publicity against the police department for the way officers chased, stopped, and frisked the innocent teenager, the Philadelphia District Attorney and Police Chief launched a joint investigation, empaneling an investigative grand jury. However, the grand jury found that the officer who frisked Darrin Manning "had acted responsibly" and she was soon back on patrol.

Apparently, the grand jury struggled with the question of whether the officer's behavior resembled aggressive policing more than criminal assault. Darrin's lawyer told the press that the young man was simply resisting an illegal sexual assault, but the grand jury believed that Darrin's resistance permitted the police officer to use force. The grand jury also found that the young man had embellished the facts when he claimed that the officer's squeeze caused life-threatening blood clots to form. In explaining why the grand jury did not perceive the female officer as a sexual aggressor, one juror noted that the Philadelphia police department permits officers to frisk persons of the opposite sex or gender.[44] Of course, even male police officers should not be squeezing boys' genitals, but this grand jury would give that a pass too, at least in terms of naming it sexual assault. The conduct fell into the ambiguous area when frisks feel like sexual assault but may not even be unreasonable, let alone criminal, in the eyes of jurors and prosecutors.

The treatment of transgender and LGBTQ civilians also illustrates the problem of confining sexual abuse to a paradigm of something male police officers do to females.

GENDER CHECKS AND WALKING WHILE TRANS

There's a phrase in the LGBTQ community: "walking while trans." In an interview with Chase Strangio of the ACLU, black transgender activist Monica Jones told how police harrassed her four times in the previous 11 months. "The police have even threatened me with 'manifestation with intent to prostitute' charge, while I was just walking to my local bar!"[45] Police are more likely to stop, frisk, and harass transgender women or gay individuals who do not conform to societal gender norms.

The *Washington Blade*, DC's gay newspaper, reported how police officers conducted a search on the street of a black lesbian, unbuttoning her "trousers." "Why are you wearing boys' underwear? Are you a dyke? Do you eat pussy?" the officers asked her.[46]

Don't jaywalk in San Antonio. Amnesty International interviewed a transgender woman who an officer stopped and frisked as she crossed a street on her way to work as a dancer. When the officer began the frisk, the woman came out as trans and told the officer she wanted to be searched by a female officer because "my breasts are real." "Let me see if you are," said the officer and he grabbed one breast. Adding further insult and injury, the officer then arrested her for jaywalking and soliciting, giving police an opportunity to search her thoroughly (twice) in detention.[47]

A report by Amnesty International noted "a pattern of officers undertaking searches which involve inappropriate touching of an individual's genitalia in order to establish a transgender man or woman's 'true' sex."[48] Transgender individuals report frisks that include being told to unzip their pants to reveal their genitals simply to satisfy the curiosity of a police officer. Others complain of offensive comments and physical abuse. Perhaps it's born of implicit bias or curiosity, or just doing a job that requires them to eliminate disorder, with recognizably transgender and queer civilians seen as part of a neighborhood's "broken windows." Whatever the cause, it feels like a violation.

"Over the past decade, law enforcement agents have consistently been among the top three categories of perpetrators of homophobic or transphobic violence against LGBTQ people reported to anti-violence organizations," concluded a 2014 report by Columbia University Law School's Center for Gender and Sexuality Law in collaboration with the Center for American Progress and other organizations. A National Gay and Lesbian Task Force survey in 2011 found that 2 percent of transgendered people who interacted with police in the prior year reported that police sexually assaulted them, 6 percent reported physical assault, and more than one out of five reported sexual harassment. Survivors of violence who report the situation to police are particularly vulnerable. Nationally, nearly half of LGBTQ survivors of violence reported police misconduct when they sought help from police.[49] While the connection between police harassment and sexual harassment may be more salient in LGBTQ complaints, the sexual misconduct extends beyond any particular group.

Former NAACP president Benjamin Todd Jealous commented in 2014: "When my brother got older, and he moved to New York City, I never knew if the cops who abused him did so because he was black, or because he was transgender, or because he was gay. I didn't really care why."[50]

"REAL RAPE"

[A]lmost no one has any difficulty recognizing the classic, traditional rape – the stranger with a gun at the throat of his victim forcing intercourse on pain of death – as just that. When the man in the hypothetical (even a stranger) "warns her to lie down" instead ... those who are certain that a "rape" has taken place decrease significantly.[51]

Serial molester Daniel Holtzclaw breaks the mold. The officer was prosecuted and convicted of rape and related crimes.[52] Ultimately, thirteen victims, all of whom were black, testified that Oklahoma City Police Officer Holtzclaw used the power of his badge to sexually abuse them. But only one of these women came forward on her own. Fortuitously, her complaint was sent to a dogged sex crimes detective. Detective Kim Davis tracked the officer's movements over the preceding months and found other victims who agreed to come forward.

For the youngest victim, the ordeal began as a Terry stop. Holtzclaw stopped a 17 year old and learned that she had an outstanding warrant for trespass. Armed with that useful information, the officer confronted her later that day, accused her of hiding drugs, and searched her. During this "search" the officer touched her breasts and slid his hands into her pants. Imagining himself immune from discovery, Officer Holtzclaw continued his sexual assault, leaving traces of her DNA on his pants, evidence that would help a prosecutor identify her as a victim.

The Holtzclaw prosecution illustrates how much power police have over civilians. Although the Supreme Court has often stated that police do not show force or coerce civilians by wearing holstered guns, these women submitted to Officer Holtzclaw without him having to unholster his weapon. A 57-year-old daycare worker testified that the officer pulled her over for a traffic violation and sought oral sex. Eyeing the officer's holstered gun, she thought "he's going to kill me." It reminded me of the scene in *Crash* described above, when the husband tries to answer his wife's accusation that he did nothing, that he tacitly permitted the officer to continue raping her. "They had guns," the husband says simply, ending the scene and possibly their marriage.

During the trial, the 17-year-old victim was cross-examined about her failure to report the rape and she answered with a deceptively simple rhetorical question. "What kind of police do you call on the police?" With that line, the unlucky teenager captured a problem that stretches far beyond Oklahoma City, that reveals why so much abuse, including police sexual abuse, goes unreported.

Matt Sedensky covered the trial for the *Associated Press*, writing that "Many of their allegations are similar, with the women saying they were accused of hiding drugs, then told to lift their shirts or pull down their pants ... Some claim to have been groped; others said they were forced into intercourse or oral sex."[53] As in the film *Crash*, what began ostensibly as an intrusive law enforcement search turned into outright sexual assault.

For the past three decades, feminists have decried rape culture. It should be no surprise, then, to find that rape culture exists within police culture, too. Just as women are "fair game" for rape if their clothes are too slutty, they can be "fair game" for stops based on suspicion they are engaged in the sex trade, especially if they look transgender or gay. And men and boys can be frisked for wearing clothing that makes them look "suspicious" in the eyes of police. Policing victims can be blamed for resisting a stop, like Eric Garner, or for "not resisting" a strip search, like Sylvia Mendenhall.

This chapter has shown that there are bad apples who intentionally abuse people during the frisks, and they usually get away with it. To rid the rape mentality from police culture, we must start by ridding police of the opportunity and excuse. We should begin by abolishing the frisk itself, except when police officers truly have no other means of staying safe during an encounter. If a person accosts a police officer and begins threatening him, that's a situation where there's a need for a patdown to take away illegal or legal weapons until the situation becomes calm. But even so, there's no need to touch around their groin area and no cause to use the frisk as a hunt for drugs. And when police hold a person's fingers so they cannot reach for anything, there's no cause to frisk. None of the frisks described in this book were necessary in any true understanding of need. Now, even police without any prurient motives must touch groin areas as an everyday task.

Even as the Court decided to allow frisks in *Terry* v. *Ohio*, the justices admitted that frisking may "inflict great indignity and arouse strong resentment." That was before second-wave feminists marched to take back the night, demanding that women and girls be able to walk on any sidewalk without fear of sexual assault. That was before the "SlutWalks" of third-wave feminism, where women took to the streets globally, asserting the right to wear whatever we want without "asking" to be raped. That was before the #MeToo movement exposed the ubiquity of sexual harassment and sexual assaults, and before sociologists exposed the harms they cause. It's time for #ThemToo for frisking victims.

Whether it's the Court or legislatures or police departments that finally reevaluate the pros and cons of stop-and-frisk policing, an honest appraisal must include a feminist recognition of the importance of keeping unwanted hands off our bodies. As the next chapter tells us, frisks leave scars, just as any unwanted sexual touching would. Abolishing the dreaded frisks will allow communities to start to heal.

7

Invisible Scars: *Terry*'s Psychological Toll

It was the most devastating discovery of my life that I had no real right to life, liberty and pursuit of happiness out of doors.

> Rebecca Solnit (writing about the pervasive threat of harassment and violence from men)[1]

Decades before sociologists studied the fallout from stop-and-frisk, James Baldwin described experiences in a way that foreshadowed what researchers would find in years to come. *The Fire Next Time*, published in 1963, starts with Baldwin's early life in New York City.

> When I was ten, and didn't look, certainly, any older, two policemen amused themselves with me by frisking me, making comic (and terrifying) speculations concerning my ancestry and probable sexual prowess, and for good measure, leaving me flat on my back in one of Harlem's empty lots.

Frisked for fun well before the Supreme Court weighed its constitutionality, Baldwin unveiled the way such sexualized aggression impacted his childhood. One could say that Baldwin's scars helped define his life and writings.

While this first encounter was in Harlem, his backyard, Baldwin also recounts another event a few years later when police enforced the invisible Manhattan color line. "I was thirteen and was crossing Fifth Avenue on my way to the Forty-Second Street library, and the cop in the middle of the street muttered as I passed him, 'Why don't you niggers stay uptown where you belong'?" Baldwin wrote this book three decades after the abuse, and readers feel the trauma's reverberations.[2]

HOW DATA CHANGES *TERRY*'S EQUATION

In other sections of this book, I argue that the Court should overturn *Terry v. Ohio* because the consent doctrine is a sham. Take away voluntary statements and voluntary consent and there goes *Terry*'s justification for allowing police to stop and frisk us without probable cause. But this chapter slings another fatal arrow into the 1968 landmark decision. To reach its decision in *Terry* v. *Ohio*, the Court balanced the government's need for stops and frisks against the harms and indignities that flow from this practice. It's been over fifty years, yet the Court has never looked at new data to decide if they estimated the correct weight on each side of the scale. This chapter shows that *Terry* was wrong about both sides of the scale.

For the side that measured the need for stop-and-frisk, the *Terry* Court imagined that society would greatly benefit from police stops based on mere reasonable suspicion. Ironically, the only reason the Supreme Court approved stop-and-frisk in the first place was because the justices believed that police needed the tactic to keep us safe.[3] Yet, this chapter will show that instead of preventing crime, stop-and-frisk actually hinders law enforcement and creates crime.

Turning to the side of the scale that measures the harms of stop-and-frisk, the Court again got it wrong. While *Terry* admitted that frisking was hardly an insignificant intrusion on a person's autonomy, the Court could not foresee the full fallout. Adding to the sexual violation of frisks described in the last chapter, there's a growing body of sociology and psychology that describes widespread harms from stop-and-frisks to both individuals and communities.

TURNING VICTIMS INTO CRIMINALS

There's an oft-repeated refrain that goes like this: Aggressive policing tactics like stop-and-frisk create distrust among African Americans, and, as a result, police can't solve crimes because community members refuse to cooperate with investigations. As the federal government documented in the Twenty-First-Century Policing Report, every American precinct relies on the community to report and help the police solve crimes, and current methods destroy trust.[4]

Of course there's no trust when police act like an occupying army, repeatedly stopping and frisking teens and twenty-somethings who venture out of their homes. When researchers asked eighteen thousand Chicago public school students about unwelcome contacts with officers, approximately half of them reported police stops and interactions where they were "told off or told to move on" by the time they reached tenth grade. About 25 percent of these unwelcome contacts included frisks and searches.[5] One study by Amanda Geller interviewed teenagers from twenty large cities across the United States and found that half were stopped once, while the top 1 percent of teens reported between fourteen and fifty stops. Nationally, Geller notes, between 15 percent and 26 percent of American youth have been arrested by age 18.[6] Other studies note the "rough manner in which officers approach citizens." "Men are often thrown to the ground or slammed to the wall during street stops" when they didn't do anything wrong.[7] Recently, a third-year Howard law school student complained to me that "officials talk about blacks *regaining* trust as if we had trust before. We never had it. Police have to create trust." Indeed, it is hard to pick up a book by Baldwin, W.E.B. Du Bois, or John Hope Franklin and think otherwise.

Distrust is a given, but that's not the half of it. Lamenting distrust because now communities won't help the police solves crimes keeps the focus on what police want. That's like criticizing Harvey Weinstein's nonconsensual encounters because he would make better movies if he didn't frighten away actresses. While accurate, it lacks a feminist concern for the victims. Missing from the distrust critique is empathy for the people who endure unwanted police frisks and a reckoning of the full scope of the harm.

When officers threw my student Richard against the wall and dug fingers into his private area, the violation triggered psychological damage more critical to society's well-being than the loss of sources for an unspecified future police investigation. Those who bemoan the lack of cooperation with police investigations should also attend to recent sociological research that demonstrates that anger, defiance, and depression flow from interactions where officers treat individuals with suspicion and disrespect.[8]

Aggressive policing can even turn law-abiding citizens into criminals. In *A Theory of African American Offending*, sociology professor James D. Unnever explains how aggressive policing actually increases crime. False accusations from law enforcement combine with other forms of racial discrimination to make the victims of these unfair stops defiant and angry. Shame, anger, hostility, and defiance are reasonable responses to criminal injustice directed at oneself. When police officers use racial invectives or other denigrating language, this also leads stop victims to believe that the force used against them was gratuitous. Professor Unnever focuses on black males because they represent the overwhelming target of violent policing and, as another researcher phrased it, "when subjects believe they were targeted because of their race," the "stress and stigma of an encounter may be compounded."[9] Because of how people react to debasement, police tactics "substantially increase the likelihood" that individuals will commit crimes.

For James Baldwin, the humiliation and danger of repeated police encounters joined similar messages at work and school to work their spell. Baldwin forthrightly recounts how his transformation to criminality began, and how he narrowly avoided this fate:

> Crime became real . . . for the first time – not as *a* possibility but as *the* possibility. . . One needed a handle, a lever, a means of inspiring fear. It was absolutely clear that the police would whip you and take you in as long as they could get away with it.
> . . . white people, who had robbed black people of their liberty . . . had the judges, the juries, the shotguns, the law – in a word, power. But it was a criminal power, to be feared but not respected, and to be outwitted in any way whatever.[10]

Luckily, James Baldwin gave the world his beautiful prose and Richard went to law school, in spite of police cruelty. Over time, some people are bound to ask, "why bother" playing by the rules? "I might as well be a criminal if that is the only thing people think that I am." The "more African Americans perceive criminal justice injustices" such as unfair stops and frisks, "the more likely they are to defiantly offend."[11] Baldwin's reflections prove that distrust is merely one consequence of aggressive and racially charged policing.

The racial breakdown of police stops on children surveyed from large cities across the United States is as follows: 45 percent of black boys reported stops, 18 percent of black girls; 26 percent of white boys and 8 percent of white girls were stopped.[12] In Youth Court in DC, almost all the teenagers were black, and approximately 80 percent were male.

Age matters. The younger they are when subjected to unwanted police stops, the more susceptible these victims become to engaging in subsequent delinquent behavior. On average, one study found, those teenagers who police had stopped at least once, were only 12 or 13 years old the first time it happened to them. At least one teenager's first stop occurred at age eight.[13]

In the television show *The Wire*, a fictional retired police major, Bunny Colvin, explains why Baltimore's at-risk teenagers don't pay attention in school and even if you "teach them every problem in some statewide test, it won't matter." These "kids," Colvin explains, "know exactly what it is everyone expects them to be." "Everyone" includes the police. "Every single one of them knows they're headed back to the corners," to sell drugs.[14] Repetitive stops and frisks send a message that no matter who they are, police will treat young black men as likely criminals, thereby encouraging them to become criminals.

If you wanted to design a system to keep people safe, this would not be it. It defies common sense to continue crime-fighting strategies that treat honest teens as second-class citizens, regardless of their actions, and increase the likelihood that they will turn to crime.

Critical race scholars argue that there is no contradiction because solving crimes is not the true goal. "The system is working the way it is supposed to."[15] Lots of people make money in a system that cages extraordinary numbers of Americans: the prison builders, CEOs, employees, and guards certainly, and arguably prosecutors, judges, and defense lawyers like me. Even with mounting proof against the drug war, "law and order" politicians still benefit from hyper-incarceration. Stop-and-frisk is the funnel, producing enough drug and "assault on a police officer" charges to feed the hungry incarceration machine, producing arrests to assure there are enough bodies to keep the machine purring.

Stop-and-frisk does for at-risk youth what bar raids did in the first half of the twentieth century for vulnerable gay men and lesbians who wanted to socialize. As LGBTQ advocates look back over the last thirty years, it is a path from criminal suspect to citizen. For decades, police regulated the performance of gender in the bars and on the streets. Butch lesbians tell of New York police officers pulling down their pants to see if they violated the rule that females wear at least three feminine garments.[16] Gay men remember bar raids where they could be arrested for dancing together. Although I've met men who laughed at running out back doors to escape arrest, they could afford to laugh now because Justice Anthony Kennedy wrote for a majority of the Supreme Court that the Constitution protects "certain personal choices central to individual dignity and autonomy."[17] In the 1950s and 1960s, police officers merely enforced the laws when they raided bars, but, in doing so, they stigmatized a segment of the population, depriving every LGBTQ person in America of their full citizenship. Perhaps the officers targeted James Baldwin because they thought him "homosexual." *Time* magazine described the gay author as "nervous, slight, almost fragile in figure" and "effeminate in manner."[18]

Advocates in some cities tell me that despite the Supreme Court marriage decisions, life hasn't improved much for at-risk LGBTQ teenagers. Young black or Latinx LGBTQ New Yorkers were particularly singled out for Terry stops even after the Supreme Court decriminalized gay sexuality and intimacy.[19] Stop-and-frisk becomes a method for police to continue to target people who officers view as part of the disorder they were hired to prevent.

Like the bar raids, Terry stops send a message about who belongs and who deserves respect and dignity. Enforced more than the sodomy laws, Terry stops exact costs and create risks for those who dare to venture out into public spaces. "Police interactions are fraught with inherent symbolic meaning concerning social identity, collective belonging and social exclusion," sociologists explain.[20] "Regulating public space and restricting the movements of certain people through that space are primary police activities," within "order maintenance policing" that include increased use of stop-and-frisk. People change their dress, change their routes, or stop visiting friends who live in highly policed areas in order to avoid police.[21] As the Center for Constitutional Rights found, "stop and frisk can leave people feeling unsafe, fearful of police, and afraid to leave their homes."[22]

Bad stops even threaten democracy. Justice Sonia Sotomayor recently observed that unfettered police power sends a message to the victims of stop-and-frisk that the government is not their government. When police can stop and check you for outstanding warrants whenever they want, this "implies that you are not a citizen of a democracy but the subject of a carceral state, just waiting to be cataloged."[23] Social science backs up the Justice's keen observation. Police encounters "form the basis" of youths' "sense of democratic belonging and obligation to the law." "Police officers are often the first and only contact that young people have with the juvenile justice system," explains researchers Jamie L. Flexon, Arthur J. Lurigio, and Richard G. Greenleaf in a study of Chicago high school students. Aggressive policing leaves "lasting impressions on youths that can affect their attitudes toward the law and legal authorities." In over-policed communities, police encounters can cause teenagers to question "democracy itself," making them less likely to vote and participate in other community strengthening behaviors. Summing up the literature, Amanda Geller and Jeffrey Fagan describe "legal cynicism" as "a state of disconnection from both community and the social and legal norms of the state." When police target neighborhoods for increased stops, summonses and arrests, this creates legal cynicism, that unravels "the social bonds that connect people to each other."[24]

It is difficult to imagine the willowy and erudite Baldwin as a drug dealer or pimp. If the talented James Baldwin considers himself lucky to escape a career in crime, it begs key questions: How many people have succumbed to criminal behavior as a result of our criminal justice messages? Once we acknowledge that aggressive policing actually increases criminality, we jettison the myth that stop-and-frisk promotes safety.

MENTAL HEALTH CONSEQUENCES

Social scientists increasingly recognize criminal injustice as a threat to physical and mental health.[25] And where there's stress and trauma, medical consequences are sure to follow. Even as he penned the *Terry* v. *Ohio* decision permitting stop-and-frisks based on mere reasonable suspicion, Justice Earl Warren recognized that "it is simply fantastic to urge that such a procedure performed in public by a policeman while the citizen stands helpless, perhaps facing a wall with his hands raised, is a 'petty indignity.'"[26] Unfortunately, social scientists only recently began studying the psychological fallout from this indignity.

Researchers who study neighborhoods where stops and frisks are prevalent found that officers often harass young men, sometimes with harsh language, and other times with violence. A study of Chicago youth by sociologist Ron Brunson described how interactions with police officers left youth feeling "dehumanized" and hopeless.[27] Another research team found that Chicago youth who suffered multiple unwanted contacts with police suffered high rates of distress.[28] Many of the participants in the study were innocent. This contrasts with advocates of programmatic stop-and-frisk, who argue that it's only a minor nuisance for those who are innocent of a crime.[29]

Brunson explains the connection between innocence and violence in a 2009 article: "Just as young men's law-abiding status failed adequately to protect them from general police harassment, it also did not insulate them from police violence. In fact, being innocent could increase young men's chances of being assaulted, as they were more likely to challenge the inappropriateness of officers' actions when they were not engaged in unlawful acts."[30]

After equating stop-and-frisk with sexual harassment, as this book does, it's no surprise to find that the harms are similar. We know that workplace sexual harassment causes psychological damage when there's repetitive unwanted conduct. When sexual harassment involves unwanted physical touching, it's especially likely to lead to lasting psychological distress. In some cases, workplace harassment leads to clinical anxiety and post-traumatic stress disorder.[31] As with workplace harassment, some victims suffer repeated Terry stops. Even for people stopped once, that encounter may be particularly aggressive and include a frisk, degrading language, violence, or a combination of these. Richard's stop included all three. Do Terry stops also impact long-term mental health?

One of the first studies to squarely examine this was undertaken by Amanda Geller, a Clinical Associate Professor of Sociology at New York University, along with Jeffrey Fagan, the Columbia law professor who served as the expert witness on statistical data analysis for the plaintiffs in *Floyd* v. *City of New York*, and Bruce Link, professor emeritus at Columbia and the director of the Center for Violence Research and Prevention. In "Aggressive Policing and the Mental Health of Young Urban Men," published in 2014 in the *American Journal of Public Health*, the authors interviewed over 1,200 men, aged 18 to 26, in New York City during the period when patrol officers stopped and frisked to meet quotas. Remember that the overwhelming majority of people targeted in New York City were innocent.[32] Eighty-five percent of the participants had been stopped at least once, while 5 percent had been stopped more than twenty-five times.

It turns out that repeated stops create anxiety long after these short detentions end. Young men stopped by police on multiple occasions "display higher levels of anxiety and trauma associated with their experiences," such as nervousness, tension, anxiety, social alienation, panic attacks, feelings of personal inadequacy and inferiority, and irrational phobic responses to a specific person, place, object, or situation. The young men's anxiety and trauma symptoms rose in correlation to the number of stops they experienced. That is, the more stops, the more likely they were to find a young man experiencing symptoms of lasting trauma.

Like workplace harassment, where fear of repeated unwelcome contact can lead to poor health outcomes, "anticipation of subsequent contact" with police "could cause or exacerbate stress and associated health problems" if "the 'dosage' of police contact is strong (meaning it involves intrusive searches or force) or individuals "believe they could be stopped again at any time."[33]

Geller and her co-authors also found that stops and frisks can lead to post-traumatic stress disorder (PTSD). To diagnose PTSD, medical professionals look for persistent symptoms such as difficulty concentrating, exaggerated startle response, and outbursts of anger – symptoms that were not present before the traumatic event. After measuring a number of variables, researchers concluded that the intensity of the stops mattered more than the number of stops. More invasive stops correlated with higher levels of trauma. Frisks were more likely to lead to PTSD than were Terry stops without the ritual search from shoulders to socks. However, Terry stops that involved physical violence, such as when participants were "thrown to the ground or slammed against walls," could also lead to PTSD symptoms.

With anxiety, depression, and especially with PTSD, it's not just the afflicted individual who suffers. Families, neighbors, and complete strangers bear the burden of these behaviors. No wonder the researchers concluded that "any benefits achieved by aggressive policing tactics may be offset by serious costs to individual and community health."

Given the mind–body split in the United States, some readers might not realize that psychological stress generally leads to physical symptoms. Even "everyday stressors produce wear and tear on the body, which has been shown to increase physiological strain and limit disease resistance."[34] Studies document how perceptions of race discrimination correlate to raised blood pressure and other negative health consequences for African Americans.[35] Racially discriminatory police practices can be viewed through this lens – another form of bias that produces physical and psychological symptoms in targeted communities. Yet racist policing policies are worse than individual biases because we're talking about how our government interacts with its people. Unlike a biased private citizen, police have the power to accuse, arrest, and incarcerate. This renders police bias more frightening and more stressful than many other forms of racially charged indignities.[36]

Consider hypervigilance, a logical by-product of aggressive policing. People remain alert, scanning their environment to protect themselves from further harm. W. E. B. Du Bois wrote about "double consciousness" at the turn of the twentieth century, a survival skill to navigate the horrors of racist violence that took its toll on every black American adult and child.[37] This double consciousness describes a form of hypervigilance. As one law student explained to me, "I always have to pay attention to how the police see me," from what he wears to where he walks and who he's with. Unhealthy side effects to hypervigilance include elevated blood pressure, increased heart rate, and the presence of biomarkers of stress, particularly among those who cope with this anxious state for extended periods of time.[38]

"After being sexually assaulted by a male officer, Tiffany described the way she tries to calm her body to resist the desire to run when she sees police," saying to herself, "You can do this, just keep walking, it's okay, you didn't do shit." Tiffany was interviewed for a study whose authors view her fortitude as a form of resistance to dehumanization because she refuses to accept the label of criminal for herself. According to the team of research psychologists, avoiding police is another form of "corporal resistance" to dehumanization.[39]

For Terry stop victims who believed that police targeted them based on race, Geller's study found an increased likelihood of anxiety, stress, or PTSD compared to participants who felt the officers acted fairly. This dovetails with multiple previous reports that describe how racial accusations of wrongdoing trigger psychological damage.[40] Let's not forget that Terry stops are by definition an accusation that the individual appears to be a criminal, dangerous, or both. Regardless of whether it's conscious or unconscious racial profiling, when police appear to select targets based on race or racial characteristics, individuals will activate their alarm systems. Such fear and anxiety describe some of the deep psychological consequences behind today's Terry stop statistics.

VICARIOUS HEALTH CONSEQUENCES

The World Health Organization (WHO) now treats violence – whether performed by the state or an individual – as a health problem.[41] In 2002, WHO reported a relationship between violence and the excessive use of force by police. On the one hand, excessive force, especially deadly force, creates physical injuries and is therefore a type of violence in itself. Additionally, when society tolerates police use of excessive force, even nondeadly force, this encourages other types of violence in a society.

When Michael Brown's body was callously left in the street in Ferguson, one civilian tweeted that the neighbors "could walk out of their homes and see a dead body in the street as it was lying there for four hours. You can preach due process to everyone but this remains a point of fact ... A lot of people were traumatized."[42] On *The New Yorker Radio Hour*, screenwriter Lena Waithe told Jelani Cobb how hearing about black bodies dropping traumatizes her.

> I am like every other black person – I am traumatized every time these stories come out.
>
> Every time these stories hit our phones, our Instagram feed, our Twitter, our TV, a piece of us dies because we know that we could be next.[43]

When *Terry* considered the negative repercussions from stop-and-frisk, the Supreme Court only looked at the indignity to the person frisked, not to on-lookers or a person's family or the community. Similarly, under the Court's latest rulings, the only person who can challenge a bad stop is the individual victim of the illegality. This standing doctrine assumes that unconstitutional policing only affects the man, woman, or child who is grabbed or groped. These legal doctrines fail to reflect the science of trauma. Psychologists have found that adults and children can become alarmed and disturbed simply by seeing another person in distress.[44] It's eminently logical that police activity would have a psychological impact beyond those individuals who experienced aggressive policing firsthand, especially when police concentrate their activities in certain neighborhoods.

The anguish from police violence and disrespect ripples outward so that even the mere perception that there is pervasive police harassment in one's neighborhood often causes residents who have not been personally policed to view police officers with trepidation. Family and neighbors may suffer trauma without being manhandled. People who have never been stopped feel anguish and anger when they witness police target others or when they learn about police abuse from family and friends. Sociologists call this "vicarious experience."

A "growing body of research suggests that vicarious experiences of the police can be as powerful in influencing one's attitudes as direct, personal experiences."[45] It's not just the person stopped or frisked who suffers. When friends and family members recount distressing police stops, this influences the listener's attitudes and emotions toward police officers. Community members who see others unfairly targeted, frisked, or hurt may become hypervigilant in order to avoid unwanted police encounters.

Disturbing media reports of violent police incidents can also cause vicarious damage. All the participants in a study of black men from California who had seen media accounts of the 2018 shooting of Stephon Clark reported what researchers termed "psychological anguish" that included the loss of "feeling safe in their existence." Researchers warned clinical psychologists to recognize the "secondary traumas that are imbedded in the psyches of black men." Even when black men don't meet the strict PTSD diagnostic criteria because they were not close to the precipitating event, the study advised, these patients may suffer from secondary traumas that may show up as "anger, sadness, avoidance, dissociation and hypervigilance."[46]

Studies like this expose the fallacy of consent searches. Once we recognize that people who have not been victimized themselves walk around afraid that police will shoot them, we can no longer accept the Court's assumption that their cooperation signals voluntary consent. Likewise, these studies should cause the Court to question its judgment that running from the police in high-crime neighborhoods justifies an officer's suspicions that the person is engaging in illegal behavior. Instead, courts should recognize that running from the police represents a form of resistance to further dehumanization. Alternatively, running might represent "avoidance or escape behavior," a trauma-driven response for those who have previously suffered an unfair Terry stop or who have simply viewed media accounts of police violence.

While Professor Geller and her co-authors focused on the recipients of unwanted and aggressive police stops, Abigail A. Sewell studied the effect of stop-and-frisk on whole communities. In one study, titled *Collateral Damage: The Health Effects of Invasive Police Encounters in New York City*, the Sewell team compared two data sets from New York City in the years 2009–12: (1) the forms police filled out recording two million stops during the three-year period, that included information about the neighborhood and about the stops, and (2) an annual random-digit-dial health survey of 10,000 New Yorkers that was subdivided by neighborhoods. Overall, the researchers' statistical analysis revealed that Terry stops, especially in neighborhoods with high levels of frisking, were "associated with poor health" even when controlling for other factors, such as access to healthcare, individual socioeconomic factors, and neighborhood income and crime levels. Physical symptoms associated with stress included "the prevalence of diabetes, high blood pressure, past year asthma episodes" as well as psychological distress.[47] In a related study, Professor Sewell and her research team found that men in high-stop neighborhoods were "more likely to report feelings of nervousness and worthlessness and more severe psychological distress" even if they had not been personally stopped.[48]

"People do not have to be inside the criminal justice system to feel the effects of the criminal justice system," concluded Professor Sewell. Aggressive police policies, the studies prove, "reach so far as to shape the health of people who have not yet entered into its gates."[49]

There is also some interesting literature on how trauma can be transmitted from one generation to the next. According to the American Psychological Association, children can inherit physical trauma symptoms through nature as well as nurture.[50]

> On the simplest level, the concept of intergenerational trauma acknowledges that exposure to extremely adverse events impacts individuals to such a great extent that their offspring find themselves grappling with their parents' post-traumatic state. A more recent and provocative claim is that the experience of trauma – or more accurately the effect of that experience – is "passed" somehow from one generation to the next through non-genomic, possibly epigenetic mechanisms affecting DNA function or gene transcription.[51]

Researchers who studied First Nations peoples in Canada found them vulnerable to the transmission of "intergenerational trauma effects," including increased depression, anxiety, substance abuse, and post-traumatic stress disorder.[52] It's not always easy to determine how trauma is passed down. These "transgenerational effects are not only psychological, but familial, social, cultural, neurobiological, and possibly even genetic as well."[53] One researcher who studies Holocaust survivors presents intergenerational trauma as a "pathway between the initial trauma, the family's history and post-trauma sociocultural milieu, the adaptational styles of survivors, and the intensity of their children's and grandchildren's reparative reactions to them."[54] Historic trauma gives context to the way later generations receive current stressors. When it comes to African Americans, Dr. Joy DeGruy argues that continued discrimination and violence extended the harmful effects of slavery, affecting the psychological and physical well-being of current generations.[55] Dr. Allen Lipsomb, who researches psychiatric epidemiology, wrote in the *Journal of Sociology and Social Work* in 2019 that there's "slim literature around the historical impact of police abuse on African Americans" but it "is likely" that the history of violence "may have translated into intergenerational effects."[56]

When black Americans give their children "the talk" to keep them safe from police, it's hard to avoid risking vicarious harm. "I told them to stand there and do as they said," explained one father, "'cause if you don't, if you breathe loud, they gonna send you on from here" (meaning they will kill you).[57] Keeping one's children safe comes with psychological risks under the *Terry* regime. Talking with sons about potential police encounters is "traumatizing for parents and it's traumatizing for kids," says Alfiee Breland-Noble, PhD, who directs the African American Knowledge Optimized for Mindfully Healthy Adolescents Project at Georgetown University.[58]

The literature on intergenerational trauma suggests that current stop-and-frisk practices are stressors that may cause negative health outcomes to both current and future generations of black Americans. The potential for serious long-lasting damage to men, women, and children makes ending stop-and-frisk policing an urgent issue.

CAUTION: STOP-AND-FRISK MAY BE HAZARDOUS TO YOUR HEALTH

Thinking back to Baldwin's childhood, it is only logical that he would experience physical and mental symptoms from an encounter with police that was both scary and demeaning. Moreover, as Baldwin explains, "one did not have to be abnormally sensitive to be worn down to the cutting edge" by repeated abuse, by the fear that police will use their "criminal power" to "whip you and take you in" whenever they wish.

As this book argues, even constitutionally approved frisking leaves lasting scars. *Terry* v. *Ohio* was wrong when it imagined that the gains in community safety outweighed the harms of watering down Fourth Amendment protections. As research now shows, this side of the scale should include: (1) psychological trauma from stress, including even PTSD for some stopped civilians; (2) vicarious psychological trauma for those who learn about aggressive stops secondhand; (3) the possibility that these stressors will be passed on to the next generation; (4) physical health consequences that flow from hypervigilance and other stress-related symptoms; (5) bad health outcomes for those who live in communities with intensive Terry-style investigations; and (6) interference in American democracy, because individuals are less likely to participate in their communities.

It took decades to recognize that tobacco creates health risks for both smokers and people around them. As with smoking, researchers have only just begun to reveal the grim costs that accompany stop-and-frisk policing. At the basic level, aggressive policing tactics harm everyone, from the person stopped to the person's neighborhood. That's what this research tells us. Stop-and-frisk encounters cause untold invisible scars. Even people who imagine that such policing reduces crime – and gain that placebo effect – end up harmed.

8

High Court Camouflage: How the Supreme Court Hides Police Aggression and Racial Animus

Imagine you are inside your home and you hear loud knocking. Police officers are banging on your door, announcing "police, police, police." This is what happened to Hollis King and two friends in Fayette County, Kentucky. Legally, you must answer the door when police demand entry, but was this a demand? Or was the banging merely an invitation?

The case went all the way to the Supreme Court, which rejected the notion that police banging "on the door as loud as [they] could" and announcing "police, police, police" could be construed as a demand to the person inside to open the door. The Court's reasoning in *Kentucky* v. *King* is emblematic of how the Supreme Court reinforces police aggression by pretending that police behavior is benign rather than coercive.[1]

Although the trial judge who heard live testimony called the knocking a "demand" for entry, a majority of justices rejected this conclusion. The majority reasoned that officers may knock as loudly as they want and yell "police" repeatedly without a reasonable occupant thinking he must open the door, as long as police do not specifically state "open up" or explicitly threaten to enter without a warrant. "There is no evidence of a 'demand' of any sort," the Court concluded.

Perhaps conservative Supreme Court justices lack experience with officers banging on their doors, but there was nothing consensual about this encounter. This was high court camouflage. Long-established precedent declares that civilians must obey orders – so when they do so, they don't waive their rights or "voluntarily" consent. Mere "acquiescence to" a police demand is not consent. The *King* case did not change this rule. Instead, the Court labeled the police behavior as nonaggressive, meaning that the civilians could choose whether or not to follow the officers' "request" for entry.

As in other "knock and talk" cases, the Court compared police coming onto private property and knocking on doors to investigate crimes as similar to door-to-door salesmen or pollsters, strangers that can be easily ignored. Knocking on front doors "is generally managed without incident by the Nation's Girl Scouts and trick-or-treaters" so when "law enforcement officers who are not armed with a warrant knock on a door, they do no more than any private citizen might do."[2]

Justice Samuel Alito further explained:

> Police officers may have a very good reason to announce their presence loudly and to knock on the door with some force ... Citizens who are startled by an unexpected knock on the door ... may appreciate the opportunity to make an informed decision about whether to answer the door to the police.[3]

By presenting officers as no more threatening than a neighbor seeking a cup of sugar or a Girl Scout selling cookies, the Court renders police power invisible. Officers don't have to inform us when we are allowed to withhold consent, because we are expected to be as comfortable refusing them as we might "any private citizen." This fiction that police are not authority figures who demand compliance with their requests permeates Fourth Amendment rules.

In fact, the police did break down Mr. King's door when no one opened it, but the police claimed they took that step only because they heard movements consistent with destroying drug evidence. Those "exigent circumstances" then excused the lack of warrant. Presumably, had the people inside stayed still, then the police would have left everyone alone, like a neighbor or Girl Scout would. By erasing the power differential in the retelling, the Court allows aggressive policing to thrive.

WHY THE COURT HIDES POLICE POWER AND AGGRESSION

Camouflaging police aggression serves many purposes for the conservative Supreme Court justices.

First, the Court's reinterpretation of facts (from coercive to benign) allows it to uphold the denial of motions to suppress evidence in the case before the Court. Mr. King was charged with drug offenses after police seized cocaine, marijuana, and evidence of distribution from inside the apartment, so his lawyer moved to exclude the evidence because police lacked a search warrant. By refusing to call the knock a demand for entry, the Court was able to endorse the admission of the drug evidence and uphold the conviction that sent Mr. King to prison for eleven years.[4]

Second, by keeping the legal rule the same and only manipulating the facts, the Court projects the false impression that people retain their rights, such as the right to be free from police knocking down your door without a warrant.

Third, prosecutors will have an easier time proving "voluntary consent" when courts pretend that police don't behave forcefully or aggressively. Consent swallows up Fourth Amendment protections because police don't need a shred of evidence to stop or search us when we "voluntarily" submit to police requests. Thanks to the fiction that people are not intimidated by police officers when they "allow" officers to take intrusive actions, there's almost no check left on police power.

Fourth, the tactic shifts the blame away from the officers who lack just cause to search and "blames the victim." Whenever a judge denies my motion to suppress because my client supposedly "consented" to the search that lands them in jail or prison, it's as if the court tells my client: "it's your fault that the officer searched you; if you had resisted him, you would be free." In an article published in 2010, I wrote:

> Just as rape victims were told they asked for it by wearing short dresses and not screaming for help, individuals are told they asked for it by extending their arms to be searched. They are told it is their fault that the police touched their thighs or looked in their pockets. They are told that they should have resisted the police incursion, even if resistance risked triggering further charges or unpleasant responses from the police. [5]

Eight years later, Justice Alito made this blame game explicit in *Kentucky v. King*. "Occupants who choose not to stand on their constitutional rights [by not answering the door when police bang on it and shout "police"] have only themselves to blame."[6]

Too often, scholars point to unconstitutional stops and frisks as the problem. Criminologists Michael D. White and Henry F. Fradella in their book, *Stop and Frisk: The Use and Abuse of a Controversial Policing Tactic*, applaud Terry stops when done in a "fair, just, and constitutional manner."[7] But White and others miss how consent creates an easy pathway to constitutional approval. Just call it "consent" and whatever the police did now survives constitutional scrutiny.[8]

Central to stop-and-frisk's long reach, the law allows police to target, pursue, and question individuals without naming it a stop. Even when police lack any justification for a stop, the Court explains,

> law enforcement officers do not violate the Fourth Amendment by merely approaching an individual on the street or in another public place, by asking him if he is willing to answer some questions, by putting questions to him if the person is willing to listen, or by offering in evidence in a criminal prosecution his voluntary answers to such questions.[9]

People who stop to answer questions have only themselves to blame when they end up behind bars.

The 1988 case of *Michigan v. Chesternut* provides an early Terry stop example of how the Court camouflages aggression. There, police chased a civilian who ran when he saw their cruiser. Police testified that "the patrol car followed respondent around the corner 'to see where he was going'" and "caught up with respondent and drove alongside him for a short distance."[10] It is difficult to imagine a more threatening act than being chased by armed men, especially men with the power to arrest and to use their weapons when making an arrest. Yet, the Supreme Court decreed that when officers engage in a chase, it must be recharacterized as "benign." According to the Supreme Court, there was nothing coercive about the police behavior here. In these circumstances, Michael Mose Chesternut, a black man walking down the sidewalks of Detroit, should consider himself free to disregard the police. "Contrary to respondent's assertion that a chase necessarily communicates that detention is intended and imminent, the police conduct involved here would not have communicated to the reasonable person an attempt to capture or otherwise intrude upon respondent's freedom of movement."[11]

Disguising police coercion as benign allows police to behave aggressively and then blame the victims of this aggression for failing to assert their rights. Court opinions hide unnecessary police aggression in order to allow it to thrive. *Michigan v. Chesternut* supports an expansive view of the "consent" stop.

It's willful blindness when the Court in *Chesternut* pretends that police "would not have communicated an attempt to ... intrude upon" a person's freedom by chasing them in a cruiser. Similarly, it's "willful blindness" when the Court in *Kentucky v. King* describes police pounding on Mr. King's door as not "a 'demand' of any sort." Remember Sylvia Mendenhall, who was singled out at the airport based on a racial profile, and was then "asked" to accompany the officers to a room where she cooperated in a strip search? When the majority interpreted Ms. Mendenhall's words "I have a flight to catch" to mean that she wanted "the search [to] be conducted quickly" rather than asking to let her go, the Court blatantly disguised the coercion, but it was a bad decision even if Ms. Mendenhall hadn't protested. To conclude that any strip search is a consensual affair, especially one where the civilian was young, female, and black, requires willful blindness.

HOW CONSENT EXCUSES RACIAL PROFILING

Law professor Devon Carbado critiqued the way the Supreme Court manipulates race in its opinions by making it appear and disappear in ways that help maintain the status quo.[12] The Court makes race invisible in two related ways. First, Court opinions omit the race of the individuals involved. Second, the Court will not suppress evidence because an officer selected his victim or undertook the search based on implicit or explicit racial bias. I add to Professor Carbado's thesis by demonstrating a direct connection between how the Court hides race and how it hides police aggression. The facts in *Drayton* help illuminate how both mechanisms support continued racial discrimination.

Christopher Drayton and Clifton Brown Jr. were two protagonists in a Supreme Court drama that demonstrates how the Court's Kafkaesque reasoning hides aggression and thereby reinforces racial profiling. The two men were crammed into seats on an interstate bus when three police officers commandeered the bus in a dragnet operation searching for drugs. One officer took the driver's seat while another stood at the back of the bus, and a third officer slowly advanced up the aisle, asking questions and searching bags. When this police officer stood inches from where Drayton and Brown sat, he told them: "We're conducting bus interdiction, attempting to deter drugs and illegal weapons being transported on the bus. We would like your cooperation." He then asked them to point out their luggage, first searching the bags and eventually the two men. Both men cooperated.[13] Next, each man submitted to a frisk.

Both Drayton and his traveling companion were black. By selecting Mr. Drayton and Mr. Brown for frisks after their luggage proved clean of any contraband, the police followed the historical practice of targeting young black and brown men for increased surveillance.[14] Racial profiling has been defined in many ways, but at heart it means that police target certain outsider groups of people for increased oversight, such as blacks or Muslims or those perceived as undocumented Mexicans. Police target young black men more than they target young white men either because implicit biases make them seem more suspicious or because their departments trained them to target certain groups for heightened policing.

True to its commitment to racial blindness, *United States* v. *Drayton* neither utters the phrase "racial profiling" nor mentions the race of Mr. Drayton and his fellow traveler. By omitting the race of the policed individuals, the Court hides the racial profiling involved. The Court's racial blindness allows the police to racially profile without fear that their actions will be scrutinized by courts.

Similarly, the *Drayton* Court stays true to its method of hiding police power and aggression. To imagine Mr. Drayton had a choice in whether to cooperate is to imagine the man was stupid, for he carried concealed narcotics that the police easily found during the frisk. Yet, when Mr. Drayton's lawyer sought to prevent the government from introducing the drugs at his trial, the government argued that both the initial stop and the frisk were consensual events. The Supreme Court agreed. When the officers boarded the bus so that the bus couldn't leave, this didn't count as a Terry stop of the passengers, the Court decided, nor did it count as a Terry stop when the police literally stood between Drayton and any exit. And when Mr. Drayton spread his arms to submit to a frisk, that was how he showed his voluntary consent to a patdown of his body.

As usual, the Court relies on nonsensical factual nuances to support its conclusion that Mr. Drayton consented to have the officer pat him down from shoulder to groin. First, Justice Anthony Kennedy put stock in how quietly the officer talked when he stood over Mr. Drayton's seat. Second, the officer testified that he addressed Mr. Drayton in language that suggested that this was voluntary, asking "Mind if I check you?" Third, although the police were armed, they kept their guns in their holsters. As the dissent pointed out, the *Drayton* Court's distinctions are absurd. Polite or rude, this drug "interdiction" was "not a consensual exercise, but one the police would carry out whatever the circumstances." "A police officer who is certain to get his way has no need to shout."[15]

Mr. Drayton's guilt complicated the Court's analysis. In reality, a person such as Mr. Drayton, with drugs strapped to his thighs, would only agree to a stop or search if the officer signaled that cooperation was mandatory. The majority elegantly side-stepped this problem of proof by explaining that the reasonable person test "presup-poses an *innocent* person." One criticism leveled at the reasonable person test is that courts fail to take into account race when deciding whether an individual would feel free to decline an officer's request.[16] Indeed, given the racial state of American black policing, a reasonable black person would fear retaliation if they refused to submit to a search. And when the Court changed the test, things got worse. What's most pernicious about Drayton's reasonable *innocent* person test is how it directs judges to ignore the person standing before them seeking redress, to ignore that they were, in fact, coerced. Now, no matter the race, gender, or sexual orientation of the accused, the Court intentionally disregards their viewpoint and renders their experience irrelevant. With these verbal gymnastics, the Court says to Mr. Drayton and to all the other individuals stopped and frisked without justification: We know you only submitted due to police pressure, but adding insult to injury, we will call your capitulation consent. As bad as rape law was for victims, it never twisted the question of consent the way the consent doctrine of the Fourth Amendment now does. Black or white or other, the reasonable *innocent* person test hides police aggression, distorts Mr. Drayton's humanity, and blames him for not resisting the officer's moves. There's a hidden racial dimension here too, for the easier it is to prove consent, the harder it is to win motions based on racial profiling.

Consent encourages racial profiling because the doctrine closes the last available door to suppressing evidence seized as a result of racial bias. Racial profiling is an improper motive, says the Court, but if an officer had reasonable suspicion to stop (or probable cause to search), the judge can't look at the motive and can't suppress the evidence. Even so, the Court still allows one small opportunity to fight racist police practices: when there's no reasonable suspicion, then racial profiling violates the Fourth Amendment.

That means that Mr. Drayton should have won because the police lacked the reasonable suspicion necessary to justify stopping him and the probable cause necessary to justify searching him. Police were not allowed to racially profile and they could not come up with any valid excuse for what they did. That's where consent comes in. Remember, police don't even need reasonable suspicion for Terry stops when stops are not called stops but are reimagined as consensual encounters. Here's how consent helps the government defeat racial profiling claims:

1. Racial profiling is improper.
2. If the officer racially profiled Mr. Drayton and his friend, the evidence cannot be used against him at court – unless the officer had reasonable suspicion for the stop-and-frisk.
3. If the officer racially profiled Mr. Drayton without reasonable suspicion, then the evidence cannot be used against him in court – unless he consented.

The two forms of camouflage – one hiding race and the other hiding aggression – work well together. Just as the Court in *Whren* v. *United States* decided that *probable cause* washes away the sins of racial profiling, the Court in *United States* v. *Drayton* decided that *consent* washes away the sins of racial profiling.[17] By hiding the police aggression that made Mr. Drayton raise his arms to be searched, the Court gives unconstitutional racial profiling a pass. The "consent" exception trumps racial profiling.

YOU THINK IT ONLY HAPPENS TO PEOPLE OF COLOR?

While it's dangerous to ignore the racial underpinning of policing throughout most of the country, it's likewise dangerous to imagine that police aggression is reserved for black people, or for Mexicans, or for Muslims – or even just for men. White people make a mistake in thinking that racist policing makes them safer and they/we are wrong to think that aggressive policing won't affect us.

"You are treating me like a f-ing black person," yelled a 59-year-old white doctor when police tackled him at an airport ticket counter.[18] The man voted for Donald Trump, who trumpeted excessive force and increased police powers (except when it involves the president and his cronies). Because the doctor believed that excessive force only harmed black men, he wasn't offended by the platform. Until it happened to him.

Recently in a coffee shop, I mentioned to a liberal white man seated at the next table that police kill more white men than black men. He said that he didn't believe that police kill that many white men. I hastened to add that, statistically, white people make up over 60 percent of the population so the chances of being shot are much lower for whites than blacks. Adjusting for population, we see that "black Americans are 2.5 times as likely as white Americans to be shot and killed by police officers."[19] The statistics were even worse for black people when one considers unarmed shootings. In fact, "unarmed black Americans were five times as likely as unarmed white Americans to be shot and killed by a police officer." Still, 51 percent of the people shot by police in the US were white, according to the statistics.[20] This man understood my comments as minimizing racism. He acted as if I were trying to erase the pain that black people experience in this country when they fear being stopped for merely walking while black or driving while black.

We can keep these two ideas alive at the same time. First, that police use violence on more white people than people of color and second, that police apply aggression unequally, in a way that terribly burdens people of color and communities of color. To deny true statistics will not benefit the people most often profiled and stopped. For those of us who define ourselves as white, the denial erases vulnerability and hides the fact that everyone benefits at some point in their life from a robust Fourth Amendment. Studies show that when white people view welfare as a program primarily for blacks, they vote for candidates who slash these benefits, even though the program helps white people also.[21] Similarly, painting unchecked police power as solely a racial issue garners support for it among many white voters.

Years ago, I snorkeled for the first time. Here were the clear blue seas off Cozumel (amazing to a New York City native), where I could see coral reefs and little fish beckon in the distance. Swimming happily toward the reefs, I spotted bags of garbage. As I watched the detritus float toward me, I started to hyperventilate for fear I would soon breathe plastic rot through the tube. In the same way, stop-and-frisk stealthily pollutes this country. Many do not feel the immediate impact of stop-and-frisk because it disproportionately affects people of color. But the harm ripples outward and can catch any of us in its stream.

Like tossed plastic that quietly coats coral reefs, we hardly notice the gradual corrosion of the Bill of Rights, a treasure that belongs to the rich as well as the poor, the privileged as well as the disenfranchised. Repeated aggressive policing causes distrust, fear, and even trauma. Trauma, in turn, can transform into post-traumatic stress. In another ripple, trauma's manifestations threaten to turn law-abiding citizens into lawbreakers. The ripples move ever outward, polluting as they go. We all swim in the same water, and the Supreme Court, prosecutors, and judges risk churning up the harm, corrupting justice, undercutting our fundamental freedoms, and damaging our relationships to one another.

When the Supreme Court takes away the rights of black and Latinx people, everyone loses those rights. That's because it's a fundamental principle of law that the pronouncements of the Court will be applied from thereon to every suspect. You cannot know whether you will ever become a suspect. More importantly, even if you never need them, those protections belong to you – those rights that the Court is busy shredding.

THE SUPREME COURT NOW BLESSES UNCONSTITUTIONAL TERRY STOPS

So far, only one stop-and-frisk case, *Utah* v. *Strieff*, has reached the Court in the twenty-first century. Unfortunately, the case did not roll back *Terry* v. *Ohio*, let alone admit that *Terry* was a built on a lie.

One day a Salt Lake City narcotics detective, Douglas Fackrell, stopped Edward Strieff on a hunch that he might be carrying drugs. It was a bad stop because the officer lacked reasonable suspicion to believe Mr. Strieff was committing a crime. Next, police ran Mr. Strieff's license, learned that he had an outstanding warrant for an unpaid traffic ticket, and arrested him on that warrant. That's when the officer searched Mr. Strieff and found a baggie of methamphetamine and drug paraphernalia that led to charges of drug possession. I'm sure Mr. Strieff never imagined that his run-of-the-mill Terry stop would be reviewed by the Supreme Court and create new law.

Although the government admitted to the courts that the stop was bad and the officer had no right to take Mr. Strieff's identification and run the warrant check, the government still wanted to prosecute him with the ill-gotten gains. Ordinarily, prosecutors can't use evidence seized during unconstitutional police stops, but the Supreme Court agreed with the government and allowed them to prosecute Mr. Strieff with the drugs seized from him. Although the officer violated Mr. Strieff's Fourth Amendment rights, Mr. Strieff lost his case because of an outstanding warrant and because the Court decided that the arresting officer was not a "bad apple."

Here's how the outstanding traffic warrant connects to the Supreme Court decision in *Strieff*. Although the stop was bad, the Court described the traffic warrant as so unexpected and unanticipated that finding a warrant interrupted the usual requirement that bars evidence found during bad Terry stops. In reality, an officer finding a warrant for an unpaid traffic ticket hardly amounts to an "extraordinary intervening circumstance."[22] As Justice Elena Kagan phrased it, "outstanding warrants do not appear as bolts from the blue."

As Chapter 1 explains, because *Terry* v. *Ohio* didn't give police the right to put their hands into pockets, police employ a variety of techniques (what I call "cheats") to help them develop probable cause to search during Terry stops. Warrant checks are one of the cheats I talked about. Police can arrest people for outstanding warrants, even if they are only unpaid traffic tickets. Once the person is arrested, police may automatically search them – what courts call a "search incident to arrest." So when officers want to see if you have drugs in your pocket, in quick succession they can move from a stop, to a warrant check, to an arrest on an outstanding warrant, followed by a search incident to arrest. But *Strieff* now pretends that outstanding warrants are an "extraordinary intervening circumstance" that sanitizes the unconstitutional stop.

As the Court saw it, the officer made two good-faith mistakes. Officer Fackrell's first "good-faith" mistake was that he lacked reasonable suspicion when he stopped Mr. Strieff and ran the warrant. Good faith because the officer was looking for drugs, not simply harassing Mr. Strieff, and perhaps the officer didn't receive enough training on what counts as "reasonable suspicion."

Justice Clarence Thomas, writing for the majority, explains the second good-faith mistake. This so-called mistake was that the officer should have described the encounter as consensual so he would not need reasonable suspicion to justify the stop. "Officer Fackrell should have asked Strieff whether he would speak with him, instead of demanding that Strieff do so ... Nothing prevented him from approaching Strieff simply to ask" questions.[23] In other words, if the officer had pretended the stop was not a stop, but a mere contact, the Supreme Court would have happily played along with the fiction that Mr. Strieff chose to answer questions and have his name run through a database. Even though consent was never in play in *Utah* v. *Strieff*, the consent fictions shape the Supreme Court's view of the unlawful stop. Chapter 2 of this book pointed out that people know that it's dangerous to leave an officer who wants to ask you questions or take your identification. The *Strieff* majority hides the power imbalance between officer and civilian. Once again, we see the consent doctrine working in tandem with stop-and-frisk to further gut constitutional rights.

After *Strieff*, we better not forget to pay a traffic ticket. If police violate our rights and then find a warrant, it's no longer enough to prove that our rights were violated. We now need to show that they were violated by a "bad cop."

JUSTICE THOMAS PLAYS THE WHITE "RACE" CARD

Race plays a pivotal role in the majority's reasoning. Even though Justice Thomas doesn't actually state that Edward Strieff was white – thereby keeping to the script of racial blindness – his opinion names the town twice, "South Salt Lake City, Utah," a majority white jurisdiction that is only 4.4 percent African American.[24]

Here's why race mattered in Justice Thomas's opinion in *Strieff*. The Department of Justice investigated Ferguson, Missouri, in the aftermath of Michael Brown's death and found that police systematically abused their arrest powers to collect fees from a black population that was hard-pressed financially.[25] Warrant checks were part of a system supported by prosecutors to help courts extract money to fund government services that benefited the whole city. Judges issued arrest warrants at alarming rates for unpaid fines. Warrants were so ubiquitous in Ferguson, Missouri, that 75 percent of the population had warrants, and 96 percent of the people arrested on outstanding warrants were African American.[26]

The Supreme Court also possessed evidence that police often employ warrant checks during illegal Terry stops. Police are trained to check warrants to look for drugs, and it's common for police to detain people for warrant checks even when there's no basis for the stop. Done on a wide scale, these warrant checks are known as "catch and release," or "fishing expeditions," with officers fishing for arrests and then releasing those without warrants. The fishing isn't bad, either. Federal and local databases nationwide show that "outstanding warrants are surprisingly common" and these sources often don't "track the ... drawers and drawers full" of warrants "for traffic violations and ordinance violations" such as the one lodged against Mr. Strieff. As Justice Kagan writes in dissent, the decision peels away protection for millions of people. "So long as the target is one of the many millions of people in this country with an outstanding arrest warrant, anything the officer finds in a search is fair game for use in a criminal prosecution."

Justice Thomas uses Mr. Strieff's whiteness to disregard the mountain of evidence before the Court about abusive warrant practices. Writing for the majority, Justice Thomas declared that "there was no indication that this unlawful stop was part of any systemic or recurrent police conduct" but rather "an isolated instance of negligence."[27] By implying that this stop took place in a white neighborhood, the Court can then treat the unlawful Terry stop in *Strieff* as if it were disconnected from the mountain of data on warrant checks laid out in court briefs.

Justice Sotomayor refused to follow the racial blindness script and made race visible. Tackling the racial angle directly, she wrote, "The white defendant in this case shows that anyone's dignity can be violated in this manner."

Divide and conquer, the majority's strategy in *Strieff*, was cynical and wrong. As every law student knows, Supreme Court decisions affect everyone stopped from here on out. There's no way to take away Mr. Strieff's Fourth Amendment remedy without affecting non-whites too. It's not even true that warrant checks are just a "Ferguson" problem (read as "just black people's problem").[28] "Salt Lake County had a 'backlog of outstanding warrants' so large that it faced the 'potential for civil liability.'" It was "routine procedure" for Salt Lake City police officers to "run warrant checks on pedestrians they detained without reasonable suspicion," said the Utah Supreme Court.[29] Even majority-white Utah is not immune from systemic criminalization and aggressive policing methods. It's dangerous for white people to imagine ourselves immune.

GENDER SPLIT ON THE COURT

The Supreme Court justices split along gender lines in *Utah* v. *Strieff* with all three women on the Court voting in favor of the civilian who was unconstitutionally stopped, while the male justices voted to increase police power. The dissenters produced two opinions that were quite different from each other in tone and substance.

Taking the traditional approach, Justice Kagan centers her discussion on the precedent and the police. Using the master's tools to tear apart the majority reasoning, Justice Kagan explains how the ruling creates the wrong "incentives for the police – indeed, practically invites them to do what [Officer] Fackrell did here," that is, make bad Terry stops and run warrant checks hoping to find drugs.

In contrast, Justice Sotomayor's dissent was overtly feminist. Notice how she speaks directly to civilians here:

> The Court today holds that the discovery of a warrant for an unpaid parking ticket will forgive a police officer's violation of *your* Fourth Amendment rights. Do not be soothed by the opinion's technical language: this case allows the police to stop *you* on the street, demand your identification, and check it for outstanding traffic warrants – even if you are doing nothing wrong.[30]

Justice Ruth Bader Ginsburg joins both dissents, except for one section where Justice Sotomayor writes only for herself. In the section where Justice Sotomayor writes only for herself, her dissent grows searing, powerful, and lyrical.

> By legitimizing the conduct that produces this double consciousness, this case tells everyone, white and black, guilty and innocent, that an officer can verify your legal status at any time. It says that your body is subject to invasion while courts excuse

the violation of your rights. It implies that you are not a citizen of a democracy but the subject of a carceral state, just waiting to be cataloged.

We must not pretend that the countless people who are routinely targeted by police are "isolated." They are the canaries in the coal mine whose deaths, civil and literal, warn us that no one can breathe in this atmosphere.

I claim Justice Sotomayor's dissent as feminist. Feminist poet Nikki Giovanni said she writes from empathy. "Empathy," explains Virginia C. Fowler in the forward to the Giovanni's poems "enables us to collapse the dualistic structures that polarize our world into 'us' and 'them.'"[31] Feminists believe in the power of empathy to transcend division, to build coalitions, to improve our democracy.

Justice Sotomayor uses "we" to describe justices on the court and communities of color: "We [the justices] also risk treating members of *our* communities as second-class citizens."[32] That's not how other justices write. In doing so, she embraces her own multiple identities, as justice and former prosecutor, along with Latina and public school graduate. Only feminist and empathetic prosecutors put themselves in the shoes of the people they prosecute. By using the empathetic "we" to include "second-class" groups that are often "othered" and referred to, if at all, as "they," Sotomayor displays an empathy that feminists cherish and that conservatives turned into a dirty word when they attacked Justice Sotomayor's nomination to the high court.

When Justice Sotomayor writes about "canaries in the coal mine," she credits *The Miner's Canary*,[33] a book written by two pioneering academics, Lani Guinier, the first woman of color to receive tenure at Harvard Law School, and law professor Gerald Torres, a critical race theorist known for championing coalitions between black, Latinx, and Native American grassroots groups to overcome structural inequalities. I assigned Justice Sotomayor's full dissent in a seminar and asked the class what the passage meant. My students did not understand the canary metaphor until I explained that miners brought a canary down into the coal mines as a method of warning them of toxic gasses. Because canaries succumbed to the hazards before the humans, a dead bird gave miners time to retreat to safety. After a moment of silence where the metaphor sank in, one student pronounced it "profound."

When Justice Sotomayor writes about the black body, about how excusing unconstitutional policing "says that your body is subject to invasion," she borrows from critical race theorist Anthony Paul Farley and even more directly from essayist Ta-Nehisi Coates's passionate book *Between the World and Me*.[34] Both critical race theory and feminism regard law's treatment of bodies as important subjects. Her recognition of the way policing literally controls bodies reminds readers of how male and female black bodies were sold and abused in slavery and how the abuse lingers on in mutated forms. Her footnotes to the quoted passage above pay tribute to several brilliant writers, including W. E. B. Du Bois. By pointing out that policing causes psychological scars, Justice Sotomayor treads where no justice has been.

You sing it, Justice Sotomayor!

HOW THE SUPREME COURT BLEW AN OPPORTUNITY TO RETHINK
TERRY V. OHIO

If readers recall, the Supreme Court arrived at its decision in *Terry* v. *Ohio* by balancing stop-and-frisk's usefulness in fighting crime against the indignity and resentment these stops would cause. It was *Terry* that acknowledged that frisks "may inflict great indignity and arouse strong resentment" but nevertheless changed the Fourth Amendment requirement so police could now frisk even when they lacked probable cause to believe the civilian had committed a crime. It was *Terry* that decided that police didn't need to know that a crime had taken place before they held someone prisoner long enough to "feel with sensitive fingers every portion of the prisoner's body . . . arms and armpits, waistline and back, the groin and area about the testicles, and entire surface of the legs down to the feet."[35]

We now know more about the lived experiences of stop-and-frisk policing than the Court did in 1968, when it refused to apply the Fourth Amendment probable cause requirement to short detentions and patdowns, instead declaring that reasonable suspicion would suffice. Ideally, the Court should conduct the balancing test again with real facts about how the practice operates and the extent of the fallout. Based on what we have learned in the past fifty years, the harms from stop-and-frisk outweigh the benefits. Balanced properly, the Court should conclude that the Fourth Amendment requires probable cause for police to order people to place their hands up against a wall or interrogate them.

In 2016, the *Strieff* case gave the Supreme Court an opportunity to give *Terry* v. *Ohio* a second look based on real facts and data about the costs of stop-and-frisk. One might expect a fresh look would lead to shoring up our constitutional rights after acknowledging that *Terry* v. *Ohio* got the policy answers wrong. But that's not what happened. Instead of repairing *Terry*'s hole in the Constitution, it enlarged it.

The 1968 Court made two fatal errors when it performed its balancing test, as Chapter 1 fully sets out. Both errors affected how the Court weighed the harms and benefits of keeping a probable cause standard for police stops. *Utah* v. *Strieff* repeated both these errors when the Court weighed the benefits and harms of suppressing the evidence taken from Mr. Strieff.

The first fatal error in *Terry* was assuming that police could protect people's constitutional rights while they turned Terry stops into valid arrests. This is what I refer to as *Terry*'s lie, a central thesis of this book. Sadly, the *Strieff* decision does not renounce the consent fiction. On the contrary, the Court bemoans the officer's failure to pretend that Mr. Strieff consented to stop and voluntarily handed over his license – that was one of the officer's two good-faith mistakes. This book has shown that people can't truly choose to exercise their right to silence during Terry stops; they will say "yes sir" to an officer's request to search their body because they fear retaliation if they don't cooperate. *Terry* was wrong to assume that police could protect people's constitutional rights and still turn short investigatory stops into arrests.

The second fatal error in *Terry* v. *Ohio* was thinking that it's rogue officers who harass black people. Things might have turned out differently back in 1968 had the Supreme Court admitted that legalizing stops and frisks without probable cause would encourage racist use of the badge. Ten months before the Court heard arguments in *Terry* v. *Ohio*, President Lyndon Johnson's Kerner Commission found that "police are not merely a spark factor" for riots that swept American cities, but its primary cause. Racist policing methods included the rampant use of stops and frisks. "To some Negroes police have come to symbolize white power, white racism, and white repression."[36] Throwing up its proverbial hands, the *Terry* v. *Ohio* Court explains: "The wholesale harassment by certain elements of the police community, of which minority groups, particularly Negroes, frequently complain, will not be stopped by the exclusion of any evidence from any criminal trial."[37] To paraphrase the Court, it's terrible, but barring the gun found on Mr. Terry from his trial won't help to solve the problem. Racist police won't care what the law says; when bad apples racially harass, they're not looking for evidence, but behaving "outside the legitimate investigative sphere."[38] The exclusionary rule (keeping out ill-gotten evidence) doesn't stop bad police officers from harassing people – or so the Court thought – so it wouldn't increase harassment if police could legally detain people on mere reasonable suspicion. That's the Court's explanation for not placing racial harassment on *Terry*'s scales.

Here's the bottom line: Mr. Terry lost because the exclusionary rule won't stop "bad cops" who violate people's constitutional rights. Mr. Strieff lost because the exclusionary rule won't stop "good cops" who violate people's constitutional rights.[39] If *Terry* was wrong about whether the exclusionary rule will stop "bad cops" from harassing minorities, that's yet another reason to jettison the original stop-and-frisk decision.

It's unfortunate that *Strieff* repeated the "bad apple" trope to blame individual offices for what's wrong with policing. In fact, over-criminalization and police abuse are not the fault of a few "bad apples." "No individual officers need harbor racial animosity for the criminal justice system to produce jails and courts filled with black and brown faces," wrote the ACLU.[40] Aggressive policing is a systemic problem and the Fourth Amendment exclusionary rule should be part of the solution. Systemic methods of fighting crime – including aggressive stops and frisks – are the problem.

This book has shown that *Terry* was wrong to assume that police could protect people's constitutional rights and still turn Terry stops into arrests. People can't truly choose to exercise their right to silence during Terry stops. They say "yes sir" to an officer's request to search their body because they fear what will happen if they resist. As the #MeToo movement reminds us, perceived consent is usually coercion when there's an imbalance in power. Often, what appears to be consensual is surely not. The Supreme Court should admit that there is no such thing as "voluntary" consent or "voluntary" answers during police interrogation. And as soon as the Court admits that, *Terry*'s crime-fighting justification implodes for, as, I have shown in this book, consent and Terry stops are solidly intertwined.

The Court should overrule *Terry* v. *Ohio* and return to the probable cause standard. Probable cause is a concept found in the Fourth Amendment that officers must learn so they can fill out search warrants. Returning stops and frisks to a probable cause standard will make it simpler for an officer like Officer Fackrell, who was apparently confused by the concept of reasonable suspicion. Jettisoning the consent doctrines will also make it easier for officers to follow the law, because the current system might confuse them into thinking there are no limits to their powers to stop, question, and search.

Even if the *Strieff* dissenters had prevailed, this would only preserve the status quo. Neither dissent seeks to reverse *Terry* v. *Ohio* and return to the probable cause standard. Although brilliant and searing, Justice Sotomayor's critique of current policing didn't even convince a majority of the justices to keep the remedy that *Terry* endorsed. I tell my law students that the Supreme Court turned the Fourth Amendment into Swiss cheese, with more holes than protection. If we see the decision in *Terry* as representing one hole in the cheese, that was just the beginning of how the Supreme Court ate through the bulk of our Fourth Amendment rights by creating new exceptions. *Strieff* continued this trend by grabbing power from civilians and giving it to the police and prosecutors. *Strieff* represents another hole in our constitutional protections.

Several scholars have called for the reversal of *Terry* v. *Ohio*, saying that the Court got the policy answer wrong when it balanced stop-and-frisk's usefulness in fighting crime against the indignity and resentment these stops would cause.[41] The Supreme Court missed an opportunity to take a fresh look at *Terry*'s policy conclusions and take into account the lasting harms that flow to individuals and communities from unwanted police stops. If the Court put all the data on the scale, it would see that the benefits of Terry stops don't outweigh their harms.

HOW TO ABOLISH STOP-AND-FRISK

Informed by feminist principles, this book calls for the dismantling of stop-and-frisk. The consent doctrine is a sham. It is simply not safe for vulnerable civilians to say no to police. We must toss out the consent doctrine. And once we get rid of the consent doctrine, *Terry* v. *Ohio* and *Utah* v. *Strieff* must fall with it. At its heart, *Terry* requires individuals to waive their rights so that police can search pockets and gather confessions during short detentions.

One need not end all police stops to make a huge difference to communities. When police have a known crime, actual victims, and probable cause (or something close to probable cause) to believe that the person they observe on the street was involved in the crime, then police are justified in detaining that individual to verify their suspicions. I'm not talking about rounding up the usual suspects because a robbery was committed by a black man, but a detailed description of the perpetrator or other information pointing to the person that police observe. Without specific information like that, Terry stops cause more harm than good.

There are some easy guidelines. Police should not use Terry stops to look for drugs because it creates massive inequality in our jails and probation offices. It's a fact that white people use and sell drugs at the same rate as people of color. Middle-class white adults don't want their college kids locked up, and if we don't let police search through the bookbags of students at private colleges looking for illegal substances (and I'm glad we don't), then police should not be searching for drugs in the pockets of young people in highly policed neighborhoods either. Reasonable suspicion or not, police should not use their valuable time and muscle to see if people are carrying drugs. Another guideline: police should not stop people because they are wearing a hoodie and appear to be avoiding the police, even if the courts say they can. Police should stop racially profiling altogether, despite how the courts tolerate the practice. And perhaps it goes without saying that police should never engage in illegal Terry stops either, such as New York's scare tactic where police throw thousands of people against the walls for frisks so everyone in those neighborhoods will get the message to leave their guns at home.

In rare instances, frisks might be justified, but not if there's more police officers than suspects and not if there are other ways for officers to stay safe. One former police officer I know told me he would hold the thumbs of the person he stopped with one hand while he questioned them and that gave him ample warning if they tried to reach into a pocket or run away. If a person's mental illness makes an officer feel unsafe, there should be back-up mental health professionals to help handle the situation. In Portland, Maine, and more recently in New York City, a mental health clinician on staff will accompany officers whenever police are dispatched to situations that involve an emotionally disturbed person. In Maine, that's in addition to every officer receiving forty hours of crisis intervention training.[42]

Even in those rare cases where frisks are necessary for an officer's safety, there's no reason for police officers to touch people's breasts or groins. If an officer holds enough power to induce a person to place their arms against a wall or raise their hands, they have already removed any possible threat and there's no need to touch them. Even patting down jacket pockets, what a court might call a run-of-the-mill frisk, might feel like a violation. Feeling intimate body parts means crossing a line. My student Lawrence accurately described police as crossing a line, taking advantage and "violating me." The current practice of frisking groins should be replaced in most instances by no frisk at all.

How does this system change? The Supreme Court could provide substantial help. With the stroke of several pens, a majority of Supreme Court justices could admit that there is no such thing as true "consent." We only need five justices to rebalance *Terry* v. *Ohio* properly, using all the existing data and employing a victim-centered perspective.

Reality check: it will take decades before the *Strieff* dissents blossom into a majority view, and it may never happen. With a Republican-controlled Senate blocking Judge Merrick Garland's 2016 nomination by President Obama and then confirming President Trump's conservative nominee Neil Gorsuch for the seat, the deck is stacked against the Fourth Amendment. The power grab by conservative Senators ensures that *Strieff's* transfer of power from civilians to the police will continue. It's much more likely that the Court will abolish the exclusionary rule in the near future than that it will abolish the consent doctrine as we know it. The Court cannot be relied upon as a guardian for the constitutional rights currently trampled by stop-and-frisk policing.

The Bill of Rights was only intended to serve as a backstop, the bare minimum protection against government overreach. States and the federal government are always free to give us greater rights. Legislatively, states can do what the Supreme Court refuses to do. States must jump into the void by creating their own "state bill of rights," a set of statutes that protect against police overreach. State statutes could prohibit police from touching suspects' bodies on the streets in order to ask them a few questions. States could also pass laws that forbid police from stopping people without probable cause. Legislation could ban claims of "consent" to excuse an otherwise unjustified stop or search. This would prevent officers from claiming they didn't need any justification to detain you because you were free to walk away from them. It would also end the blame game where police lack probable cause, but claim you chose to subject your body or belongings to a search. At the very least, we must end the consent fiction for anyone too young to legally buy a beer.

State-by-state ballot initiatives represent another route to changing these harmful practices. Legislation and ballot initiatives are not a quick fix like the Supreme Court overturning *Terry* v. *Ohio*, but these legislative routes have a better chance of success if we can convince people that current practices harm all our communities.

Every state must also create remedies for police violations. We can no longer count on the Fourth Amendment case law to bar evidence tainted by police wrongdoing. Civil remedies for victims of police abuse are likewise inadequate, as we saw when the Supreme Court ruled that teenager Savanah Redding was illegally strip searched at school and yet, she still lacked the right to sue. State exclusionary rules could give us remedies for police behaviors that the Court already labels as unconstitutional, such as contempt of cop arrests or breaking down our front doors without warrants. As states pass laws to broaden individual liberties – such as abolishing so-called consent – these laws should also contain a remedy for criminal and civil courts. That way, the officers who pounded on Hollis King's door will no longer think they may pound loudly on all our doors without a warrant and call it a consent search when people let them in. That way, a state trial judge could not blame someone like Sylvia Mendenhall for submitting to a strip search. With state exclusionary rules, victims of unjustified stops and searches will no longer be tried and punished because they cooperated with police.

Even legislation that doesn't fully abolish stop-and-frisk can make a big impact. If legislators believe that officers may need to detain people without probable cause when there's been a report of a violent crime and there's some evidence suggesting an individual may be involved or may know something, that's only a sliver of stop-and-frisk activity. If state laws prevent stops on mere suspicion of misdemeanors and drug offenses, that will still go far in curbing the way that stop-and-frisk funnels individuals into the mass incarceration machinery.

Some states have started to downgrade nonviolent criminal offenses, turning felonies into misdemeanors and downgrading misdemeanors into civil infractions, akin to a parking offense.[43] This impacts stop-and-frisk policing by making it harder for officers to turn Terry stops into arrests. You may remember that when experts crunched the numbers back during the heyday of stop-and-frisk in New York City, possession of marijuana topped the charts. Those stops would have worked out differently had there been a state law making marijuana possession a mere civil infraction. Why bother setting up a confrontation when their suspicions – even if confirmed – won't support an arrest? As I write this, twenty-two states and the District of Columbia statutorily downgraded the possession of small amounts of marijuana, and others are debating it.[44] When states diminish the arsenal of charges available during Terry stops, this encourages police to prioritize solving murders, rapes, and other violent crimes over petty quality-of-life offenses, such as carrying a red cup that might contain alcohol (why police stopped my law student Lawrence) or walking across a park after dark (leading to Linda Dominguez's nightmare arrest). Even small legislative fixes can offer police desirable alternatives to arrest when a mentally ill woman walks too close to cars or shouts to imaginary foes.

The key to legislative change lies with the voters' attitudes and views. There is a growing awareness in the country that our experiment with mass incarceration was a dismal failure and that it drains money away from housing, education, and employment opportunities. Jails are where we put people awaiting trial or after conviction for minor offenses – I'm talking about the type of arrests that typically flow from a "successful" stop-and-frisk – offenses such as drug possession or resisting arrest.[45] Less expensive than prisons, jails can still cost taxpayers as much as $191 per day for one inmate, according to the Vera Institute. Total funding of prisons and jails across the United States clocks in at $80 billion a year, and when researchers added in the social costs from incarceration, they determined that the full cost exceeds $1 trillion per year.[46] There are many efforts across the country to reduce the number of people behind bars, including the First Step Act that President Trump signed in 2018, modest, bipartisan legislation that reduces federal drug sentencing. More than half of states accept federal Justice Reinvestment funding, requiring them to use data-driven approaches to reduce crime by shifting resources toward more cost-effective strategies. Results from the program's first seven years reveal that states spent one-third of the funds on community programs, primarily substance abuse treatment and mental health services.[47]

Abolishing stop-and-frisk must be recognized as part of the work currently underway to dismantle the New Jim Crow, which includes ending the drug war, mass incarceration, racial profiling, and the killing of unarmed civilians. Black and brown bodies have borne the brunt of these policies, and to achieve racial equity will require us to end all of them. Since widespread stop-and-frisk practices provide a gateway to this full array of harms and inequalities, it makes sense to close the gate.

After Freddie Gray's death, the Baltimore Police Department instituted a new use of force policy that requires officers to try to de-escalate conflicts before using deadly force. When the Use of Force Project reviewed 100 police departments in the United States, they found that forty-four departments now require officers to de-escalate situations, when possible, before using force and a similar number require officers to exhaust all reasonable alternatives before resorting to deadly force.[48]

Police culture is notoriously resistant to change. How officers behave on the job turns more on the reward system, including overtime pay, rather than ethics or skills trainings. Imagine if police were evaluated based on how often they helped people find drug treatment or mental health services? Imagine if customer satisfaction by poor neighborhood residents determined pay. Imagine a police force where people rose up through the ranks because they engaged in de-escalation techniques and made exceptionally few arrests. That's the type of policing that should replace Terry stops.

"No American should be afraid to call the police for fear of becoming victimized by the very people sent to protect them," wrote the Congressional Black Caucus in their open report to President Trump in 2018.[49] The Caucus calls for increased funding for training in de-escalation tactics, proper use of force, implicit bias, and sensitivity training, along with money for mandatory body cameras. The report also calls for a new focus where police work with communities to solve problems rather than focusing on crime and punishment. All of these efforts could improve policing, improve lives, and help police transition to new models of policing once we legislatively end stop-and-frisk and consent searches.

Alex Vitale, in his book, *The End of Policing*, recommends a different approach than the Caucus. Society turns to police to fix problems that the profession is ill-suited for, explains Vitale, a professor of sociology and the coordinator of the Policing and Social Justice Project at Brooklyn College. Vitale's answer to policing abuse is more services and less policing. "Ending the war on drugs, abolishing school police, ending broken windows policing [including stop-and-frisk], developing robust mental healthcare, and creating low-income housing systems will do much more to reduce abusive policing," than increasing technology or putting more police on the streets in the name of "community policing."[50]

Looking at the neighborhoods with the most crime and violence, Vitale addresses these "pockets of intense poverty," where jobs are scarce and public services are inadequate. These pockets are the result of a history of racism and inequitable government policy and neglect. Think about the issues that are central to a community's well-being. More police officers won't solve malnourishment, poor schools, unemployment, housing shortages, chemical addiction, physical and mental illness. It may not be a zero-sum game, but in the era of stop-and-frisk, police budgets expand while other needs remain unaddressed.

Current officers who like the masculine image of the police – officers who Vitale describes as "obsessed with the use of threats and violence to control the poor and socially marginal" – won't transition easily to problem-solving methods that are often viewed as a softer or feminine approach. For departments to start hiring officers based on their problem-solving prowess would require a change in the top brass, a new kind of police chief. As long as we continue to put the same types of leaders at the top of police departments, there will be no meaningful change. If police culture shifts, officers won't be engaged in much stopping and frisking. And if police don't change, then we must find other ways to reduce the number of police interactions. The fewer the interactions, the safer we will all be.

PROGRESSIVE PROSECUTORS CAN MAKE A DIFFERENCE

There's another way to battle the pernicious consent doctrine. Progressive prosecutors should take up this issue. There's a wave of prosecutors voted into office by constituents who want to eliminate over criminalization and racist outcomes. These prosecutors are making headway. For example, Baltimore stopped prosecuting marijuana cases in February 2019, even though the crime was still on the books in Maryland.[51] In taking this step, Marilyn Mosby of Baltimore joined district attorneys Larry Krasner of Philadelphia, Kimberly Foxx of Chicago, Cyrus Vance Jr. of Manhattan, and Eric Gonzalez of Brooklyn. Elected district attorneys can't actually control police department policy – that's generally set by a chief who is appointed by the mayor – and they can't reward good policing nor punish misconduct. Nevertheless, police chiefs should see themselves as part of a team and deploy their resources in a manner that supports the local community and the mission and priorities of the elected prosecutor. In Boston, progressive District Attorney Rachael Rollins won't prosecute disorderly conduct, disturbing the peace and approximately thirteen other nonviolent misdemeanors unless there are exceptional circumstances.[52] Mr. Krasner, perhaps the most progressive of the first wave of progressive prosecutors, developed a "do-not-call list" of Philadelphia police officers with a history of lying, racial bias, or brutality. He is not alone. Prosecutors around the United States keep such lists. In St. Louis, after Kimberly Gardner was elected chief prosecutor for the city, the progressive prosecutor dropped more than 100 cases that relied on statements from officers who were on the list because of their history of lying, abuse, or corruption. Gardner's office also refuses to accept new cases or search warrant requests from officers whose names appear on the list.[53] In this way, prosecutors help shape the role of police in our courtrooms.

Just as progressive prosecutors seek to prevent perjury by keeping known liars from testifying, they should also be honest about the power imbalance that turns consent searches into fictions. Progressive prosecutors could treat "consent" the way they treat other testimony that's suspect. They can ensure that their prosecutors won't argue consent as a defense to Fourth Amendment violations. Let's see how this would work in practice. Imagine Sylvia Mendenhall were arrested at the Philadelphia train station and tried in state court. District Attorney Krasner's office would not allege that she was free to leave or that she consented to a strip search. Instead, line prosecutors might claim in court papers that police had probable cause to search her. At the hearing, police would need to convince the judge that the Terry stop was based on objective incriminating facts, not racial profiling, and that officers then developed probable cause for the search. In this way, honest prosecutors will make our courtrooms more honest.

Then there's the equally troubling fiction of "voluntary" statements when individuals answer questions during Terry stops. I'm thinking of the drug users I've represented who admit to carrying needles so the officer won't accidently prick themselves during a search. Currently the government will use these incriminating statements to justify the search (even though my clients seem sure that police would have searched them anyway) and to persuade a jury to convict. Even though the Supreme Court calls these statements "voluntary," readers know they are not. Under the new regime, neither drugs nor statements could be used to convict.

Ending the fiction of voluntary answers to police questioning during Terry stops won't prevent police from solving crimes. The proposed change recognizes that people can't assert a right to silence during Terry stops and it prevents courts from using their cooperation against them at trial.[54] Logically, once police stop punishing victims of Terry stops by arresting them when they cooperate, it might actually encourage people to cooperate with detectives who are working to solve serious crimes.

Instead of pretending that there was a consent stop or voluntary conversation or consent search, we must change the law to reflect the truth. Progressive prosecutors should recognize that civilians can't exercise their right to silence during stops any more than they can refuse consent. Ending the consent fiction means that prosecutors will no longer use the drugs found during consent searches as evidence at trial. Ending consent as an excuse for lawless searches will affect more than just street stops, for the law currently recognizes consent searches of cars and even consent searches of homes.

At noon, one of my favorite members of the Youth Court staff walks into the courtroom and warmly congratulates the participants on finishing their first day, reminding them to come back in two weeks. As the teenagers happily leave the courtroom to resume their interrupted lives, I always wonder what will happen if an officer stops them this week or the next. In the end, what we taught them boils down to three phrases that we have put onto one side of a business card:

Am I free to leave?

I never consent to searches.

I want a lawyer.

On the other side of the card is the phone number for lodging a complaint about their treatment with DC's independent body that investigates civilian complaints. That's how the teenagers and their families can become part of the solution. Enough complaints and the officer might find themselves on a do-not-call list.

What's not on the card – what the Supreme Court has thrown into the trash – is free speech, the right to walk away and not answer questions, dignity, and bodily integrity.

It will take time for us to recoup our constitutional rights, whether it comes through legislative fixes, new Supreme Court justices, or a change in prosecution and police cultures. For now, what will these teens remember? What will they do next time? Did we inspire a teen or motivate him to report abuses? Fortunately, these *Know Your Rights* trainings ignite a passion for justice within my law students. I expect that many Howard law students will go on to lead the efforts to dismantle an unjust criminal system, including aggressive stops and invasive searches.

CONCLUSION

It's time to dismantle a system of policing that blames civilians when we give up our rights. You don't have to be versed in feminist theory to recognize that police officers hold all of the power during a stop, and, even if we know our rights on paper, it's simply not safe to exercise them. With this bright line fix, police will only stop and interrogate us when they have probable cause to believe we have committed a crime. Police will stop frisking except when there is truly no safe alternative available to a lone officer who needs to talk to a civilian. With this simple fix, we end the invasive sidewalk patdown where officers put their hands on breasts and groins. Ending stops and frisks as we know them will protect many men, women, and children from bodily and psychological harm that accompanies the *Terry* type of sexual harassment.

> At the end of one Know Your Rights training in Chicago, an eighth-grade student ran up to my brother who supervised the student teacher in that class. "Dr. Ross," he said, slightly out of breath. "I want to be a lawyer. How do I do that?" According to my brother, this was a young man who had never shown much interest in school before, so his response was, "That's great, but you would have to go to college first." "Okay," the teenager nodded. "I will go to college."

Even though I see all the ways that the Supreme Court has taken away civilian power, the teenager is filled with hope. He sees knowledge as power. And indeed, knowledge is a form of power, even if what we learn is how little power we have. Until readers know what we lose through Terry stops and how so much of the constitutional bulwark against oppressive government has been dismantled, we will never turn around and change it. Fifty years after *Terry* v. *Ohio*, it's time to abolish stop-and-frisk.

Notes

1 *I am Not Your Negro*, directed by Raoul Peck, USA: Magnolia Pictures, 2016. The film is based on James Baldwin's unfinished manuscript, *Remember This House*, which is a memoir of Baldwin's personal experiences during the civil rights era.

INTRODUCTION

All URLS were last accessed on February 2, 2020.

1 George C. Thomas III, "Terrorism, Race and A New Approach to Consent Searches," 73 Miss. L.J. 525, 541 (2003).

2 Alicia Garza, Patrisse Cullors, and Opai Tometi created the hashtag after Trayvon Martin was essentially "placed on trial for his own murder and the killer, George Zimmerman was not held accountable." Alicia Garza, "A HerStory of the #BlackLivesMatter Movement," *Black Lives Matter*, October 7, 2014, https://blacklivesmatter.com/herstory/. George Zimmerman was acquitted of murdering Trayvon Martin in February 2012.

3 Gabriel, interview with the author, December 2015.

4 The following investigations under 42 U.S.C §14141 (and a federal court decision) all found that police used stop- and-frisk intensively in certain areas of the city and consistently violated the constitutional rights of civilians:

For New Orleans: U.S. Department of Justice Civil Rights Division, "Investigation of New Orleans Police Department" (March 16, 2011), www.justice.gov/sites/default/files/crt/legacy/2011/03/17/nopd_report.pdf.

For New York City: *Floyd* v. *City of New York* (*Floyd Liability Opinion*), 959 F. Supp. 2d 540 (S.D.N.Y. 2013) *appeal dismissed* (September 25, 2013).

For Ferguson, Missouri: Civil Rights Division, U.S. Department of Justice, "Investigation of the Ferguson Police Department" (March 4, 2015), www.justice.gov/sites/default/files/opa/press-releases/attachments/2015/03/04/ferguson_police_department_report.pdf.

For Baltimore: Civil Rights Division, Civil Rights Division, "Investigation of the Baltimore City Police Department," *August* 10, 2016, www.Justice.gov/opa/file/883366/download.

5 The data show that the NYPD overwhelmingly targeted young men of color for stops. From 2004 to 2012, New Yorkers were subjected to police stops and street interrogations more than 4.4 million times and the overwhelming target of these tactics were young Black and Latinx males. Fifty-two percent of the persons stopped were black, 31 percent were Hispanic, and only 10 percent of those stopped were white – *Floyd* v. *City of New York*, 959 F. Supp. 2d 540, 558–59 (S.D.N.Y. 2013); see also New York Civil Liberties Union, "Stop and Frisk Data," //www.nyclu.org/en/Stop-and-Frisk-data (this website is continuously updated). Since 2014, while the number of stops decreased radically, young black and Latino males continue to be the targets of a hugely disproportionate number of stops. New York Civil Liberties Union, "Stop-and-Frisk In the de Blasio Era," 2019.

6 Erin Fitzgerald, Sarah Elspeth Patterson, Darby Hickey, and Cherno Biko, *Work: Transgender Experiences in the Sex Trade* (National Center for Transgender Equality, 2015); Osman Ahmed and Chai Jindasurat, *Lesbian, Gay, Bisexual, Transgender, Queer, and HIV-Affected Hate Violence in 2014* (National Coalition of Anti-Violence Programs, 2015).

7 Using statistics from New York City, police arrested 6 percent of the people they stop and summonsed another 6 percent to court, with most of the arrests for misdemeanors. Next, prosecutors don't charge all the cases that police hand to them; "42% of all summonses in 2010 resulted in either dismissal or adjournment in contemplation of dismissal." *Floyd* v. *City of New York*, 959 F. Supp. 2d 540, 573–76 (S.D.N.Y. 2013); Issa Kohler-Hausmann, "Managerial Justice and Mass Misdemeanors," 66 Stan. L. Rev 611, 693 (2014). When prosecutors charge defendants with misdemeanors, fewer than 1 in 500 individuals go to trial. Jenny Roberts, "Crashing the Misdemeanor System," 70 Wash. & Lee L. Rev. 1089, 1131 and n. 17 (2013) (using statistics from 2011 in New York City).

What these numbers suggest is that even if prosecutors charged every person who police arrested, there would only be one or two individuals heading to trial for every five thousand stops. But the number of motions to suppress are actually lower than the number of trials because lawyers only file them when the government seeks to use physical evidence or statements that police gathered during the stop. For example, with charges such as resisting arrest and disturbing the peace, there is generally no evidence to try to suppress, Kohler-Hausmann, "Managerial Justice and Mass Misdemeanors," 611, 693.

Both sides know that prosecutors "win 80 to 90% of the small number of motions that are made." Therefore, while it's possible for criminal defendants to demand a suppression hearing and then plead guilty when they lose, most lawyers file motions to suppress as part of a plea negotiation strategy, and the most lenient deals usually require giving up the suppression hearing. George C. Thomas III, "Judges Are Not Economists (Fn1) and Other Reasons to Be Skeptical of Contingent Suppression Orders: A Response to Professor Dripps," 38 Am. Crim. L. Rev. 47, 50–51, 55 (2001).

8 Joanna L. Grossman, "Moving Forward, Looking Back: A Retrospective on Sexual Harassment Law," 95 B. U. L. Rev. 1029, 1034–35 (2015) discusses the development of sexual harassment law. In 1979, Catharine MacKinnon published her "game-changing book" *Sexual Harassment of Working Women* 26 (Yale University Press, 1979), and in 1980, her "framework was adopted virtually wholesale by the EEOC, which published its first guidelines on sexual harassment." For a discussion of state statutes that mirror or expand Title VII, see Rachel Farkas, Brittany Johnson, and Ryann McMurry, "State Regulation of Sexual Harassment," 20 Geo. J Gender & L. 421, 424–25 (2019)("forty-seven states and Washington DC have implemented anti-discrimination statutes that either expressly or impliedly prohibit sexual harassment in the private workplace.")

9 *Meritor Sav. Bank, FSB v. Vinson*, 477 U.S. 57, 78 (1986) (deciding that sexual harassment violates Title VII of the Civil Rights Act of 1964 and recognizing that either sexual or non-sexual conduct is capable of producing hostile work environments).

10 "Constructive discharge" occurs "when an employer deliberately makes an employee's working conditions intolerable and thereby forces her to quit their job, and a plaintiff must prove (1) deliberateness of the employer's action and (2) intolerability of the working conditions. Civil Rights Act of 1964, § 701 et seq., 42 U.S.C.A. § 2000e et seq., *Blakes v. City of Hyattsville*, 909 F. Supp. 2d 431 (D. Md. 2012)." Deborah F. Harris, *Circumstances in Title VII employment discrimination cases (42 U.S.C.A. § 2000e et seq.) which warrant finding of "constructive discharge" of discriminatee who resigns employment*, 55 A.L.R. Fed. 418, 421.

11 More on the literature on sexual harassment in Chapter 6.

12 *Safford Unified Sch. Dist. No. 1 v. Redding*, 557 U.S. 364, 374–75 (2009).

13 A number of judicial doctrines, including the standing doctrine, and the doctrine of qualified immunity, limit plaintiffs' ability to successfully sue law enforcement for misconduct under civil rights statutes. Barry Friedman and Maria Ponomarenko, "Democratic Policing," 90 N.Y.U.L. Rev. 1827, 1868 (2015). Qualified immunity shields certain government officials, including law enforcement from civil liability, unless they violated a "federal statutory or constitutional right," and the unlawfulness of their conduct was "clearly established" at the time of their conduct." *Ashcroft v. al-Kidd*, 563 U.S. 731, 735 (2011). This standard creates an enormous hurdle for civil rights plaintiffs "because the courts have required not just a clear legal *rule*, but a prior case on the books with functionally identical *facts*." Jay Scheikert, "Qualified Immunity: The Supreme Court's Unlawful Assault on Civil Rights and Police Accountability," *Cato Institute: At Liberty*, March 5, 2018, www.cato.org/blog/qualified-immunity-supreme-courts-unlawful-assault-civil-rights-police-accountability. There's also standing problems. For example, *City of Los Angeles v. Lyons*, 461 U.S. 95 (1983) decided that the plaintiff who was choked by the LAPD lacked standing to challenge the LAPD's use of chokeholds, even though they had injured and killed several arrestees, because the plaintiff could not show with sufficient certainty that he would be subjected to a chokehold in the future.

14 Through "consciousness-raising sessions" in the 1970s, women gathered and told their life stories and recognized that their individual exploitation was part of a pattern, a system. In fact, the term "sexual harassment" arose out of a consciousness-raising session that a feminist professor at Cornell held with her female students to discuss their work experiences. Lin Farley came up with the term that would be broad enough to encapsulate both physical and emotional abuse. Erin Blakemore, "Until 1975, 'Sexual Harassment' Was the Menace with No Name," *History*, January 8, 2018, www.history.com/news/until-1975-sexual-harassment-was-the-menace-with-no-name.

15 MacKinnon, *Sexual Harassment of Working Women*.

16 Lisa A. Crooms, "Stepping into the Projects: Lawmaking, Storytelling, and Practicing the Politics of Identification," 1 *Mich. J. Race & L.* 1, 9–10, 42 (1996). The article builds on Professor Regina Austin's ideas about "the politics of identification" in the black community, in Regina Austin, "The Black Community, Its Lawbreakers, and a Politics of Identification," 65 *S. Cal. L. Rev.* 1769 (1992). Professor Crooms-Robinson teaches Gender and the Law (along with other courses) and serves as director of Howard University School of Law's Constitutional Law Center.

17 Denene Millner, "The Movement & the Future: Tarana Burke," *Essence*, October 25, 2018, www.essence.com/magazine/tarana-burke-profile-november-2018/.

18 Milano tweeted: "If all the women who have been sexually harassed or assaulted wrote 'Me too' as a status, we might give people a sense of the magnitude of the problem." @Alyssa_Milano, Twitter (October 15, 2017 4:21 p.m.). As of July 2019, the hashtag #MeToo has been used over 19 million times on Twitter, and 2,123,667 times on Instagram.

19 Paul Butler, *Chokehold*, 32 (The New Press, 2017); Devon Carbado, "[E]racing The Fourth Amendment," 100 *Mich. L. Rev.* 946, 968–70 (2002). For Carbado, "the perpetrator perspective" means recognizing that race plays a role even when a police officer does not exhibit "overtly racist behavior" so is not "obviously a perpetrator of racism." The "victim perspective," in contrast, "is explicitly race-conscious."

20 Phyllis Goldfarb, "A Theory-Practice Spiral: The Ethics of Feminism and Clinical Education," 75 *Minn. L. Rev.* 1599, 1644 (1991).

21 Launched in December of 2014 by the African American Policy Foundation, the hashtag campaign #sayhername "calls to attention police violence against Black women, girls and femmes." Available at http://aapf.org/shn-campaign. Law professor Kimberlé Crenshaw of UCLA and Columbia Law School co-founded the AAPF with Dr. Luke Charles Harris of Vassar College.

22 *Lawrence v. Texas*, 539 U.S. 558 (2003) (striking down laws that criminalize sexual conduct between consenting same-sex partners). "The State cannot demean their existence or control their destiny by making their private sexual conduct a crime," wrote Justice Anthony Kennedy for the majority, treating private and intimate choice as part of overarching principles of autonomy, dignity and respect. Stigma, Jane Schacter notes, animates the majority opinion, and the concept of stigma "has been pivotal in the domain of racial and gender classifications." Jane S. Schacter, "*Lawrence v. Texas* and the Fourteenth Amendment's Democratic Aspirations," 13 *Temple Political & Civil Rights L. Rev.* 733, 750–51 (2004). For a discussion of substantive due process from *Roe v. Wade* to *Lawrence*, see Cass R. Sunstein, "Liberty After Lawrence," 65 *Ohio St. L. J.* 1059, 1060–61 (2004).

23 Mary Anne C. Case, "Disaggregating Gender from Sex and Sexual Orientation: The Effeminate Man in the Law and Feminist Jurisprudence," 105 *Yale L.J.* 1, 68 (1995) referring to the case of *Oncale v. Sundowner Offshore Services Inc.*, 523 U.S. 75 (1988) (a gay man was entitled to prove that the torment he received at the hands of other male employees constituted harassment "based on sex" under Title VII).

24 Bridget J. Crawford, Kathryn M. Stanchi, and Linda L. Berger, "Feminist Judging Matters: How Feminist Theory and Methods Affect the Process of Judgment," 47 U. Balt. L. Rev. 167, 167–68 (2018).

25 For "full-blown searches" (when police move beyond the patdown of a person's outer clothing, into pockets or searching bags), police need "probable cause" to believe they will find evidence of a crime in the place they are looking.

26 Catherine Hanssens, Aisha-Moodie Millis, Andrea Ritchie, Dean Spade and Urvashi Vaid, *A Roadmap for Change: Federal Policy Recommendations Addressing the Criminalization of LGBT People and People Living with HIV* 19 (The Center for Gender & Sexuality Law, 2014) (quoting testimony by Trina Braxton, a Youth Leader with Streetwise & Safe (SAS) during a city council meeting during which the NYPD's discriminatory use

of 'stop-and-frisk' practices were a subject of discussion. SAS is a New York City-based organization focused on LGBTQ youth of color's experiences of policing and helped create a brochure to teach other youth their rights. SAS's training pamphlet for police stops is available at http://welcometocup.org/Store?product_id=102.

27 Human Rights Watch found that police in New York City, Los Angeles, Washington, DC, and San Francisco confiscate condoms when they stop, search, and arrest people identified or profiled as sex workers. "Sex Workers at Risk: Condoms as Evidence of Prostitution in Four US Cities," *Human Rights Watch*, July 19, 2012, www.hrw.org/report/2012/07/19/sex-workers-risk/condoms-evidence-prostitution-four-us-cities. Due to public pressure, in 2014 the NYPD modified its policy of allowing officers to seize condoms as evidence of prostitution. Advocates argue that condoms simply display an intent to practice safe sex. However, the policy still authorizes officers to seize condoms in cases involving the promotion of prostitution or sex trafficking. See Martha Kempner, "The NYPD Finally Changes Condoms-as-Evidence Policy, But Leaves Giant Loophole," *Rewire News*, May 13, 2014, rewire.news/article/2014/05/13/nypd-finally-changes-condoms-evidence-policy-leaves-giant-loophole/. For similar legislation in California, see E. J. Dickson, "California Just Passed A Landmark Law Protecting Sex Workers' Rights," *Rolling Stone*, July 31, 2019, www.rollingstone.com/culture/culture-features/california-condom-landmark-law-protecting-sex-workers-rights-865740/.

28 Estelle B. Freedman, *Redefining Rape: Sexual Violence in the Era of Suffrage and Segregation* 7 (Harvard University Press, 2013).

29 Andrea Dworkin, "Rape Atrocity and the Boy Next Door" (1975) (a lecture delivered at select colleges) reprinted in Johanna Fateman and Amy Scholder, eds., *Last Days at Hot Slit: The Radical Feminism of Andrea Dworkin*, 84–111 (The MIT Press, 2019).

30 *Floyd v. City of New York* (*Floyd Liability Opinion*), 959 F. Supp. 2d 540, 561 & 662 (S.D.N.Y. 2013); *Floyd v. City of New York* (*Floyd Remedy Order*), 959 F. Supp. 2d 668, 680 (S.D.N.Y. 2013).

31 Michael D. White and Henry F. Fradella, *Stop and Frisk: The Use and Abuse of a Controversial Policing Tactic*, 147 (New York Press, 2016).

32 Katharine T. Bartlett, "Feminist Legal Methods," 103 *Harv. L. Rev.* 829, 836–37 (1990) ("When feminists 'do law,' they do what other lawyers do" plus the less conventional methods mentioned above).

33 Bennett Capers, "Real Rape Too," 99 *Calif. L. Rev.* 1259, 1308, and 1295 (2011) citing Catharine A. MacKinnon, "Feminism, Marxism, Method, and the State: Toward Feminist Jurisprudence," *Signs* 7 (1982): 515, at 544.

34 Barbara Ransby, *Making All Black Lives Matter*, 228, 566–68, and 804 (University of California Press, 2018). Ransby is a distinguished professor of African American Studies, Gender and Women's Studies, and History at the University of Illinois at Chicago. Black Lives Matter (BLM) was formed by three women; Alicia Garza and Patrisse Khan-Cullors who Ransby identifies as politically engaged and openly queer, while she describes the third founder, Opal Tometi, as an emerging feminist. BLM represents "the first time in the history of US social movements that Black feminist politics have defined the frame for a multi-issue, Black-led mass struggle that did not primarily or exclusively focus on women," Ransby writes and she also chronicles how many smaller organizations within the umbrella of Black Lives Matter embrace the queer label and seek to operate through a "Black queer feminist lens."

35 Angela Y. Davis, *Women, Race & Class*, 177, 193–201 (Vintage Books, 1983).

36 *Terry* v. *Ohio*, 392 U.S. 1, 34 (1968) (White, J. concurring) ("the person stopped is not obliged to answer, answers may not be compelled, and refusal to answer furnishes no basis for an arrest, although it may alert the officer to the need for continued observation.")

37 *City of Houston* v. *Hill*, 482 U.S. 451 (1987) (striking down as "unconstitutionally overbroad" a statute making it a crime to oppose or "interrupt any policeman in the execution of his duty.")

38 Ta-Nehisi Coates, *Between the World and Me*, 6 (Spiegel & Grau, 2017).

39 See discussion in Chapter 4.

1 WAIVE YOUR RIGHTS: THAT'S HOW STOPS AND FRISKS WERE MEANT TO WORK

1 Richard is not his real name. This former student read and approved the use of his story in this book.

2 A report by the New York Civil Liberties Union found that between 2014 and 2017, NYPD stopped 73,055 innocent people. Of the innocent, 64 percent were frisked, and 24 percent had force used against them. New York Civil Liberties Union, "Stop-and-Frisk in the De Blasio Era," March 14, 2019, www.nyclu.org/en/publications/stop-and-frisk-de-blasio-era-2019. In many cases, more than one act of force was used. In Devon W. Carbado, "From Stop and Frisk to Shoot and Kill: Terry v. Ohio's Pathway to Police Violence," 64 *UCLA L. Rev.* 1508, 1551 (2017) the author argues "the stop-and-frisk doctrine is an important part of the police violence problem because that body of law allows police officers to force engagements with African Americans based on little or no justification." Moreover, "the frequency of those engagements overexposes African Americans not only to surveillance, discipline, and social control, but also to arrests and the possibility of violence, including serious bodily injury and death."

3 *Terry* v. *Ohio*, 392 U.S. 1, 27 (1968). The quote "verify or dispel the officer's suspicion" comes from *U.S.* v. *Sharpe*, 470 U.S. 675, 711–12 (1985) (Judge Brennan, dissenting) citing to *Florida* v. *Royer*, 460 U.S., 491 505 (1983) (plurality opinion by White, J.).

4 Ekow N. Yankah, "Pretext and Justification: Republicanism, Policing and Race," 40 *Cardozo L. Rev.* 1543, 1574–75 (2019) (citing the suppression hearing and trial transcripts from the *Terry* case); *Terry* v. *Ohio*, 392 U.S. at 4–8.

5 Carbado, "From Stop and Frisk to Shoot and Kill," 1517.

6 *Terry* v. *Ohio*, 392 U.S. at 17.

7 Ibid., 22. "One general interest is of course that of effective crime prevention and detection; it is this interest which underlies the recognition that a police officer may in appropriate circumstances and in an appropriate manner approach a person for purposes of investigating possibly criminal behavior even though there is no probable cause to make an arrest." *Terry* described a second interest that relates only to the frisk: "the more immediate interest of the police officer in taking steps to assure himself that the person with whom he is dealing is not armed with a weapon that could unexpectedly and fatally be used against him."

8 Canvassing the literature, researchers found that "Aggressive maintenance order strategies that target individual disorderly behaviors do not generate significant crime reductions." By contrast, "community and problem-solving solutions were more successful." Anthony Braga, Brandon C. Welsh, and Cory Schnell, "Can Policing Disorder Reduce Crime?:

A Systematic Review and Meta-Analysis" *J. Res. Crime Delinq.* 52 (2015): 567–88 at 580. One study of New York City impact zones, where police saturate areas of high crime, found that investigative stops "had no measurable effect on crime"; that is, Terry stops did not play a statistically significant role in reducing crime. The authors saw better results for stops based on probable cause, the standard which would replace reasonable suspicion if *Terry* v. *Ohio* were overruled. John MacDonald et. al., "The Effects of Local Police Surges on Crime and Arrests in New York City," *Columbia of Public Law* [Research Paper No. 14–468] (2016) and Jeffrey Fagan, "Terry's Original Sin," *University of Chicago Legislative Forum* 43, 45 (2016): 43–97 at 45. For a discussion in how aggressive police stops increase crime, more on this in Chapter 7.

9 David A. Harris, "Across the Hudson: Taking the Stop and Frisk Debate Beyond New York City," 16 N.Y.U. *J. Legis. & Pub. Pol'y* 853, 863 (2013).

10 *Floyd* v. *City of New York* (*Floyd Liability Opinion*), 959 F. Supp. 2d 540 (S.D.N.Y. 2013) *appeal dismissed* (Sept. 25, 2013).

11 Graham A. Rayman, *The NYPD Tapes* (Palgrave Macmillan, 2013); Graham A. Rayman, "Bed-Stuy cops ordered: Turn this place into a ghost town," *Village Voice*, May 12, 2010. The tape was also introduced into the *Floyd* trial. *Floyd*, 959 F. Supp. 2d at 597.

12 *Floyd* v. *City of New York*, 959 F. Supp. 2d 540, 599–600 (S.D.N.Y. 2013).

13 New York Civil Liberties Union, "Stop and Frisk Data" www.nyclu.org/en/stop-and-frisk-data (data from 2011 showed 88 percent are innocent).

14 "The rate of arrests arising from stops is low (roughly 6 percent), and the yield of seizures of guns or other contraband is even lower (roughly 0.1 percent and 1.8 percent respectively)." *Floyd* v. *City of New York*, 959 F. Supp. 2d 540, 559 (S.D.N.Y. 2013). Kate Taylor, "Stop-and-Frisk Policy 'Saves Lives,' Mayor Tells Black Congregation," *New York Times*, June 10, 2012. Bloomberg said, "If the kid is on the street with a gun, we've got to get that gun out of his hands, and we've got to make the kids believe that the likelihood of being stopped is so great that they shouldn't carry a gun." Bloomberg also said, "making it 'too hot to carry,' the NYPD is preventing guns from being carried on our streets . . . That is our real goal – preventing violence before it occurs"). Dana Rubenstein, "Bloomberg on the New York murder rate: 'we just are not going back,'" *Politico*, July 13, 2012, www.politico.com/states/new-york/city-hall/story/2012/07/bloomberg-on-the-new-york-murder-rate-we-just-are-not-going-back-000000.

15 Tonya Simpson and Lucien Bruggeman, "Videos contradict Bloomberg's apologies to black voters," *ABC News*, February 11, 2020, https://abcnews.go.com/US/videos-contradict-bloombergs-apologies-black-voters/story?id=68915337.

16 Kami Chavis Simmons, "The Legacy of Stop and Frisk: Addressing the Vestiges of a Violent Police Culture," 49 *Wake Forest L. Rev.* 849, 851 (2014) ("Clearly, New York's stop-and-frisk policy has evolved into a tactic whose purpose is to intimidate and harass vulnerable classes of individuals—poor, racial, and ethnic minorities.")

17 *Floyd* v. *New York*, 959 F. Supp. 2d 540, 560, and 667 (S.D.N.Y. 2013).

18 Shane Goldmacher, "Michael Bloomberg Pushed 'Stop-and-Frisk' Policing. Now He's Apologizing," *New York Times*, November 17, 2019, www.nytimes.com/2019/11/17/us/politics/michael-bloomberg-speech.html.

19 On the campaign trail, then candidate Donald Trump argued that stop and frisk "worked incredibly well" in New York and advocated the strategy for other American cities.

Michael Barbaro, Maggie Haberman, and Yamiche Alcindor, "Donald Trump Embraces Wider Use of Stop-and-Frisk by Police," *New York Times,* September 21, 2016, www .nytimes.com/2016/09/22/us/politics/donald-trump-don-king-black-voters.html. For a history of coded racial language in American politics, see Ian Haney Lopez, *Dog Whistle Politics: How Coded Racial Appeals have Reinvented Racism and the Wrecked Middle Class* (Oxford University Press, 2014), and Josh Zeitz, "How Trump is Recycling Nixon's 'Law and Order' Playbook," *Politico,* July 18, 2016, www.politico.com/magazine/story/2016/ 07/donald-trump-law-and-order-richard-nixon-crime-race-214066.

20 These statements were made to an audience of police officers at Suffolk County Community College in Brentwood, New York in July of 2017. Brian M. Rosenthal, "Police Criticize Trump for Urging Officers Not to Be 'Too Nice' With Suspects," *New York Times,* July 29, 2017, www.nytimes.com/2017/07/29/nyregion/trump-police-too-nice.html.

21 "Trump's comments came three days after a jury convicted white Chicago police officer Jason Van Dyke of second-degree murder in the death of black teenager Laquan McDonald." Deb Riechmann and Michael Tarm, "Trump Calls on Chicago to Embrace Stop-and-Frisk Policing," *Associated Press,* October 8, 2018, www.apnews.com/ 015e2e6ba3e44119a5c79beb99d2cf81.

22 "A quarter million Chicagoans were stopped without finding any criminal activity during just three months in the summer of 2014, the ACLU reported." Curtis Black, "Chicago Tried Stop-and-Frisk. It Didn't Work.," *The Chicago Reporter,* September 29, 2016, www .chicagoreporter.com/chicago-tried-stop-and-frisk-it-didnt-work/; Politicians and law enforcement spread misinformation about the effectiveness stop-and-frisk in Chicago, Black, "The Chicago Police Union's 'Alternative Facts' On Police Reform," *The Chicago Reporter,* May 2, 2019, www.chicagoreporter.com/the-chicago-police-unions-alternative-facts-on-police-reform/; Radley Balko, "Jeff Sessions Blames the ACLU for Chicago's Homicide Rate. He's Wrong," *The Washington Post,* May 15, 2018, www.washingtonpost .com/news/the-watch/wp/2018/05/15/jeff-sessions-blames-the-aclu-for-chicagos-homicide-rate-hes-wrong/. Following a scathing report by the American Civil Liberties Union (ACLU) in 2015, the ACLU of Illinois and the Chicago Police Department (CPD) entered a landmark agreement to reform the practice of stop-and-frisk. Stops plummeted by 80 percent beginning the following year, Josh McGhee, "Stop-and-frisk down 80% in Chicago but Black and Latinx people still hit the hardest, judge finds," *The Chicago Reporter,* October 29, 2019, www.chicagoreporter.com/stop-and-frisk-down-80-in-chicago-but-black-and-latinx-people-still-hit-the-hardest-judge-finds/ For more on the agreement, see Investigatory Stop and Protective Pat Down Settlement Agreement (ACLU, 2015) linked at the bottom of this page: www.aclu-il.org/en/press-releases/landmark-agreement-reached-investigatory-stops-chicago.

23 Laurel Wamsley, "New York City Had Its First Weekend Without A Shooting in 25 Years" *NPR,* October 17, 2018, www.npr.org/2018/10/17/658084556/new-york-city-had-its-first-week end-without-a-shooting-in-25-years/. The Brennan Center found that the murder rate fell, while the number of stops declined, when New York City ended its programmatic use of stop-and-frisk. James Cullen and Ames Grawert, "Fact Sheet: Stop and Frisk's Effect on Crime in New York City," *Brennen Center,* October 7, 2016, www.brennancenter .org/our-work/research-reports/fact-sheet-stop-and-frisks-effect-crime-new-york-city.   For other studies on the failure of programmatic stop and frisks, see n. 8 above.

24 *Crime + Punishment*, directed by Stephen Maing (2018; USA: HULU, 2018); Josephine Livingstone, "Crime + Punishment Examines the Scourge of Police Quotas," *New Republic*, August 30, 2018,
https://newrepublic.com/article/150963/crime-punishment-examines-scourge-police-quotas. One of the NYPD 12 says: "They're retaliating against me because of my numbers. I would have to massively write summons and arrest people to come up with the number close to the number that they want to come up with."

25 Sheryl Gay Stolberg and Eric Lichtblau, "Sweeping Federal Review Could Affect Consent Decrees Nationwide," *New York Times*, April 3, 2017, www.nytimes.com/2017/04/03/us/justice-department-jeff-sessions-baltimore-police.html (Describing the Sessions Memorandum of March 31, 2017, requiring a review of all existing DOJ agreements in light of the new administration's principles.) There were fourteen outstanding consent decrees, 4 out-of-court agreements and six opening or continuing investigations, including Baltimore. In addition, in one his first acts in office, Attorney General Sessions sought unsuccessfully to delay the implementation of a Baltimore consent decree to reform the police department based on a "searing 163-page report in August [of 2017] condemning police practices in Baltimore." Lynh Bui and Peter Hermann, "Baltimore mayor, police commissioner pledge to move forward on reform efforts," *Washington Post*, April 4, 2017, www.washingtonpost.com/local/public-safety/baltimore-police-commissioner-pledges-reform-despite-justice-dept-action/2017/04/04/5b745ce8-b88b-4b5e-a14b-4f9f84376168_story.html.

   In a last-minute act before President Trump fired him, Attorney General Sessions limited the scope and duration of consent decrees by mandating they be "narrowly tailored to remedy alleged violations and are not used to extract greater relief from state or local government than the Department could obtain through litigation." Office of Public Affairs, "Justice Department Releases Memorandum on Litigation Guidelines for Civil Consent Decrees and Settlement Agreements," (U.S. Department of Justice, 2018); Katie Benner, "Sessions, in Last-Minute Act, Sharply Limits use of Consent Decrees to Curb Police Abuses," *New York Times*, November 8, 2018, www.nytimes.com/2018/11/08/us/politics/sessions-limits-consent-decrees.html.

26 A Rasmussen poll in 2016 found that 41 percent of likely US voters favor stop-and-frisk, while 47 percent oppose it. This poll was in response to the first 2016 presidential debate where Donald Trump proposed allowing police to stop-and-frisk anyone they considered suspicious. Ritlka Gupta, "Poll: Over 40 Percent of Voters Favor Stop-and-Frisk," News Max, September 28, 2016, www.newsmax.com/newsfront/voters-favor-stop-and-frisk-law/2016/09/28/id/750625/. One Howard law student argued that grass-roots efforts were as important as the courts in changing the NYPD stop-and-frisk practices. Brittany Williams, "Courts and the Political Process - How Activists Can Implement Social Change," 58 *How. L.J.* 637, 639 (2015).

27 *Floyd* v. *City of New York*, 959 F. Supp. 2d at 557. Judge Scheindlin emphasizes that it is not her task to reconsider the constitutionality of stop-and-frisk as a policing tool, but to decide whether police conduct amounted to unlawful stop and frisks predicated on racial discrimination rather than reasonable suspicion, writing, "this case is not about the effectiveness of stop and frisk in deterring or combating crime. This mandate is solely to judge the constitutionality of police behavior," and "whether the City has

a policy or custom of violating the Constitution by making unlawful stops and conducting unlawful frisks."

28 John Q. Barrett, "Deciding the Stop and Frisk Cases: A Look Inside the Supreme Court's Conference," 72 *St. John's L. Rev.* 749 (1998). For the unconstitutional methods in Baltimore, see U.S. Department of Justice, Civil Rights Division, "Investigation of the Baltimore City Police Department" (August 10, 2016), www.justice.gov/crt/file/883296/download.

29 *Adams v. Williams*, 407 U.S. 143, 161–62 (1972) (Marshall, J., dissenting).

30 *Terry v. Ohio*, 392 U.S. at 39 (Douglas, J., dissenting).

31 *Illinois v. Wardlow*, 528 U.S. 119, 122 (2000).

32 *Terry v. Ohio*, 392 U.S. at 34 (White, J. concurring).

33 *Berkemer v. McCarty*, 468 U.S. 420, 439 (1984).

34 The officer's "justifiable suspicion afforded a proper constitutional basis for accosting Terry, restraining his liberty of movement briefly, and addressing questions to him. . . ." *Terry*, 392 U.S. at 6. "One general interest is of course that of effective crime prevention and detection; it is this interest which underlies the recognition that a police officer may in appropriate circumstances and in an appropriate manner approach a person for purposes of investigating possibly criminal behavior." *Terry*, 392 U.S. at 22.

35 *Floyd v. City of New York*, 959 F. Supp. 2d 540, 557 (S.D.N.Y. 2013) ("6% of all stops resulted in an arrest, and 6% resulted in a summons. The remaining 88% of the 4.4 million stops resulted in no further law enforcement action.").

36 Evidence law derides "bootstrapping." *Glasser v. United States*, 315 U.S. 60, 62 (1942).

37 *Florida v. Royer*, 490 U.S. 491, 498–500 (1983); *Berkemer v. McCarty*, 468 U.S. 420, 439 (1984) (explaining that Terrry stops and traffic stops are similarly noncoercive and the "comparatively nonthreatening character of detentions of this sort explains" why police don't have to give Miranda warnings before asking questions).

38 Possession of marijuana was the primary crime charge during the height of New York's stop and frisk, *Floyd v. New York*, 959 F. Supp. 2d 540, 576 n. 131; *Minnesota v. Dickerson*, 508 U.S. 366, 373 (1993) (citing *Sibron v. New York*, 392 U.S. 40, 65–66 (1968) ("If the protective search goes beyond what is necessary to determine if the suspect is armed, it is no longer valid under *Terry v. Ohio*, 392 U.S. 1." The "sole justification" of the *Terry* frisk is the "protection of the police officer and others nearby."), *Dickerson*, 508 U.S. at 378. Feeling a lump to see if it was drugs "therefore amounted to the sort of evidentiary search that *Terry* expressly refused to authorize," *Dickerson*, 508 U.S. at 378. Annie Fisher, "The Myth of the Terry Frisk," 14 *U. Pa. J. Const. L.: Heightened Scrutiny* 1, 1–2 (2012) ("It is one thing when a *Terry* frisk is done and a weapon is actually recovered, but in tens of thousands of misdemeanor cases in Philadelphia, the *Terry* frisk is merely a mechanism to get into the defendant's pocket[.]"); David A. Harris, "Frisking Every Suspect: The Withering of Terry," 28 *U. Cal. Davis L. Rev.* 1, 5–6 (1994). Confessions can create probable cause for a search, while consent searches create an exception to the probable cause requirement. Tracey Maclin, "The Good and Bad News About Consent Searches in the Supreme Court," 39 *McGeorge L. Rev.* 27, 29 (2008).

39 *Utah v. Strieff*, 136 S. Ct. 2056, 2060–63 (2016). The "incident to arrest" doctrine allows police to search arrestees thoroughly without any specific suspicion or fear. (For a further discussion of the Strieff opinions, see Chapter 8.)

40 *Terry* v. *Ohio*, 392 U.S. at 20. The outstanding warrant is just another excuse to arrest. As Justice Sotomayor stated, the outstanding warrant was "part and parcel of the officer's illegal 'expedition for evidence in the hope that something might turn up.'" *Strieff*, 136 S. Ct. at 2066 (Sotomayor, J., dissenting). (Chapter 8 describes the widespread warrant check practice.)

41 *Escobedo* v. *Illinois*, 378 U.S. 478, 490 (1964).

42 *Moran* v. *Burbine*, 475 U.S. 412, 458 (1986) (Stevens, J., dissenting) (citing, *Escobedo* v. *Illinois*, 378 U.S. 478, 490 (1964)); *Berghuis* v. *Thompkins*, 560 U.S. 370, 410 (2010).

43 Ronan Farrow, "From Aggressive Overtures to Sexual Assault: Harvey Weinstein's Accusers Tell Their Stories," *New Yorker*, October 10, 2017, www.newyorker.com/news/news-desk/from-aggressive-overtures-to-sexual-assault-harvey-weinsteins-accusers-tell-their-stories; Megan Twohey et al., "Weinstein's Complicity Machine," *New York Times*, December 5, 2017, www.nytimes.com/interactive/2017/12/05/us/harvey-weinstein-complicity.html.

44 Mary Newman, "Barnes v. City of Cincinnati: Command Presence, Gender Bias, and Problems of Police Aggression," 29 *Harv. J.L. & Gender* 485, 490–91 (2006); Frank Rudy Cooper, "Who's the Man?": *Masculinities Studies, Terry Stops, and Police Training*, 18 *Colum. J. Gender & L.* 671, 693 (2009).

45 Valorie K. Vojdik, "Gender Outlaws: Challenging Masculinity in Traditionally Male Institutions," 17 *Berkeley Women's L.J.* 68, 100 (2002) ("Hazing incidents at both The Citadel and VMI often targeted the testicles and groin area.").

46 Frank Rudy Cooper, "A Genealogy of Programmatic Stop and Frisk: The Discourse-to-Practice-Circuit," 73 *U. Miami L. Rev.* 1, 75 (2018).

47 *Maryland* v. *Pringle*, 540 U.S. 366 (2003) (defining probable cause).

48 *New York* v. *Quarles*, 467 U.S. 649 (1984)(exigent circumstances allowed police to question a person in custody about the location of a gun without first giving him Miranda warning); *Brigham City* v. *Stuart*, 547 U.S. 398, 405 (2006) (allowing entry into a home without a warrant when an officer had an objectively reasonable basis for believing that an injured civilian inside the home needed help and reasonably believed that the violence was escalating).

2 THE MOST DANGEROUS RIGHT: WALKING AWAY FROM AN OFFICER

1 *Florida* v. *Royer*, 460 U.S. 491, 497–98 (1983) (citing concurring opinions by Justice Harlan and Justice White in *Terry* v. *Ohio* 392 U.S. at 32–33, 34.)

2 The cell-phone video of the incident is available at Jacquellena Carrero and Alex Johnson, "McKinney, Texas, Cop Placed on Leave After Pulling Gun on Teens at Pool Party," *NBC News*, June 8, 2015, www.nbcnews.com/news/us-news/mckinney-texas-officer-leave-after-wild-pool-party-video-surfaces-n371281 and in Azadeh Ansari, "Texas Teen Tackled by Police Officer at Pool Party Files Federal Lawsuit," *CNN*, January 5, 2017, www.cnn.com/2017/01/05/us/texas-mckinney-pool-party-officer-lawsuit/index.html. According to DAB's lawsuit, McKinney Police Corporal "Eric Casebolt was senior of a total of twelve officers who arrived on the scene." *Bakari* v. *Casebolt*, 2017 WL 5177593 (E.D.Tex.). The officer was suspended but ultimately resigned and was able to retain his pension and other benefits. Barnes filed a lawsuit against the police officer for excessive force, seeking

$5 million in damages. Christine Hauser, "Texas Teenager Sues Officcer Who Threw Her to the Ground at Party," *New York Times*, January 5, 2017, www.nytimes.com/2017/01/05/us/mckinney-pool-party-cop-lawsuit.html?login=email&auth=login-email.   The   parties reached a settlement agreement in which Barnes was rewarded $148,850. Steve Pickett, "Settlement Agreement eached in Mckinney 'Pool Party' Lawsuit," May 29, 2018, https://dfw.cbslocal.com/2018/05/29/settlement-agreement-mckinney-pool-party-lawsuit/.

3 Malcolm Sparrow, *Handcuffed: What Holds Policing Back and the Keys to Reform* 34–35 (Brookings Institution Press, 2016); Kimberly Kindy, Jennifer Jenkins, Steven Rich, Keith L. Alexander, and Wesley Lowery, "Fatal Police Shootings in 2015 Approaching 400 Nationwide," *Washington Post*, May 30, 2015, www.washingtonpost.com/national/fatal-police-shootings-in-2015-approaching-400-nationwide/2015/05/30/d322256a-058e-11e5-a428-c984eb077d4e_story.html. ("Running is such a provocative act that police experts say there is a name for the injury officers inflict on suspects afterward: a foot tax.")

4 See the video of the confrontation between a police officer and Charlena Michelle Cooks in Barstow, California, at Micahel Martinez and Kyung Lah, "Police Video Shows 'Horrifying' Arrest of Pregnant Woman, ACLU Says," *CNN*, May 29, 2015, www.cnn.com/2015/05/28/us/barstow-california-police-video-pregnant-woman-arrest/ and Morgan Whitaker, "Cameras Capture Police Throwing 8-month Pregnant Woman to the Ground," *AOL*, May 28, 2015, www.aol.com/article/2015/05/28/cameras-capture-police-throwing-8-month-pregnant-woman-to-the-gr/21188497/.

5 *Hiibel v. Sixth Judicial Dist. Court of Nevada, Humboldt County*, 542 U.S. 177, 187–88 (2004) affirmed an arrest for failing to give a name under a Nevada "stop and identify" statute during a Terry stop based on reasonable suspicion. The Court claimed not to overrule *Brown v. Texas*, 443 U.S. 47, 49 (1979) that reversed a conviction under a "stop and identify" statute when officers detained the individual without reasonable suspicion of wrongdoing. *Hiibel* appeared to further limit arrests to situations where the request for identification was "reasonably related to the circumstances justifying the stop," did not extend the length of the stop, and for statutes that didn't require people to turn over a driver's license or documentation. Despite these limitations, "the Hiibel Court effected a dramatic moment in the expansion of the Terry doctrine, and, in the process, jarred the previously stalwart notion of an absolute right to not speak in public." E. Martin Estrada, "Criminalizing Silence: Hiibel and the Continuing Expansion of the Terry Doctrine," 49 *St. Louis U. L.J.* 279, 293–94 (2005). (The Hiibel case is discussed in Chapter 5.)

6 Kimberlé Crenshaw, "Demarginalizing the Intersection of Race and Sex: A Black Feminist Critique of Antidiscrimination Doctrine, Feminist Theory and Antiracist Politics," 1989 *U. Chi. Legal F.* 139 (1998). "Crenshaw was one of the first scholars to examine the consequences of anti-discriminatory laws' tendency to treat race and gender as mutually exclusive categories," Yvette N. A. Pappoe, "The Shortcomings of Title VII for the Black Female Plaintiff," 22 *U. Pa. J.L. & Soc. Change* 1, 8 (2019).

7 Andrea Ritchie, *Invisible No More*, 35 (Beacon Press, 2017).

8 A federal appeals court panel dismissed the federal civil rights lawsuit based on the officers' qualified immunity but allowed Malika Brooks to proceed on assault and battery claims under state law. The majority found the officers behaved unreasonably when, knowing she was pregnant, they "tased her three times within less than one minute, inflicting extreme pain on Brooks." Dissenting from the finding of excessive force, Chief Judge Alex Kozinski

wrote that Brooks "breached the covenant of cooperation by refusing to comply with police orders" and Seattle should award the officers "commendations for grace under fire." *Mattos v. Agarano*, 661 F.3d 433, 456 (9th Cir. 2011)(Kozinski, J. concurring in part, dissenting in part). Bill Meares, "Justices decline case of taser use on pregnant woman," *CNN*, May 29, 2012, www.cnn.com/2012/05/29/justice/scotus-taser-shocks/index.html.

9 Elizabeth Bruenig, "Michael Bloomberg and the Long History of Misogyny Toward Mothers," *New York Times*, February 28, 2020.

10 Cathy J. Cohen, Punks, "Bulldaggers, and Welfare Queens: The Radical Potential of Queer Politics?," *Gay and Lesbian Quarterly*, 437–65 (1997); Dorothy Roberts, *Killing the Black Body: Race, Reproduction and the Meaning of Liberty* (Vintage Books, 1997); Ritchie, *Invisible No More* at 165–82.

11 *Florida v. Royer*, 460 U.S. 491, 497 (1983)(plurality opinion): "law enforcement officers do not violate the Fourth Amendment by merely approaching an individual on the street or in another public place, by asking him if he is willing to answer some questions, by putting questions to him if the person is willing to listen, or by offering in evidence in a criminal prosecution his voluntary answers to such questions." *Royer* cites *Terry v. Ohio*, 392 U.S. at 32–33 (Harlan, J., concurring): "ordinarily the person addressed [by an officer] has an equal right to ignore his interrogator and walk away; he certainly need not submit to a frisk for the questioner's protection." Justice Potter Stewart articulated the free to leave test to separate out stops from consensual encounters this way: "a person has been 'seized' within the meaning of the Fourth Amendment only if, in view of all the circumstances surrounding the incident, a reasonable person would have believed that he was not free to leave," *United States v. Mendenhall*, 446 U.S. 544, 554 (1980) (Stewart, J., in Section II-A writing for himself and one other). This language was adopted by the Court in later opinions.

12 Baltimore State's Attorney Marilyn Mosby charged six officers in the arrest, transport, and death of Freddie Gray, none of whom were convicted. Prosecutors alleged that there was no probable cause to arrest Mr. Gray because the knife clipped to his belt was legal as a matter of state law. Prosecutors also made a novel legal argument that police committed misdemeanor assault against Mr. Gray when they handcuffed him without probable cause. Justin Fenton, "Prosecutors to Test Novel Legal Theory in Trial of Officer Charged in Freddie Gray Case," *The Baltimore Sun*, May 9, 2016, www.baltimoresun.com/maryland/baltimore-city/bs-md-ci-freddie-gray-statements-20150505-story.html. The defense disputed the legality of the knife, pointing to the Baltimore City Code that prohibits a broader range of knives than the state statute. Justin George and Justin Fenton, "Officer Requests to See Knife as Part of Defense in Freddie Gray Case," *The Baltimore Sun*, May 5, 2015, www.baltimoresun.com/maryland/baltimore-city/bs-md-ci-freddie-gray-statements-20150505-story.html.

13 *Illinois v. Wardlow*, 528 U.S. 119, 124 (2000).

14 Ben Grunwalk and Jeffrey Fagan, "The End of Intuition-Based High-Crime Areas," 107 *Cal. L. Rev.* 345, 369, 396 (2019); *United States v. Montero-Camargo*, 208 F. 3d 1122, 1138 (9th Cir. 2000) (Kozinski, J., concurring).

15 For similar advice, see "Who, What, Why: What should you do if you encounter a bear?," *BBC News*, June 30, 2015, www.bbc.com/news/magazine-33334431.

16 This presupposes a good system for monitoring complaints, which we have in the District of Columbia. It also helps if the police body camera records and preserves the footage.

17 According to the DOJ report on the Chicago Police Department, the "jumpout" technique "involves groups of officers accelerating up to a group of pedestrians, screeching to a halt a few feet away, and jumping out with their guns drawn." The tactic causes people to panic and flee. "The officers then zero-in on the fleeing person, often with one officer tasked with chasing him on foot," the report states. "Some of the most problematic shootings occurred when that sole officer closed in on the subject, thus greatly increasing the risk of a serious or deadly force incident." U.S. Department of Justice Civil Rights Division, "Investigation of the Chicago Police Department" (January 13, 2017), www .justice.gov/opa/file/925846/download.

18 Lenese Herbert, "Can't You See What I'm Saying: Making Expressive Conduct a Crime in High-Crime Areas," 9 *Geo. J. on Poverty L. & Pol'y* 135, 153 (2002). Howard law professor Herbert writes that "reactive flight may be the most effective way for residents to communicate their distaste of the police and to exercise their choice to remove themselves from police presence."

19 *Decker* v. *Tinnel*, No. 2:04-CV-227, 2005 U.S. Dist. LEXIS 38559 (N.D. Ind. Dec. 20, 2005). The federal lawsuit alleged constitutional violations under the Fourth Amendment and Due Process Clause. The judge dismissed all claims. It is difficult for some judges to equate sexual impropriety with traditional Fourth Amendment abuses of power. The Fourth Amendment considers the reasonableness of an officer's conduct rather than a police officer's subjective intentions. I found this case from reading a draft of a student law review article, Jon Ostrowsky, "#metoo's Unseen Frontier: Law Enforcement Sexual Misconduct and the Fourth Amendment Response," 67 *UCLA L. Rev.* 258, 296 (2020). As bad as the Fourth Amendment may seem for plaintiffs seeking remedies for unwanted sexual abuse by police, it's worse when courts take a Due Process approach because only egregious assaults satisfy that standard. Ostrowsky explains that many courts eschew the Fourth Amendment altogether, making it even more difficult for people to bring suits for sexual misconduct.

20 *Florida* v. *Bostick*, 501 U.S. 429, 432, and 437 (1991). Although "one officer carried a zipper pouch containing a pistol," the majority calls this "the equivalent of carrying a gun in a holster." Important facts in this case that showed this was a consensual contact rather than a Terry stop, include that "the gun was [not] ever removed from its pouch, pointed at Bostick, or otherwise used in a threatening manner."

21 *U.S.* v. *Drayton*, 536 U.S. 194, 198, 211 (2002) and *Florida* v. *Bostick*, 501 U.S. 429, 431–32 (1991).

22 *Bostick*, 501 U.S. at 430.

23 Mark Makela, "Transcript: Donald Trump's Taped Comments About Women," *The New York Times*, October 8, 2016, www.nytimes.com/2016/10/08/us/donald-trump-tape-transcript.html. During the 2016 presidential election, the "Hollywood tape" from 2005 came to light. Trump was recorded making comments about women, including: "I just start kissing them. It's like a magnet. Just kiss." Referring to women, he then goes on to say "I don't even wait. And when you're a star, they let you do it. You can do anything."

24 *Florida* v. *Bostick*, 501 U.S. 429, 434 (1991) citing *California* v. *Hodari D.*, 499 U.S. 621, 628 (1991).

25 Margaret Raymond, "The Right to Refuse And The Obligation To Comply: Challenging The Gamesmanship Model Of Criminal Procedure," 54 *Buff. L. Rev.* 1483, 1492 (2007).

26 *Price Waterhouse* v. *Hopkins*, 490 U.S. 228 (1989).

27 L. Song Richardson, "Implicit Racial Bias and Racial Anxiety: Implications for Stops and Frisks," 15 *Ohio St. J. Crim. L.* 73, 80 (2017); L. Song Richardson, "Cognitive Bias, Police Character, and the Fourth Amendment," 44 *Ariz. St. L.J.* 267, 272 (2012); Andrew E. Taslitz, "Police are People Too: Cognitive Obstacles to, and Opportunities for, Police Getting the Individualized Suspicion Judgment Right," 8 *Ohio St. J. Crim. L.* 7 (2010); Katherine B. Spencer, Amanda K. Charbonneau, and Jack Glaser, "Implicit Bias and Policing," *Social and Personality Psychology Compass* 50 (2016).

28 The *Washington Post*'s independent database for police shootings recorded 752 killings by police in 2019 (as of October 31, 2019), 32 percent of those killed were killed while fleeing either by car (133 deaths or 17 percent) or by foot (110 deaths or 15 percent). The percentage of people killed while fleeing has remained fairly consistent, 32 percent in 2018 and 34 percent in 2017. "National Police Shootings," *Washington Post* (updates continue), www .washingtonpost.com/graphics/2019/national/police-shootings-2019.

29 George Lardner Jr., "McDuffie Death: It Seemed to Be Open–Shut Case," *The Washington Post*, May 21, 1980, www.washingtonpost.com/archive/politics/1980/05/21/mcduffie-death-it-seemed-to-be-open-shut-case/181a3552-c09d-4652-afb1-a9f4f0998a23/?utm_term= .616352e38814; David Smiley, "McDuffie Riots: Revisiting, Retelling Story – 35 Years Later," *Miami Herald*, May 16, 2015, www.miamiherald.com/news/local/community/ miami-dade/article21178995.html. (In the Brownsville suburb of Miami, the "consequences of the damage have lasted decades. 'It certainly isn't the way it once was and it never will be.'")

30 Michael S. Schmidt and Matt Apuzzo, "South Carolina Officer Is Charged With Murder of Walter Scott," *New York Times*, April 7, 2015, www.nytimes.com/2015/04/08/us/south-carolina-officer-is-charged-with-murder-in-black-mans-death.html. After a local jury deadlocked on a murder charge, the Justice Department under Loretta Lynch indicted Officer Slager, who pleaded guilty to a federal civil rights violation. Categorizing the killing as second-degree murder, the federal judge sentenced him to twenty years. Dustin Waters, "I Was Scared: S.C. Officer on Trial for Murder in Shooting of Unarmed Black Man Takes the Stand," *Washington Post*, November 29, 2016, www.washingtonpost.com/ news/post-nation/wp/2016/11/29/i-was-scared-s-c-officer-on-trial-for-murder-in-shooting-of-unarmed-black-man-takes-the-stand/?utm_term=.e48d109b8dbf.

31 Matt Stevens, Melissa Gomez, and Christina Caron, "Police Killing of Antwon Rose, 17 in East Pittsburg Prompts Protests," *New York Times*, June 21, 2018, www.nytimes.com/2018/ 06/21/us/antwon-rose-police-killing-protests.html. Antwon Rose wrote the poem quoted at the top of this chapter, a poem that repeats the line "I am confused and afraid." A. T. Williams, "What Antwon Rose's Poetry Tells Us About Being Black in America," *New Yorker*, July 4, 2018, www.newyorker.com/culture/culture-desk/what-antwon-roses-poetry-tells-us-about-being-black-in-america ("His words bring into focus the cruel irony of what it feels like to be a young black man in America, a country in which he is told that he is free but is treated like a 'statistic.'")

32 Lauren Gold, "Pasadena Police Reports Detail Kendrec McDade Shooting," *Pasadena Star-News*, September 26, 2014, www.pasadenastarnews.com/2014/09/26/pasadena-police-reports-detail-kendrec-mcdade-shooting/; Elizabeth Day, "Kendrec McDade Died in a Hail of US Police Bullets in 2012. His Mother Still Seeks Justice," *Guardian*, October

17, 2015, www.theguardian.com/us-news/2015/oct/17/black-student-kendrec-mcdade-shot-us-police-review-withheld. ("I taught him his rights," said Kendrec McDade's mother.)

33 These names appear in a database compiled by the *Washington Post* of fatal police shootings. The *Post* continues to update this database because the government statistics are woefully inadequate, relying on police departments to voluntarily relay data to the FBI. Police have shot and killed approximately 1,000 people each year since the *Post* began tracking this. "Fatal Force: 2019 police shootings database," *Washington Post*, July 15, 2019, www.washingtonpost.com/graphics/2019/national/police-shootings-2019/?utm_term=.1e0ef41a1c65.

34 History professor Ibram Kendi advocates the term "racist policy" over "structural racism" or "systemic racism." "'Racist policy' is more tangible and exacting," Ibram X. Kendi, *How to Be an Anti-Racist*, 18 (Random House, 2019).

35 Joe Fox Adrian et al., "What We Learned About Police Shootings 5 Years After Ferguson," *Washington Post*, August 9, 2019, www.washingtonpost.com/nation/2019/08/09/what-weve-learned-about-police-shootings-years-after-ferguson/?arc404=true.

36 Ibid. In 2018, police shot and killed 449 white people, 229 black people and 165 Hispanics out of a total of 992 people. Overall, whites represent 61 percent of the population while blacks represent 13 percent. "Fatal Force: 2019 police shootings database," *Washington Post*, July 15, 2019, www.washingtonpost.com/graphics/2019/national/police-shootings-2019/?utm_term=.1e0ef41a1c65.

37 Jon Swaine, Oliver Laughland, Jamiles Lartey, and Ciara McCarthy, "Young Black Men Killed by US Police at Highest Rate In Year of 1,134 Deaths," *Guardian*, December 31, 2015, www.theguardian.com/us-news/2015/dec/31/the-counted-police-killings-2015-young-black-men. More recent reports find that the risk of being killed by police is 2.5 times higher for black men than for white men. Frank Edwards, Hedwig Lee and Michael Esposito, "Risk of Being Killed by Police Use of Force in the United States by Age, Race-Ethnicity, and Sex," *Proceedings of the National Academy of Sciences* (2019): 1–12 at 3 (putting the number of deaths from police at 3.4 per 100,000 thousand deaths of black males aged 25 to 29, and noting, "police violence was one of the leading causes of death in the years 2013 to 2018").

3 CONSENTING TO SEARCHES: WHAT WE CAN LEARN FROM FEMINIST CRITIQUES OF SEXUAL ASSAULT LAWS

1 Susan Estrich, *Real Rape*, 83 (Harvard University Press, 1987); Estrich, "Rape," 95 *Yale L. J.* 1087, 1150 (1986).

2 Lawrence, interview with the author, January 2020. Alanna Vagianos, "Bloomberg's Stop-And-Frisk Was 'State-Sanctioned Sexual Assault' of Men of Color," *Huffington Post*, March 2, 2020.

3 For the 2020 the student body at Howard University School of Law, nearly 82 percent of the students are black; the remaining 18 percent are Hispanic/Latino, Asian, White, or multiracial. "Howard law welcomes the class of 2020" (2017), http://law.howard.edu/content/howard-law-welcomes-class-2020. Generally, I have about five white students in a class of fifty students.

4 *United States* v. *Drayton*, 536 U.S. 194, 199 (2002). ("Mind if I check you?" the officer testified he asked Mr. Drayton, who was seated on a bus. "Drayton responded by lifting his hands about eight inches from legs. Lang conducted a patdown of Drayton's thighs.")

5 *United States v. Mendenhall*, 446 U.S. 544, 547–48 (1980). This was a plurality decision where Stewart, J., announced the judgment of the Court. A plurality opinion means that a majority of the justices agreed that the federal agents did not violate her rights, but disagreed on how to reach this result. There were three published opinions in all.

6 The text paraphrases the testimony. As Justice White explained, Mendenhall was "informed that the officers wanted her to come with them to the DEA office" and the agent testified at the hearing that "if Ms. Mendenhall wanted to leave at that point she would have been forcibly restrained." *United States v. Mendenhall*, 446 U.S. at 576 (1980) (White, J. dissenting). A majority of justices agreed that this was a Terry stop.

7 *United States v. Mendenhall*, 1979 U.S. S. Ct. Briefs LEXIS 1094 at 36.

8 *Mendenhall*, 446 U.S. at 559 (1980).

9 "Between 1970, when the feminist movement first started to talk about rape, and 1979, when the militance had receded, every state in the union went through a serious reevaluation of its rape codes and made significant adjustments." Susan Brownmiller, *In Our Time: Memoir of a Revolution* (Dial Press, 1999).

10 Jill Filipovic, "Offensive Feminism: The Conservative Gender Norms That Perpetuate Rape Culture, and How Feminists Can Fight Back," in Jaclyn Friedman and Jessica Valenti, eds., *Yes Means Yes: Visions of Female Sexual Power & A World Without Rape* 13, 26–27 (Seal Press, 2008). ("we must emphasize a pleasure-affirming vision of female sexuality where saying yes and no are equally valid moral decisions... We need to situate sexual assault within the greater cultural battles over women's bodies.") Filipovic is a feminist, millennial journalist, author, and lawyer whose work appears in the *New York Times*, *Huffington Post*, and *Cosmopolitan*. Amandla Stenberg, "Amandla Stenberg on Sexual Assault and Coping With Trauma," *Teen Vogue*, October 6, 2018, www.teenvogue .com/story/amandla-stenberg-writes-about-sexual-assault. In an essay discussing her own experience with sexual abuse, Stenberg writes, "I had not consented, but I had not said no. So I did not consider what I had experienced an assault. I figured it was just an inherent part of sexual exploration as a teenage girl; the conundrum of compliance. And even in the throes of my discomfort, I prioritized the male ego. In both instances, I excused the behavior because I had been taught to." Stenberg is an actress and social justice activist who was named "Feminist of the Year" by the Ms. Foundation of Women in 2015.

11 Estelle B. Freedman, *Sexual Violence in the Era of Suffrage and Segregation*, 42-43 (Harvard University Press 2018).

12 Catharine MacKinnon, *Toward a Feminist Theory of the State*, 180 (Harvard University Press, 1991).

13 *Schneckloth v. Bustamonte*, 412 U.S. 218 (1973). While both men's surnames derive from Spain, it's unclear if the officers would have perceived them as non-white.

14 Ibid., 220, 227.

15 *Bumper v. North Carolina*, 391 U.S. 543, 548–49 (1968).

16 *Mendenhall* 446 U.S. at 559; Dissent at 566 (White, J. dissenting)(emphasis added)

17 Andrea Dworkin, *Our Blood: Prophesies and Discourse on Sexual Politics*, 58 (Harper & Row, 1976); Susan Brownmiller, *Against Our Will: Men, Women and Rape* 8 (Fawcett Books, 1975).

18 Catharine A. MacKinnon, "Feminism, Marxism, Method and the State: Toward Feminist Jurisprudence," *Signs* 8 (1983): 635–58 at 650; Josephine Ross, "Blaming the Victim:

Consent within the Fourth Amendment and Rape Law," 26 *Harv. J. of Racial & Ethnic Just.* 1 (2010) (introducing a feminist critique of consent into the framework of policing and criminal procedure.)

19 Janet E. Ainsworth, "In a Different Register: The Pragmatics of Powerlessness in Police Interrogation," 103 *Yale L.J.* 259, 283–84 (1993) citing Robin T. Lakoff, *Talking Power: The Politics of Language in our Lives* 205 (Basic Books, 1990).

20 Ibid., 285.

21 Dana Patton and Joseph L. Smith, "Lawyer, Interrupted: Gender Bias in Oral arguments at the US Supreme Court," *Journal of Law and Courts* 5 (2017). (Examining three decades of oral arguments, the researchers found that female lawyers are interrupted more frequently than male lawyers, allowed to speak for less time in-between interruptions, and subjected to longer speeches by the justices.)

22 Juliet Eilperin, "White House Women Want to be in The Room Where It Happens," *Washington Post, September* 13, 2016, www.washingtonpost.com/news/powerpost/wp/2016/09/13/white-house-women-are-now-in-the-room-where-it-happens/.

23 Catharine MacKinnon, *Feminism, Marxism, Method and the State*, 96 (Harvard University Press, 1989)("bad girls, like wives, are consenting, whores, unrapable."). As one court phrased it in 1915, "no impartial mind can resist the conclusion that a female who had been in the recent habit of illicit intercourse with others will not be so likely to resist as one spotless and pure," Estrich, *Real Rape*, 47. In the South, slaves could not testify in court against their owner. Estelle B. Freedman writes "In the rare instances when free black women accused white men of rape, courts assumed that they had consented. Between the Revolution and the Civil War, when popular and legal construction of rape continued to narrow to require a chaste white female victim and nonwhite male perpetrator for conviction." Estelle B. Freedman, *Sexual Violence in the Era of Suffrage and Segregation*, 19, 21, and n. 24.

24 Anne M. Coughlin, "Sex and Guilt," 84 *Va. L. Rev.* 1, 28 (1998).

25 MacKinnon, *Feminism, Marxism, Method and the State*, 648.

26 Dorothy E. Roberts, "Rape, Violence and Women's Autonomy," 69 *Chi.-Kent L. Rev* 359, 379 (1993). Anti-miscegenation laws prohibited marriage and intimacy between white and non-white individuals. Stephanie M. Wildman, "Interracial Intimacy and the Potential for Social Change," 17 *Berk. W. L. J.* 153, 156 (2002). In the Jim Crow era many Southern states routinely prosecuted white men and women with fornication and adultery for having engaging in sexual relationships with blacks. On the other hand, a black man would often be charged with the more serious offense of rape for having sex – even if it was consensual – with a white woman. Martha Hodes, *White Woman, Black Man* 3, 4 (Yale University Press, 1997).

27 David Jaros, "Criminal Doctrines of Faith," 59 *B.C. L. Rev.* 2203, 2258 (2018); Joëlle Anne Moreno, "Rights, Remedies and the Quantum and Burden of Proof," 3 *Va. J. Crim. L.* 89, 98–100 (2015); *Utah v. Strieff*, 136 S. Ct. 2056, 2063–64 (2016) (discussed in Chapter 8).

28 John M. Burkoff, "Search Me?," 39 *Tex. Tech. L. Rev.* 1109, 1114 (2007).

29 *Florida. v. Bostick*, 501 U.S. 429, 437–38 (1991). The reasonable innocent person test determines whether a person is free to leave, but from its inception it's been entangled with consent to search. "We do reject, however, Bostick's argument that he must have been seized because no reasonable person would freely consent to a search of luggage that

he or she knows contains drugs. This argument cannot prevail because the 'reasonable person' test presupposes an *innocent* person." Initially, for "consent" searches, judges were told to consider the point of view of the person searched as well as objective factors. *Schneckloth v. Bustamonte*, 412 U.S. 218 (1973). In a departure from Bostick, *Ferguson v. City of Charleston*, 532 U.S. 67. 84–85 (2001) uses the term "knowing waiver" of constitutional rights to describe whether there's true consent when pregnant women agree to drug testing.

30 *United States v. Drayton* 536 US 194, 205 (2015) (Justice Kennedy, writing for the majority).

31 In contrast to the Supreme Court's theory "that innocent people do not feel overly threatened by brief encounters with police," for many minorities "the sight of an officer in uniform evokes a sense of fear and trepidation, rather than security," writes law professor Robert Ward, arguing that courts should consider a person's race when ascertaining whether a person consented to a stop or search. Robert V. Ward, "Consenting to a Search and Seizure in Poor and Minority Neighborhoods: No Place for a Reasonable Person," 36 *How. L.J.* 239, 247 (1993). Chapter 8 discusses how the innocent person test relates to racial discrimination.

32 Janice Nadler, "No Need to Shout: Bus Sweeps and the Psychology of Coercion," 2002 *Sup. Ct. Rev.* 153, 188–90 (2002) (discussing social science literature).

33 *United States v. Drayton*, 536 U.S. 194, 208 (2002) (Souter, J., dissenting).

34 Estrich, "Rape," 95 *Yale L. J.* 1087, 1118 (1986).

35 *Floyd*, 861 F. Supp. 2d 274 (S.D.N.Y. 2012) (Order on Expert Testimony), Appendix B (Blank UF-250 Form).

36 *U.S. v. Drayton*, 536 U.S. 194, 207 (2002).

37 *Schneckloth v. Bustamonte*, 412 U.S. 218, 227–8 (1973) (announcing the rule that consent may be valid even when people don't know they have a right to say no).

38 Yale Kamisar, "Mapp v. Ohio: The First Shot Fired in the Warren Court's Criminal Procedure 'Revolution,'" in Carol Streiker, ed., *Criminal Procedure Stories*, 45 (Foundation Press, 2006). *Mapp v. Ohio*, 367 U.S. 643 (1961). In 1949, the Supreme Court in *Wolf v. Colorado*, 338 U.S. 25 (1949) decided that the Fourth Amendment constraints on federal officials applied to state and local police officers too, but nothing changed. Then in 1961, the police departments started massive reforms when the Supreme Court ruled that state courts must exclude evidence that police gathered in violation of the Fourth Amendment. *Mapp* launched the "criminal procedure revolution" when it declared that states were bound by the exclusionary rule. As Eric J. Miller notes, traditional wisdom claims that the revolution in individual rights began with *Mapp* and ended seven years later with *Terry v. Ohio*. Miller argues for a different view of the trajectory. With *Terry*, the Supreme Court did not seek to shrink privacy rights as much as it wanted to regulate and set some standards on the pre-arrest detentions in crime-heavy urban environments. Eric Miller, "The Warren Court's Regulatory Revolution in Criminal Procedure," 43 *Conn. L. Rev.* 1, 56 (2010).

39 Susan Brownmiller, *Against Our Will*, 15, 18, and 209: "A female definition of rape can be contained in a single sentence. If a woman chooses not to have intercourse with a specific man and the man chooses to proceed against her will, that is a criminal act of rape . . . [However,] this is not and never has been the legal definition . . . Rape could not

be envisioned as a matter of female consent or refusal . . . [or on] a female's right to her bodily integrity."

40 Sarah Maslin Nir, "Brooklyn Prosecutors Investigating Rape Charge Against Detectives," *New York Times*, October 1, 2017, www.nytimes.com/2017/10/01/nyregion/nypd-detectives-accused-of-raping-teen.html; Jan Ransom and Alan Feuer, "She Accused 2 Police Officers of Rape. Then Her Testimony Was Questioned," *New York Times*, March 9, 2019, www.nytimes.com/2019/03/06/nyregion/nypd-rape-brooklyn.html.

41 Maria Silvestri, "New York's Slimiest: How One Case Is Bringing National Attention to Police-Perpetrated Rape," *Truth Out*, November 13, 2017, https://truthout.org/articles/new-york-s-slimiest/.

42 Natasha Lennard, "Police Reportedly Claim a Brooklyn Teen Consented to Sex in Custody. That's Impossible," *The Intercept*, October 20, 2017, https://theintercept.com/2017/10/20/brooklyn-teen-police-rape-consent/; D. Watkins, "NYC cops skate on probation after admitting sexual assault: 'F**k the justice system,'" *Salon*, September 4, 2019, www.salon.com/2019/09/04/nyc-cops-skate-on-probation-after-admitting-sexual-assault-fk-the-just ice-system/. For another editorial critical of the defense, see Adrienne Mahsa Varkiani, "NYPD cops are smearing a victim accusing them of rape to avoid indictment," *ThinkProgress*, October 22, 2017, https://archive.thinkprogress.org/anna-chambers-nypd-cops-attack-credibility-38ec1d7f9c22/.

43 Alan Feuer, "Aggressive Defense Continues in Case of Detectives Accused of Rape," *New York Times*, March 19, 2018, www.nytimes.com/2018/03/19/nyregion/detectives-rape-defense-new-york.html; Associated Press, "NY works to prohibit cops from having sex with people in custody," *PIX 11*, https://pix11.com/2018/02/14/ny-works-to-prohibit-cops-from-having-sex-with-people-in-custody/.

44 S7708; Section 130.05 Subdivision 3 of New York Penal Code, enacted in March of 2018. Jessica Chia, "State lawmakers pass bill barring cops from having sex with detainees," *Daily News*, March 31, 2018, www.nydailynews.com/new-york/ny-passes-bill-barring-cops-sex-detainees-article-1.3906874.
New York joined fourteen other states who have passed similar legislation that prohibit police from having sex with detainees. Albert Samaha, "New York Just Passed A Bill Banning Cops from Having Sex with People in Custody," *BuzzFeed News*, March 30, 2018, www.buzzfeednews.com/article/albertsamaha/new-york-police-rape-sex-custody-banned-nypd.

45 This was count #50 in the grand jury indictment against Detectives Richard Hall and Eddie Martins. Eventually, the officer pled guilty to lesser charges of misconduct and receiving a bribe, and received probation. Edgar Sandoval, "After Rape Case Unravels, Ex-Detectives Plead Guilty to Lesser Crimes," *New York Times*, August 29, 2019.

46 Al Baker, Alan Feuer, and Joseph Goldstein, "Indictment Issued in Case of 18-Year-Old Who Said 2 Officers Raped Her," *New York Times*, October 27, 2017, www.nytimes.com/2017/10/27/nyregion/indictment-in-brooklyn-rape-investigation.html?action=click&module=RelatedCoverage&pgtype=Article&region=Footer. ("She was petrified, so she showed it," said her lawyer.)

47 Elizabeth N. Brown, "Cops Claim Teen Consented to Sex in Their Custody, Point Prosecutors to Her 'Provocative' Selfies," *Reason*, October 23, 2017, https://reason.com/2017/10/23/nypd-slut-shames-teen-who-says-she-was-r/.

48 Megan McLemore, *In Harm's Way: State Response to Sex Workers, Drug Users and HIV in New Orleans* (Human Rights Watch, 2013), www.hrw.org/report/2013/12/11/harms-way/state-response-sex-workers-drug-users-and-hiv-new-orleans (noting that over one million people in the United States are living with HIV.)

4 PUNISHING DISRESPECT: NO FREE SPEECH ALLOWED HERE

1 "Head of the Civil Rights Division Vanita Gupta Delivers Remarks at the Howard University School of Law Annual Wiley A. Branton Symposium," *U.S. Department of Justice*, October 14, 2016, www.justice.gov/opa/speech/head-civil-rights-division-vanita-gupta-delivers-remarks-howard-university-school-law. Note that I added in "every time" from when I heard her speak on the subject at an earlier event at the Justice Roundtable.
2 New York University law professor Peggy C. Davis described a "microaggression" as the "subtle, stunning, automatic, and non-verbal exchanges which are 'put downs' of Blacks" that 'contribute to relative paralysis of action, planning, and self-esteem.' Psychiatrists who have studied black populations view them as 'incessant and cumulative' assaults on black self-esteem." Peggy C. Davis, "Law as Microaggression," 98 *Yale L. J.* 1559, 1565 (1989).
3 Bryan Smith, "An American Tragedy," *Chicago Magazine*, December 14, 2015, www.chicagomag.com/Chicago-Magazine/January-2016/Sandra-Bland/. The Waller County Sheriff's Department released the entire footage captured by the officer's dashcam. Texas Department of Public Safety, *Sandra Bland Traffic Stop*, YouTube video, 8:35, posted by "Texas Department of Public Safety," July 22, 2015, www.youtube.com/watch?time_continue=514&v=CaWo9Ymr2BA.
4 For a transcript of Sandra Bland's arrest, see Ryan Grim, "The Transcript of Sandra Bland's Arrest Is As Revealing As The Video," *Huffington Post*, July 22, 2015, www.huffpost.com/entry/sandra-bland-arrest-transcript_n_55b03a88e4b0a9b94853b1f1. For Sandra Bland's cell phone recording of the incident, see David Montgomery, "Sandra Bland, It Turns Out, Filmed Traffic Stop Confrontation Herself," *New York Times*, May 7, 2019, www.nytimes.com/2019/05/07/us/sandra-bland-video-brian-encinia.html.
5 Brian Collister, "Trooper Fired for Sandra Bland Stop: 'My safety was in jeopardy,'" *Texas Tribune*, September 16, 2017, www.texastribune.org/2017/09/16/trooper-fired-sandra-bland-stop-my-safety-was-jeopardy/. Notably, the trooper who arrested Sandra Bland was fired because of his behavior toward her, but not for using excessive force.
6 Although the suicide ruling was disputed by Sandra Bland's family and some civil rights activists, law school dean Camille A. Nelson, an expert on the intersection of critical race theory and cultural studies, wrote that "any latent mental vulnerabilities" that Ms. Bland suffered "were no doubt exacerbated by her arrest and jailing." Moreover, "this is not the first time that Waller County Jail has been investigated" for failing to follow proper procedures for at-risk inmates. Camille A. Nelson, "Frontlines: Policing at the Nexus of Race and Mental Health," 43 *Fordham Urban L.J.* 615, 624, and 681 (2016).
7 *City of Houston v. Hill*, 482 U.S. 451, 462 (1987). (Striking down as "unconstitutionally overbroad" a statute making it a crime to oppose or "interrupt any policeman in the execution of his duty.")
8 *Hartman v. Moore*, 547 U.S 250, 256 (2006).

9 *City of Houston* v. *Hill*, 482 U.S. 451, 463 (1987) (citing to *The King* v. *Cook*, 11 Can. Crim. Cas. Ann. 32, 33 (B.C. County Ct. 1906)).

10 *Lewis* v. *City of New Orleans*, 415 U.S. 130, 135 (1974) (Powell, J., concurring) The case invalidated an "ordinance making it unlawful 'to curse or revile or use obscene or opprobrious language toward or with reference to' a police officer while in performance of his duties."

11 *Whren* v. *United States*, 517 US 806 (1996). In *Atwater* v. *City of Lago Vista*, 532 US 318 (2001) the Court approved an arrest for a misdemeanor seatbelt violation where the maximum punishment was a fine.

12 *City of Houston* v. *Hill*, 482 U.S. at 463.

13 Even when your state law specifically says "police cannot arrest for this," the retaliatory arrest satisfies the Fourth Amendment as long as many other states in the United States permit such arrests. That ruling came in a Virginia case where the police officers learned that the driver lacked a valid license. Problem was, Virginia's law directed officers to issue a summons rather than making an arrest for driving on a suspended license. Nevertheless, the Supreme Court upheld the arrest. Unbelievably, the Supreme Court ruled unanimously that it's objectively reasonable under the Fourth Amendment for a police officer not to follow the laws of his particular state in making an arrest. *Virginia* v. *Moore*, 553 U.S. 164 (2008).

14 *Nieves* v. *Bartlett*, 139 S. Ct. 1715 (2019). For a recitation of the facts, read the district court judge's order. *Bartlett* v. *Nieves*, 4:15-CV-00004-SLG, 2016 WL 3702952, at 1-2 (D. Alaska July 7, 2016).

15 The President's Task Force on Twenty-First Century Policing, "Final Report of the President's Task Force on Twenty-First Century Policing," 1 (2015). ("Law enforcement culture should embrace a guardian – rather than a warrior –mindset to build trust and legitimacy both within agencies and with the public.")

16 *Nieves* v. *Bartlett*, 2018 WL 6171874 (U.S.), 47 (U.S. Oral. Arg., 2018).

17 Studies suggest de-escalation techniques can be effective for crisis intervention and may also reduce police use of force and officer injury. Robin S. Engel, Hannah D. McManus, and Tamara D. Herold, "The Deafening Demand for De-escalation Training: A Systemic Review and Call for Evidence in Police Use of Force Reform," *The Annals of the American Academy of Political and Social Sciences* 687 (2020): 146–65 www.theiacp.org/sites/default/files/IACP_UC_De-escalation%20Systematic%20Review.pdf; Janet R. Olivia, Rhiannon Morgan, and Michael T. Compton, "A Practical Overview of De-Escalation Skills in Law Enforcement: Helping Individuals in Crisis While Reducing Police Liability and Injury," *Journal of Police Crisis Negotiations* 10 (2010): 15–29 at 15.

18 Yuri R. Linetsky, "What the Police Don't Know May Hurt Us: An Argument for Enhanced Legal Training of Police Officers," 48 N.M. L. Rev. 1, 4–5 (2018).

19 Ann C. McGinley and Frank Rudy Cooper, *Masculinities and the Law*, 6–7 (NYU Press, 2012) (the Introduction).

20 Ann C. McGinley, "Policing and the Clash of Masculinities," 59 How. L.J. 221, 242 (2015) (citing James W. Messerschmidt, *Masculinities and Crime: Critique and Reconceptualization of Theory*, 79–81 (Rowman & Littlefield, 1993)).

21 Cara Rabe-Hemp, *Thriving in an All-Boys Club: Female Police and Their Fight for Equality* (Rowman & Littlefield, 2017).

22 Leigh Goodmark, "Hands Up at Home: Militarized Masculinity and Police Officers Who Commit Intimate Partner Abuse," 2015 *BYU L. Rev.* 1183, 1186 (2016) (citing Kimberly A. Lonsway, "Policies on Police Officer Domestic Violence: Prevalence and Specific Provisions Within Large Police Agencies," *Police Quarterly*, 9 (2006): 397–422 at 399–400; Leigh Goodmark, *Decriminalizing Domestic Violence: A Balanced Policy Approach to Intimate Partner Violence* (U.C. Press, 2018).

23 W.A. Westley, *Violence and the Police: A Sociological Study of Law, Custom and Morality* (MIT Press, 1970); Kristian Williams, *Our Enemies in Blue: Police and Power in American* 44 (3rd Ed., AK Press, 2015) ("The experience and the feeling [of conflict with the community] give rise to a collective emphasis on secrecy, an attempt to coerce respect from the public, and a belief that almost any means are legitimate in completing an important arrest. These are for the policeman basic occupational values.")

24 Lawrence W. Sherman, "Learning Police Ethics," *Criminal Justice Ethics*, 1 (1982): 10–19 at 10, 14 and n. 2; Josephine Ross, "Warning: Stop and Frisk May Be Hazardous to Your Health," 25 *Wm. & Mary Bill Rgts J.* 689, 724 (2016).

25 Angela P. Harris, "Gender, Violence, Race, and Criminal Justice," 52 *Stan. L. Rev.* 777, 797 (2000).

26 *Ta-Nehisi Coates on Police Brutality, the Confederate Flag, and Forgiveness*, Fresh Air Podcast (July 13, 2015), www.npr.org/2015/07/13/422554778/ta-nehisi-coates-on-police-brutality-the-confederate-flag-and-forgiveness [https://perma.cc/SE63-W8RD].

27 Frank Rudy Cooper, "'Who's the Man?': Masculinities Studies, Terry Stops, and Police Training," 18 *Colum J. Gender & L.* 671 (2009): 671–79 and 709–20.

28 McGinley, "Policing and the Clash of Masculinities," 59.

29 A. J. Willingham, "How the iconic 'Whose streets? Our streets!' chant has been co-opted," *CNN*, September 20, 2017, www.cnn.com/2017/09/19/us/whose-streets-our-streets-chant-trnd/index.html; Ezekiel Edwards, "St. Louis Police's Chants of 'Whose Streets? Our Streets!' Once Again Reveal the Warped Mindset Infecting Too Many Departments," *ACLU*, September 21, 2017, www.aclu.org/blog/criminal-law-reform/reforming-police-practices/st-louis-polices-chants-whose-streets-our; Frank Cooper, "Training to Reduce 'Cop Macho' and 'Contempt of Cop' Could Reduce Police Violence," *The Conversation*, December 18, 2015, https://theconversation.com/training-to-reduce-cop-macho-and-contempt-of-cop-could-reduce-police-violence-51983. Cooper writes, "we have found that police officers' interactions with blacks tend to be more fraught, not only in terms of disproportionate outcomes (as previous work has shown) but also interpersonally, even when no arrest is made and no use of force occurs." The "disparities we observe here cannot be explained by a small number of extreme officers."

30 Frank Rudy Cooper, "'Who's the Man?," 671 (2009).

31 Rob Voigt et al., "Language from police body camera footage shows racial disparities in officer respect," *Proceedings of the National Academy of Sciences*, 114 (2017): 6521–26.

32 Police culture not only echoes masculine values, but often the two are inextricable. Criminologists have found that police officers often "associate their police authority with their masculine authority," and use their roles as officers to "boost their individual masculine esteem" by using force or degrading language to assert their dominance. Frank R. Cooper, "Masculinities, Post-Racialism and the Gates Controversy: The False

Equivalence between Officer and Civilian," 11 *N.V.L.J.* 1, 20 (2010). While some argue that anti-masculinist training may shift the occupational culture of police departments, Cooper, "'Who's the Man?'," 671, 732–33, and other theorists suggest that merely changing the norms will not suffice. Rather, minimizing police violence requires "altering the rules of gender [and masculinity] itself" which is no easy feat, Harris, "Gender, Violence, Race, and Criminal Justice," 777, 803. While changing police culture and its profound connection to masculine performance may be difficult, training officers to recognize "the damage that excessive hypermasculine behaviors and attitudes can create" may yield change.

McGinley, "Policing and the Clash of Masculinities," 59.

33 Tina Fey, *Bossypants*, 14–15 (Little, Brown & Company, 2011).

34 Rebecca Solnit, *Recollections of My Non Existence: A Memoir* 55 (Viking, 2020); Erica Schwiegershausen, "Most Women Are Catcalled Before They Turn 17," *The Cut*, May 28, 2015, www.thecut.com/2015/05/most-women-are-catcalled-before-they-turn-17 .html. (Linking to an international study affiliated with Cornell University that shows that 85 percent of girls in the United States are harassed on the street before they turn 17, and 72 percent of US Women report taking different transportation due to harassment.)

35 Trystan Cotten lives in Berkeley. Tara Bahrampour, "Crossing the Divide," *Washington Post*, July 20, 2018, www.washingtonpost.com/news/local/wp/2018/07/20/feature/crossing-the-divide-do-men-really-have-it-easier-these-transgender-guys-found-the-truth-was-more-complex/?utm_term=.8a4205552e37.

36 "Every State Line." Track # 4 on *Imperfectly*. Righteous Babe, CD. Ani DiFranco, 1992.

37 *Ravina* v. *Columbia University*, 16-cv-2137, 2019 WL 1450449, at 2, 6 (S.D.N.Y. Mar. 31, 2019); Sydney Maki, "Columbia Bias Suit Jury to Decide if Professor Crossed the Line," Bloomberg News, July 25, 2018.

38 Traci Jan, "Racial talk swirls with Gates' arrest," *Boston Globe*, July 21, 2009, http://archive.boston.com/news/education/higher/articles/2009/07/21/racial_talk_swirls_ with_gates_arrest/; Abby Goodnough, "Sergeant Who Arrested Professor Defends Actions," *New York Times*, July 23, 2009, www.nytimes.com/2009/07/24/us/24gates.html.

39 The police report for the arrest of Henry Louis Gates is available at *Missed Opportunities, Shared Responsibilities*, 55–56 (Appendix C) (Cambridge Review Committee, 2010), http://media.washingtonpost.com/wp-srv/politics/documents/cambridgereview063010.pdf.

40 *Commonwealth* v. *Sholley*, 739 N.E.2d 236, 241 (Mass. 2000); *Commonwealth* v. *Feigenbaum*, 404 Mass. 471, 473–74 (1989). The misdemeanor crime of being a "disorderly person" is set forth Mass. Gen. Laws G.L. c. 272, § 53. The statute reads: (a) Common night walkers, common street walkers, both male and female, *persons who with offensive and disorderly acts* or language accost or annoy another person, lewd, wanton, and lascivious persons in speech or behavior, keepers of noisy and disorderly houses, and persons guilty of indecent exposure *shall be punished by imprisonment in a jail or house of correction for not more than 6 months, or by a fine of not more than $200, or by both such fine and imprisonment.*

41 *Commonwealth* v. *Sholley*, 739 N.E.2d at 242–44.

42 *Commonwealth* v. *Lopiano*, 805 N.E.2d 522, 525 (Mass. App. 2004); *Commonwealth* v. *LePore*, 666 N.E.2d 152 (Mass. App. 1996). (The defendant's conduct, namely, flailing his arms and shouting at police after being told to leave area by police, did not amount to

"violent or tumultuous behavior" within the scope of disorderly conduct statute, absent any evidence that the defendant's flailing arms were anything but a physical manifestation of his agitation or that the noise and commotion caused by the defendant's behavior was extreme.)

43 If the officer had probable cause, it would make more sense for him to issue a summons rather than arresting him given that the officer knew the name and address of his "suspect" and even knew by that point that Professor Gates worked at Harvard. Ironically, fifteen days before the sergeant arrested the professor, the maximum penalty for the misdemeanor was reduced from six months to a fine of $150. Instead of charging Professor Gates, the City of Cambridge released a statement calling Gates's arrest "regrettable and unfortunate." Associated Press, "Officer Won't Apologize For Gates Arrest, Despite Criticism," WBUR, July 23, 2009, www.wbur.org/news/2009/07/23/harvard-scholar-disorderly.

44 Paul Butler, "The System is Working the Way it is Supposed To: The Limits of Criminal Justice Reform," 104 *Geo. L.J.* (2016): 1419.

45 "When asked who, if anyone, was more at fault in the conflict between Henry Louis Gates and Officer James Crowley, 27 percent say Gates and 25 percent say Crowley. Nearly half say they don't know (36 percent), or blame both (10 percent) or neither (3 percent) parties. The balance tilts slightly toward faulting Gates among whites (29 percent vs. 22 percent who blame Crowley) though 10 percent blame both and another 39 percent do not assign blame to either." More people disapprove (41 percent) than approve (29 percent) of President Obama's handling of the situation. And by a margin of about two-to-one, more whites disapprove (45 percent) than approve (22 percent). "Obama's Ratings Slide Across the Board," *Pew Research Center*, July 30, 2009, www.people-press.org/2009/07/30/section-2-henry-louis-gates-jrs-arrest/.

46 Devon Carbado, "(E)Racing the Fourth Amendment," 100 *Mich. L. Rev.* 946, 953, 966 (2002). For a discussion of race as performance, see Anthony Paul Farley, "The Black Body as Fetish Object," 76 *Or. L. Rev.* 457, 465 (1997).

47 Danielle Meitiv, conversation with the author, March 2015. Some of this also appears in Sarah Wildman, "The 'Free-Range Mom' Is About to Hit the Big Time," *Washingtonian*, August 25, 2015, www.washingtonian.com/2015/08/25/maryland-free-range-mom-danielle-meitiv-is-about-to-hit-the-big-time/.

48 This is what Judith Butler refers to as "performativity." "Performativity must be understood … as the reiterative and citational practice by which discourse produces the effect it names," Judith Butler, *Bodies That Matter: On the Discursive Limits of "Sex,"* 2 (Routledge, 1993); Elena Loizidou, *Judith Butler: Ethics, Law, Politics*, 27, 36 and 41 (Routledge, 2007).

49 Emily Hoerner and Rick Tulsky, "Cops Around the Country Are Posting Racist And Violent Comments On Facebook," *InjusticeWatch*, www.injusticewatch.org/interactives/cops-troubling-facebook-posts-revealed/. Philadelphia lawyer Emily Baker-White of the Plain View Project "examined accounts of about 2,900 officers from departments across the country," finding that about 20 percent (or 1 in every 5 officers) posted offensive matter, and, for retired officers, the number was doubled, to about 40 percent (or every 2 in 5 officers). Emily Hoerner, "Cops Across the US Have Been Exposed Posting Racist and Violent Things on Facebook. Here's the Proof," *BuzzFeed News*, June 1, 2019, updated July 23, 2019 (published in collaboration with Injustice Watch); Shaila Dewan,

"When Police Officers Vent on Facebook," *New York Times,* June 3, 2019, www.nytimes
.com/2019/06/03/us/politics/police-officers-facebook.html.

50 The Bureau of Justice Statistics released the 2015 policing data: "When police initiated an
interaction, they were twice as likely to threaten or use force against Black and Hispanic
residents than white residents." Alexi Jones, "Police stops are still marred by racial
discrimination, new data shows" Prison Policy Initiative, October 12, 2018, www
.prisonpolicy.org/blog/2018/10/12/policing/; "National Police Shootings," *Washington Post,*
February 11, 2020 (updates continue), www.washingtonpost.com/graphics/2019/national/
police-shootings-2019/.

51 Judith Butler, *Precarious Life: The Powers of Mourning and Violence,* 59, 67 (Verso, 2004).
Unlike indefinite detentions at Guantanamo that Butler analyzes, courts may review
police stops. Nevertheless I argue that because courts mostly abdicate that responsibility,
police function like "petty sovereigns" and "the law becomes the instrument of power,"
Elena Loizidou, *Judith Butler: Ethics, Law, Politics,* 115–16.

5 BEYOND MIRANDA'S REACH: HOW STOP-AND-FRISK UNDERMINES THE RIGHT TO SILENCE

1 Levy, interview with the author, January 2016. Bronx Defender Scott Levy coordinated
the marijuana arrest project. He told me that police sometimes ask youth to show them the
marijuana and sometimes they just go into their pockets without asking. He called
these "manufactured misdemeanors." Under Section 221.10 of the New York Penal Code,
police could only charge for marijuana that was in public view, not in a person's pocket. Ray
Rivera, "Federal Suit Claims Police Distort Marijuana Searches to Create Misdemeanors,"
New York Times, May 1, 2013, www.nytimes.com/2013/05/02/nyregion/5-in-bronx-contend-
police-distorted-marijuana-searches-to-create-misdemeanors.html; *Analysis Finds Racial Disparities, Ineffectiveness in NYPD Stop-and-Frisk Program; Links Tactic to Soaring Marijuana
Arrest Rate* (New York Civil Liberties Union, 2013), www.nyclu.org/en/press-releases/analysis-
finds-racial-disparities-ineffectiveness-Nypd-stop-and-frisk-program-links. In 2012, more than
"26,000 people were stopped for alleged marijuana possession by the NYPD. "Stop-and-Frisk
2012," NYCLU Briefing, www.nyclu.org/sites/default/files/releases/2012_Report_NYCLU.pdf.

2 The American Civil Liberties Union of the Nation's Capital analyzed all marijuana-related
arrests in the District between 2000 and 2010. "Slightly more than half of the population of
the District was black in 2010. Yet, 91% of all marijuana arrests during that year were of
black people, despite roughly equal marijuana usage rates between black and white
populations." Police made "nearly 15 arrests per day" for possession of marijuana that year.
Seema Sadanandan, Esq., "The ACLU-NCA Presents Testimony on the Metropolitan
Police Department," *ACLU DC,* March 11, 2015, www.acludc.org/en/node/43332; Benjamin R. Freed, "D.C. Leads the Nation in Marijuana Arrests," *The DCist,* June 4, 2013,
https://dcist.com/story/13/06/04/dc-leads-nation-in-marijuana-arrest/ ("While the city's white
arrest rate for simple marijuana possession was 185 per 100,000 in 2010, it was 1,489 per
100,000 – or 8.05 times as frequently – for DC's black residents.").
This is a national problem. *The War on Marijuana in Black and White* (American Civil
Liberties Union, 2013), www.aclu.org/files/assets/aclu-thewaronmarijuana-rel2.pdf; Dylan
Mathews, "The Black/White Marijuana Arrest Gap, In Nine Charts," *Washington Post,*

June 4, 2013, www.washingtonpost.com/news/wonk/wp/2013/06/04/the-blackwhite-mari juana-arrest-gap-in-nine-charts/?utm_term=.e82a366d45ab. (explaining the extent of the disparity between the rate of arrest and the rate of use for white and black Americans.)

3 *Edwards* v. *Arizona*, 451 U.S. 477 (1981); "Custodial Interrogations," 48 *Geo. L.J. Ann. Rev. Crim. Proc.* 223, 246–47 (2019). ("Further interrogation without counsel present is barred 'unless the accused himself initiates further communication, exchanges, or conversations with the police,' and subsequent events indicate that the accused waived the right to counsel.")

4 Joseph Goldstein, "'Testilying' by Police a Stubborn Problem," *New York Times*, May 18, 2018, www.nytimes.com/2018/03/18/nyregion/testilying-police-perjury-new-york .html (quoting a NYPD officer saying, "Behind closed doors, we call it testilying.") Investigators for the Mollen Commission found that police used the term "testilying" broadly, to include all false testimony on the stand: "The practice [of police perjury] – by officers either legitimately interested in clearing the streets of criminals or simply eager to inflate statistics – ... is prevalent enough in the department that it has its own nickname: 'testilying.'" Joe Sexton, "New York Police Officers Often Lie Under Oath, Report Said," *New York Times*, April 22, 1994, www.nytimes.com/1994/04/22/us/new-york-police-often-lie- under-oath-report-says.html?pagewanted=all&module=inline (reporting on a draft of the Mollen Commission Report that found widespread perjury in the New York City Police Department). Christopher Slobogin, "Testilying: Police Perjury and What to Do About It," 67 *U. Colo. L. Rev.* 1037, 1040 (1996); Laurie Magid, "Deceptive Police Interrogation Practices: How Far Is Too Far?" 99 *Mich. L. Rev.* 1168, 1210 (2001).

5 Megan Crepeau et. al., "Three Chicago Cops Indicted in Alleged Cover-up of Laquan McDonald Shooting Details," *Chicago Tribune*, June 28, 2017, www.chicagotribune.com. Chicago prosecuted three senior officers for conspiring to cover up incriminating details of the death of Laquan MacDonald in an effort to protect the shooter. These Chicago police officers, David March, Joseph Walsh, and Thomas Gaffney were acquitted on all charges. In Baltimore, an officer was convicted of fabricating evidence but remained on the force under Baltimore Police Department rules because it was a misdemeanor offense. Kevin Rector, "Baltimore Police Officer Found Guilty of Fabricating Evidence in Case Where His Own Body Camera Captured the Act," *Baltimore Sun*, November 9, 2018, www .baltimoresun.com/news/maryland/crime/bs-md-ci-pinheiro-ruling-20181109-story.html.

6 Steven Drizin and Richard A. Leo, "The Problem of False Confession in the Post-DNA World," 82 *N.C.L. Rev.* 891 (2004). Kristin Henning wrote: "Indeed, youth is a significant risk factor for police-induced false confessions. The very features of adolescence that make youth vulnerable to peer influence and poor decision making also make youth susceptible to police coercion," Kristin Henning, "Criminalizing Normal Adolescent Behavior in Communities of Color: The Role of Prosecutors in Juvenile Justice Reform," 98 *Cornell L. Rev.* 383, 441 (2013).

Gender may also play a part in susceptibility. Women are more likely to confess to crimes than men. In a controlled experiment, 47 percent of men signed a written confession, while 75 percent percent of women signed confessions under the same circumstances. Not only are girls vulnerable because of their age, but some researchers suggest that girls are socialized to be more suggestible, talkative, and cooperative than boys which may be related to higher rates in false confessions, Krista D. Forest, "The Role of Preexisting Stress on False Confessions: An Empirical Study," *The Journal of Credibility Assessment and Witness Psychology*, 3 (2002): 23–45 at 23, 34; Kaitlyn Thomsen, "*Adolescent Rights Comprehension: The Influence of Age, Intelligence, and Interrogative Suggestibility*," (M.A. Thesis, Simon Fraser University), 14–16 (2006); Barry C. Feld, "Questioning Gender: Police Interrogation of Delinquent Girls," 49 *Wake Forest L. Rev.* 1059, 1099 (2014).

7 *Making a Murderer*, Netflix, December 18, 2015, written by Laura Ricciardi and Moira Demos. Dassey appealed his conviction, arguing that he involuntarily confessed to the crime as a result of coercive interrogation tactics by law enforcement. While a lower federal court agreed and vacated his conviction, the Seventh Circuit Court of Appeals reversed and remanded, finding it was not unreasonable to determine that the confession was made voluntarily. To this judgement, dissenting judges described the interrogation as, "Psychological coercion, questions to which the police furnished the answers, and ghoulish games of '20 Questions,'" in which Brendan Dassey guessed over and over again before he landed on the "'correct' story," *Dassey* v. *Dittmann*, 877 F.3d 297, 201, 319 (7th Cir. 2017) (Wood, C. J., joined by Royner and Williams, dissenting). The US Supreme Court refused to hear Brendan Dassey's appeal, *Dassey* v. *Dittmann*, 138 S. Ct. 2677 (2018) (denying petition for writ of certiorari) and Dassey remains behind bars for the murder of Teresa Halbach. www.reuters.com/article/us-usa-court-murderer/supreme-court-turns-away-making-a-murderer-case-appeal-idUSKBN1JL1P5.

8 Samuel R. Gross, "Exonerations in the United States, 1889 through 2003," 95 *J. Crim. L. & Criminology* 523, 547. (2005). Gross studied 340 exonerations, he found that individuals under the age of 18 were three times more likely to falsely confess than adults. "Exonerations by Contributing Factor," (The National Registry of Exonerations), www.law.umich .edu/special/exoneration/Pages/ExonerationsContribFactorsByCrime.aspx; Samuel R. Gross and Michael Shaffer, "*Exonerations in the United States, 1989–2012: Report by the National Registry of Exoneration*," 2–4 (National Registry of Exonerations, 2012), www.law .umich.edu/special/exoneration/Documents/exonerations_us_1989_2012_full_report.pdf (listing exonerations). A leading study of 125 proven false confession cases found that 63 percent of false confessors were under the age of 25 and 32 percent were under 18, Bluhm Legal Clinic, "Wrongful Conviction of Youth," *Northwestern School of Law* n.d., www.law.northwestern.edu/legalclinic/wrongfulconvictionsyouth/understandproblem/

9 *Terry* v. *Ohio*, 392 U.S. 1, 34 (1968) (White, J. concurring).

10 *Pennsylvania* v. *Muniz*, 496 U.S. 582, 596 (1990) (At its core, the privilege reflects our fierce "unwillingness to subject those suspected of crime to the cruel trilemma of self-accusation, perjury or contempt"). Susan R. Klein, "Transparency and Truth During Custodial Interrogations and Beyond," 97 *B.U.L. Rev.* 993, 1020–21 (2017). ("The ban on compelled statements under oath prevents moral and psychological torture – the cruel trilemma between self-accusation, perjury, or contempt.")

11 *Schmerber* v. *California*, 384 U.S. 757, 763 (1966).

12 *Salinas* v. *Texas*, 570 U.S. 178, 193-94 (2013) (Breyer, J. dissenting).

13 The United Kingdom changed the rules. Beginning in April 1995, suspects may refuse to answer an officer's questions, but the government made it clear that silence can be used against the suspect. The court may draw inferences based on their silence. Criminal Justice and Public Order Act 1994, c. 33 (U.K.), www.legislation.gov.uk/ukpga/1994/33/section/36.

14 *Berguis v. Thompkins*, 560 U.S. 370, 391 (2010) (Sotomayor, J. dissenting). *Berguis* eliminated the pre-arrest right to silence. Readers, silence will protect you after police read you your Miranda warnings. Then you don't have to say anything to be safe, although asking for a lawyer is better because it ends the questioning.

15 Ibid., 370, fn. 9 (2010) (Sotomayor, dissenting) (these examples all come from this footnote).

16 *Salinas*, 570 U.S. at (Breyer, J. dissenting).

17 *Hiibel v. Sixth Judicial District Court*, 542 US 177 (2004) (This was a 5–4 decision).

18 Ibid., 199 (Breyer, J. dissenting). Compare *Berkemer v. McCarty*, 468 U.S. 420, 421 (1984), which decided that police don't have to give Miranda rights during traffic stops because they are usually brief. "Moreover, the typical traffic stop is conducted in public, and the atmosphere surrounding it is substantially less 'police dominated'" than in other kinds of interrogations.

19 Ritchie, *Invisible No More* at 135, citing Dean Spade, *Normal Life: Critical trans Politics* 137–69 (South End Press, 2011); *Stonewalled: Police Abuse and Misconduct Against Lesbian, Gay, Bisexual, and Transgender People in the U.S.* 18 (Amnesty International, September 21, 2005), www.amnesty.org/download/Documents/84000/amr511222005en.pdf.

20 Gabriel Arkles and Bobby Hodgson, "A Trans Woman was Charged with False Personation for Giving the NYPD her Real Name," *ACLU*, January 24, 2019, www.aclu.org/blog/lgbt-rights/transgender-rights/trans-woman-was-charged-false-personation-giving-nypd-her-real.

21 Andrea Ritchie, *Invisible No More: Police Violence Against Black Women and Women of Color* (Beacon Press, 2017), at 133.

22 *Koch v. City of Del City*, 660 F.3d 1228 (10th Cir. 2011).

23 Ms. Cooks initiated a lawsuit against the city of Barstow, California, alleging false arrest without probable cause and thereby violating her rights under the Fourth and Fourteenth Amendment of the Constitution. She also alleged assault and battery by police. The details of the settlement have not been made public. *Charlena Michelle Cooks v. City of Barstow et al.*, 5:15CV01153 (2019). Shortly before police tackled Charlena Michelle Cooks, the same police department "reached a settlement agreement with the ACLU Foundation of Southern California (ACLU SoCal) on behalf of two brothers who were arrested for refusing to identify themselves to police officers. The agreement calls for training Barstow officers to recognize that a refusal to identify is rarely sufficient reason to make an arrest," "City of Barstow and ACLU Settlement Seeks to End 'Stop and Identify'Arrest," *ACLU of Southern California*, May 22, 2015; Areva Martin, "Smarter, More Sophisticated Policing a Must,"Areva Martin (blog) June 10, 2016 (detailing Cooks' and other African Americans' encounters with law enforcement agencies), https://arevamartin.com/smarter-sophisticated-policing-must/.

24 It began with the "free to leave" doctrine. The judge ruled that Vicki Koch had not been free to walk inside her house, away from the officer. *Koch*, 660 F.3d at 1241–42. Although the tenth circuit court accepted this finding, it's erroneous, since the officer lacked any reason to suspect Ms. Koch of committing a crime. Even detained people may not be compelled to speak, however, so this erroneous finding cannot be blamed for the way that the appellate court abrogated the right to silence.

25 *Wooley v. Maynard*, 430 U.S. 705, 714 (1977).

26 *Koch*, 660 F.3d at 1243–44.

27 *Alexander* v. *City of Round Rock*, 854 F.3d 298, 302 (5th Cir. 2017). Note that in the Fourth Circuit, a federal trial judge also followed this line of reasoning, refusing to find a right to sue under the First Amendment for retaliation against an individual who declined to speak to police officers during a criminal investigation. *McFayden* v. *Duke Univ.*, 786 F. Supp 2d 887, 949 (M.D.N.C. 2011). For a circuit court that goes the other way, see *Veiga* v. *McGee*, 26 F.3d 1206, 1213 (1st Cir. 1994). (It would be unlawful "for a police officer to detain Mr. Viega for refusing to answer their questions" during a traffic stop.)

28 *Janus* v. *AFSCME, Council 31*, 138 S. Ct. 2488 (2018) (all union dues are a form of protected expressions that may not be compelled). The case overturned *Abood* v. *Detroit Bd. of Educ.*, 431 U.S. 209 (1977), a case that allowed unions to compel dues to pay for collective bargaining, while barring unions from spending mandatory dues on lobbying efforts.

29 *Masterpiece Cakeshop, Ltd.* v. *Colo. Civil Rights Comm'n*, 138 S. Ct. 1719 (2018) (Thomas, J. concurring).

30 B. Jessie Hill, "Sex, Lies, and Ultrasound," 89 *U. Colo. L. Rev.* 421, 430, 432, and 437 and n. 31 (2018). (Describing law from South Dakota and other states that force doctors to tell patients information that most doctors believe are misleading or false.)

31 *Planned Parenthood* v. *Casey*, 505 U.S. 833, 884 (1992). ("To be sure, the physician's First Amendment rights not to speak are implicated, but only as part of the practice of medicine, subject to reasonable licensing and regulation by the State.")

32 *Nat'l Inst. of Family & Life Advocates* v. *Becerra*, 138 S. Ct. 2361 (2018). (Holding that crisis pregnancy centers cannot be forced to post signs advertising abortion services.)

33 Women's Health and Reproductive Rights Groups Launch End the Lies Campaign to Expose Deceptive Practices by Fake Women's Health Centers, *End The Lies*, February 28, 2018, https://endthelies.com/press-release/womens-health-reproductive-rights-groups-launch-end-lies-campaign-expose-deceptive-practices-fake-womens-health-centers/ (End the Lies is a "new campaign" by "a coalition of women's health and reproductive rights groups from across the country led by NARAL Pro-Choice America" that "seeks to expose the deceptive and dangerous practices of fake women's health centers.") NARAL stands for National Abortion Rights League.

34 "SCOTUS Turns Its Back on Women," *Prochoice America*, June 26, 2018, www.prochoiceamerica.org/2018/06/26/scotus-turns-its-back-on-women/. See also, Ilyse Hogue and Amy Everitt, "CPCs, Pseudo-Clinics, Should Have to Post Women's Rights," *Mercury News*, October 7, 2015, www.mercurynews.com/2015/10/07/ilyse-hogue-and-amy-everitt-cpcs-pseudo-clinics-should-have-to-post-womens-rights/. ("It is time to recognize CPCs for what they are: a grave threat to a woman's right to control her own body and autonomy. While CPCs have every right to exist in a free country, they do not have the right to deceive women seeking medical assistance.")

35 *Becerra*, 138 S. Ct. at 2385 (Breyer, J., dissenting) (emphasis added).

36 One scholar calls these scripts "compelled private lies," B. Jessie Hill, "Sex, Lies, and Ultrasound," 89 *U. Colo. L. Rev.* 421, 429 (2018).

37 *United States* v. *Drayton*, 536 U.S. 194, 207 (2002).

38 In *JDB* v. *North Carolina*, 564 U.S. 261 (2011), a 13-year-old boy was removed from his class and brought to a room where he was interrogated, without Miranda, by a police officer

with the help of school officials. The Court did not say that JDB "was deprived of his freedom of action in some significant way" (the test for whether someone is in custody). It simply allows judges to consider a young child's age when determining whether they were in custody.

39 In places that follow *Koch v. City of Del City*, 660 F.3d 1228 (10th Cir. 2011) from the tenth circuit and *Alexander v. City of Round Rock*, 854 F.3d 298 (5th Cir. 2017) from the fifth circuit discussed in this chapter.

40 *Whren v. United States*, 517 U.S. 806 (1996). This case is discussed in Chapter 4.

41 *Nieves v. Bartlett*, 139 S. Ct. 1715 (2019) (see discussion of case in Chapter 4).

42 In Baltimore, police charged 1,350 people with making a false statement to an officer, from 2010 to 2014, and 89 percent were African American, U.S. Department of Justice Civil Rights Division, "Investigation of the Baltimore City Police Department," 5 (August 10, 2016), www.justice.gov/opa/file/883366/download (analyzing stops from January 2010 to May 2015).

In 1998, the Supreme Court rejected the argument that punishing a person who lies to federal investigators creates a "cruel trilemma" of admitting guilt, remaining silent, or falsely denying guilt." "This 'trilemma' is wholly of the guilty suspect's own making, of course. An innocent person will not find himself in a similar quandary," *Brogan v. U.S.*, 522 U.S. 398, 404 (1998) (upholding federal conviction of union officials for making false statements to federal investigators, even when the statement was mere denial of wrongdoing.)

43 *The Handmaid's Tale*, Hulu, April 26, 2017, produced by Margaret Atwood (a television series based on Atwood's novel, Margaret Atwood, *The Handmaid's Tale* (McClelland and Stewart, 1985). At the 2017 Women's March, one participant's sign read: "Make Margaret Atwood Fiction Again," illustrating the power of both the novel to reveal insights in the current age. Michelle Goldberg, "Margaret Atwood's Dystpia, and Ours," *New York Times*, September 14, 2019, www.nytimes.com/2019/09/14/opinion/sunday/margaret-atwood-the-testaments-handmaids-tale.html.

6 THE FRISK: "INJURIES TO MANHOOD" AND TO WOMANHOOD

1 Seth W. Stoughton, "*Terry v. Ohio* and the (Un)Forgettable Frisk," 15 *Ohio St. J. Crim. L.* 19, 29 (2017); *Terry v. Ohio*, 392 U.S. 1, 17 n. 13 (1968). This is not a new technique. In *Terry v. Ohio*, 392 U.S. 1, 17 n. 13 (1968) the Court cited a police manual that read "[T]he officer must feel with sensitive fingers every portion of the prisoner's body. A thorough search must be made of the prisoner's arms and armpits, waistline and back, the groin and area about the testicles, and entire surface of the legs down to the feet."

2 *Police Officer Appears to Sexually Assault a Suspect... During a Stop and Frisk*, YouTube video posted by "CC mob," September 30, 2017, www.youtube.com/watch?v=jAYieOK FY9c. It appears to be a Terry stop because the civilian confidently states: "You are not going to find anything on me."

3 Paul Butler, *Chokehold*, 98 (The New Press, 2017).

4 Ibid.

5 *Floyd v. New York*, 959 F. Supp. 2d 540, 558 (S.D.N.Y. 2013). ("52 percent of all stops were followed by a protective frisk for weapons. A weapon was found after 1.5 percent of these frisks. In other words, in 98.5 percent of the 2.3 million frisks, no weapon was found.")

6 Seth W. Stoughton, "*Terry v. Ohio*, 28–29. (As an officer, "in practice I did very little 'patting.' Instead, I would slide my hand (or hands) over the area of suspect's body that I was searching, moving them in small circles as I did so, so that my fingertips and palms might detect any protuberance in or under the suspect's clothing.")

7 The Federal Law Enforcement Training Center suggests that officers may be able to establish their recognition of drugs by testifying that they have practiced frisking officers who have baggies of drugs in their pockets. Steven L. Argiriou, "*Terry* Frisk Update: The Law, Field Examples and Analysis," *Federal Law Enforcement Training Centers*, www.fletc .gov/sites/default/files/imported_files/training/programs/legal-division/downloads-articles-and-faqs/research-by-subject/4th-amendment/terrystopupdate.pdf; David A. Harris, "Frisking Every Suspect: The Withering of Terry," 28 *U.C. Davis L. Rev* 1, 26–27 (1994)(citing cases where "anyone involved in any drug transaction – including the purchaser/user – may be frisked automatically.")

8 David J. Goodman and Viviana Yee, "Death of a Man in Custody Adds Fuel to a Dispute Over a Policing Strategy," *New York Times*, July 20, 2014, www.nytimes.com/2014/07/21/ nyregion/death-of-a-man-in-custody-adds-fuel-to-a-dispute-over-a-policing-strategy.html. The video is available at: 'I can't breathe': Eric Garner in chokehold by NYPD officer – video, *The Guardian*, December 4, 2014, www.theguardian.com/us-news/video/2014/dec/04/i-cant-breathe-eric-garner-chokehold-death-video.

9 The "broken windows" theory "argues that close police surveillance and well-ordered maintenance of high-crime urban environments reduce criminal activity. Having zero tolerance for low-level crime (e.g., panhandling, public urination, public drunkenness, loitering) and quickly mending visual representations of criminal activity such as broken windows or graffiti are thought to prevent further defacement and an escalation to more serious crimes." This theory is generally seen as a driving principle behind New York's aggressive policing policies. Brett G. Stoudt, Michelle Fine, and Madeline Fox, "Growing Up Policed in the Age of Aggressive Policing Policies," 56 *N.Y.L. Sch. L. Rev.* 1331, 1332 (2012). For a history of broken windows and how it relates to Eric Garner's death, see Matt Taibbi, *I Can't Breathe: A Killing on Bay Street*, 57–63 (Spiegel & Grau, 2017).

10 Ali Winston, "Eric Garner Death Was 'Not a Big Deal,' Police Commander Said," *New York Times*, May 16, 2019, www.nytimes.com/2019/05/16/nyregion/eric-garner-pantaleo-trial .html

11 Moore, interview with the author, December 2017. Jonathan C. Moore represented the family in their dispute with New York City and negotiated the $5.9 million settlement. J. David Goodman, "Eric Garner Case Is Settled by New York City for $5.9 Million," *New York Times*, July 13, 2015, www.nytimes.com/2015/07/14/nyregion/eric-garner-case-is-settled-by-new-york-city-for-5-9-million.html.

12 Police had stale information that Mr. Garner had loitered and been among a group selling untaxed cigarettes, but the person of interest was only described to the police as "Eric," so it made out reasonable suspicion but not probable cause to arrest, Al Baker, J. David Goodman and Benjamin Mueller, "Beyond the Chokehold: The Path to Eric Garner's Death," *New York Times*, June 13, 2015, www.nytimes.com/2015/06/14/nyregion/eric-garner-police-chokehold-staten-island.html (A landlord complained of a group loitering in March of 2014, "[t]hough police officials understood the Eric of his complaint to be Mr. Garner,

[the landlord] said he was referring to someone else."). Moreover, selling or possessing untaxed cigarettes are not misdemeanors found in the penal code. Rather they are regulatory infractions. New York State Public Health Law, Article–F–Regulation of Tobacco Products, Herbal Cigarettes and Smoking Paraphernalia; Distribution to Minors, § 1399–bb (McKinney 2003). The New York Code permit police to perform stops based upon a reasonable suspicion of a felony or misdemeanor, but not for mere violations. "Had the legislature intended to include violation level offenses, it most certainly would have done so." *People* v. *Brukner*, 43 N.Y.S.3d 851, 853 (N.Y. Co. Ct. 2016).

13 *People* v. *De Bour*, 352 N.E.2d 562, 571–72 (N.Y. 1976). The case articulates the standard for contacts, stops, and frisks under New York law.

14 *Terry*, 392 U.S. at 34.

15 Shaun King, "Copy of the Heartbreaking Civil Rights Lawsuit Eric Garner Filed Against the NYPD in 2007," *Daily Kos*, April 15, 2015, www.dailykos.com/stories/2015/4/15/1377940/-Copy-of-the-heartbreaking-civil-rights-lawsuit-Eric-Garner-filed-against-the-NYPD-in-2007. Garner's complaint read: "On September. 1, 2007, at approx. 7:30 p.m. on the corner of Castleton Ave & Heberton Ave [a police officer] and his team stopped me for reasons of their own."

16 Susanna Capelouto, "Eric Garner: The Haunting Last Words of a Dying Man," CNN, December 8, 2014, www.cnn.com/2014/12/04/us/garner-last-words; *NYPD Publicly Executes Eric Garner for Illegal Cigarettes*, YouTube video, posted by "African Diaspora News Channel," July 22, 2014, www.youtube.com/watch?v=g-xHqf1BVE4.

17 When Eric Garner says "I told you the last time," he does not refer to the sexual assault seven years previously. Eric Garner was stopped several times after he filed that lawsuit. Also, the person named in Mr. Garner's complaint was not among the officers who stood around him the day he died. Daniel Pantaleo, the officer who applied the chokehold to Eric Garner, was a repeat offender. In the two years before Officer Pantaleo "put Garner in the chokehold, the records show, he had seven disciplinary complaints and 14 individual allegations lodged against him. Four of those allegations were substantiated by an independent review board." Even a conservative reading of the documents indicates Pantaleo had among the worst CCRB disciplinary records on the force." Carimah Townes and Jack Jenkins, "EXCLUSIVE DOCUMENTS: The Disturbing Secret History of the NYPD Officer Who Killed Eric Garner," *ThinkProgress*, March 21, 2017, https://archive.thinkprogress.org/daniel-pantaleo-records-75833e6168f3/(Officer Pantaleo's information was leaked from the Civilian Complaint Review Board).

18 The police violated the constitution by tackling Eric Garner. The settlement was for $5.9 million. J. David Goodman, "Eric Garner Case Is Settled by New York City for $5.9 Million," *New York Times*, July 13, 2015, www.nytimes.com/2015/07/14/nyregion/eric-garner-case-is-settled-by-new-york-city-for-5-9-million.html. Nevertheless, the tackle still fell under the Terry regime that directs officers to seek evidence of a crime based on suspicion. No officers were indicted or prosecuted, but the Police Commissioner fired Officer Daniel Pantaleo more than five years after Mr. Garner's death for violating a department ban on chokeholds.

19 Emily Hoerner, "Cops Across the US Have Been Exposed Posting Racist and Violent Things On Facebook. Here's the Proof," *BuzzFeed News*, June 1, 2019, updated July 23, 2019, www.buzzfeednews.com/article/emilyhoerner/police-facebook-racist-violent-posts-comments-philadelphia (Published in collaboration with Injustice Watch.)

20 Kate Dailey, "TSA Screenings Worry Sexual-Assault Survivors," *Newsweek*, November 17, 2010, www.newsweek.com/tsa-screenings-worry-sexual-assault-survivors-70029 ("After a sexual assault, it seems that many survivors have difficulty having their bodies touched by other people, says Shannon Lambert, founder of a nonprofit organization that provides support and information to survivors of rape and sexual abuse.")

21 In both instances, Eric Garner was a pedestrian and a team of police officers came up to him in a cruiser. Matt Tabbi, *I Can't Breathe: A Killing on Bay Street*, 35–36.

22 The officer who killed Eric Garner, Daniel Pantaleo, was previously sued for degrading searches of other men. Kevin McCoy, "Choke-Hold Cop Sued in Prior Misconduct Cases," *USA Today*, December 4, 2014, www.usatoday.com/story/news/nation/2014/12/04/choke-hold-cop-pantaleo-sued/19899461/. (lawsuit alleged "humiliating strip searches in public view"). Civil rights attorney John Burris describes a case he brought where a judge stopped the Oakland police from strip searching African American men in public. John L. Burris, "Life as A Civil Rights Lawyer in the San Francisco Bay Area," 47 *Golden Gate U.L. Rev.* 133, 140 (2017).

23 Andrea Ritchie, *Invisible No More: Police Violence Against Black Women and Women of Colour* (Beacon Press, 2017), 7–8 & 121.

24 *National Police Misconduct Reporting Project, 2010 Annual Report* (Cato Institute, 2010), www.leg.state.nv.us/Session/77th2013/Exhibits/Assembly/JUD/AJUD338L.pdf (9.3 percent of the complaints involved sexual misconduct of some type).

25 Matt Sedensky, "AP: Hundreds of Officers Lose Licenses Over Sex Misconduct," *AP News*, November 1, 2015, https://apnews.com/fd1d4d05e561462a85abe50e7eaed4ec/ap-hundreds-officers-lose-licenses-over-sex-misconduct. The AP obtained records from 2009 through 2014 from forty-one states on police decertification, an administrative process in which an officer's law enforcement license is revoked.

26 Matthew Spina, "When a Protector Becomes a Predator," *Buffalo News*, November 22, 2015, https://s3.amazonaws.com/bncore/projects/abusing-the-law/index.html.

27 *Addressing Sexual Offenses by Law Enforcement: Executive Guide* (The International Association of Chiefs of Police, 2011), www.evawintl.org/Library/DocumentLibraryHandler.ashx?id=1021.

28 Ibid., 4 (addressing sexual offenses by law enforcement). "Though the guide was completed in 2011, it's not clear if it actually led to changes within individual police forces." Zoe Carpenter, "The Police Violence We Aren't Talking About," *Nation*, August 27, 2014, www.thenation.com/article/archive/police-violence-we-arent-talking-about/.

29 Peter Kraska and Victor Kappeler, "To Serve and Pursue: Exploring Police Sexual Violence against Women," *Justice Quarterly*, 12 (1995): 86–111 at 91. The Nation calls the National Decertification Index, which lists officers who've lost their certification, "a leaky sieve" because participation is voluntary. Zoe Carpenter, *The Police Violence We Aren't Talking About*, Nation, August 27, 2014, www.thenation.com/article/police-violence-we-arent-talking-about/.

30 The Cato report used FBI statistics for comparison. *National Police Misconduct Reporting Project, 2010 Annual Report* (Cato Institute, 2010), www.leg.state.nv.us/Session/77th2013/Exhibits/Assembly/JUD/AJUD338L.pdf.

31 Peter B. Kraska, "To Serve and Pursue: Exploring Police Sexual Violence Against Women," in Victor E. Kappeler, *The Police and Society: Touchstone Readings*, 2nd ed.,

325, 326 (Waveland Press, 1999); Allen D. Sapp, "Sexual Misconduct by Police Officers," in Thomas Barker and David L. Carter eds., *Police Deviance*, 2nd ed., 139. (Anderson Publishing Co., 1991); Samuel Walker and Dawn Irlbeck, *Police Sexual Abuse of Teenage Girls: A 2003 Update on "Driving While Female*, 4 (Police Professionalism Initiative, 2003), https://samuelwalker.net/wp-content/uploads/2010/06/dwf2003.pdf.

32 Phillip Stinson, John Liederbach, Steven L. Brewer, and Mathna E. Brooke, "Police Sexual Misconduct: A National Scale Study of Arrested Officers," *Crim. Justice Policy Rev.* 26 (2015): 665–90 at 665. From 2005 to 2007, the police officers arrested for sexual misconduct were overwhelmingly male and most involved victims younger than 18 years old. Over 200 of these 548 cases involved charges of forcible rape or sodomy, followed by fondling or statutory rape. While most child victims were abused by off-duty officers, three-quarters of the adults were abused while the officer was on duty. Ibid., 674–76.

33 Ibid., 675–78. Victims were male in only 8 percent of police prosecutions for sexual misconduct. Even when police are arrested for sexually assaulting male victims, Stinson found that most of the male victims were children or teens. The inclusion of young male victims was not included in prior empirical research on police sexual misconduct.

34 Oddly, Stinson theorizes that this proves that the inherent power differential between police officers and females extends to male children and male teens more than it does to adult men. Stinson builds on an earlier feminist definition of police sexual violence and agrees that "sex crimes often result from encounters involving young females because of an inherent power differential and the interplay between issues of power and gender that work to produce opportunities for sex crimes." Ibid., 686 n. 2. (citing Peter B. Kraska and Victor E. Kappeler, "To Serve and Pursue: Exploring Police Sexual Violence Against Women," and Allen D. Sapp, "Sexual Misconduct by Police Officers.") This definition may have influenced Stinson's conclusions.

35 Stinson, et al., "Police Sexual Misconduct," 683.

36 Valorie K. Vojdik, "Sexual Violence Against Men and Women in War: A Masculinities Approach," 14 *Nev. L.J.* 923, 927, 946, 951 (2014). One prison inmate told Human Rights Watch why he didn't tell authorities he was raped: "You know that if it is degrading for a woman, how much more for a man." *No Escape: Male Rape in U.S. Prisons*, "Anomaly or Epidemic" (Human Rights Watch, 2001), www.hrw.org/reports/2001/prison/report.html ("The terrible stigma attached to falling victim to rape in prison … discourages the reporting of abuse. Deeply ashamed of themselves, many inmates are reluctant to admit what has happened to them, particularly in situations in which they did not put up obvious physical resistance"); James E. Robertson, "A Clean Heart and an Empty Head: The Supreme Court and Sexual Terrorism in Prison," 81 *N.C. L. Rev.* 433, 443–44 (2003).

37 In New York City, the police Civilian Complaint Review Board (CCRB) began investigating complaints of sexual misconduct in February 2018. Only thirteen months later, CCRB had "received 83 complaints containing 126 allegations of sexual harassment, sexual or romantic propositions, sexual humiliation and sexually motivated strip searches." Rich Calder, "Sexual misconduct complaints flood police watchdog" *New York Post*, March 19, 2019, https://nypost.com/2019/03/19/sexual-misconduct-complaints-flood-police-watchdog/.

38 While police chiefs estimated that 20 percent of their officers participated in some form of sexual misconduct while on duty, they "reported that on average only 2.7% of all officers

engage in serious forms of this behavior" such as "rape, sexual assault, and sex with a juvenile," Timothy M. Maher, "Police Chiefs' Views on Police Sexual Misconduct," *Police Practice and Research*, 9 (2008): 239–50 at 240. "In unjustified traffic stops, where the officer pulls over someone who appears attractive, an officer may do this just to get a better look at them, just to 'go fishing' is the phrase that refers to this activity," Maher, "Cops on The Make: Police Officers Using Their Job, Power, And Authority to Pursue Their Personal Sexual Interests," *Journal of the Institute of Justice & International Studies*, 7 (2007): 32–39 at 33.

39 David Garrick, "San Diego paying out $350K in sexual assault case," *San Diego Union-Tribune*, June 29, 2019, www.sandiegouniontribune.com/communities/san-diego/story/2019-06-21/san-diego-paying-out-350k-in-sexual-harassment-assault-case (Officer Christopher Hays, whose alleged sexual misconduct and inappropriate touching have cost taxpayers more than $2 million.)

40 Christina Cocca and Gadi Schwartz, "Civil Rights Lawsuit Alleges Deputies Burned Man's Genitals with Taser," *NBC News*, February 8, 2014, www.nbclosangeles.com/news/national-international/civil-rights-lawsuit-la-sheriffs-deputies-daniel-johnson-taser/58297/.

41 *Amaechi v. West*, 237 F.3d 356 (4th Cir. 2001).

42 *Sims v. Labowitz*, 877 F. 3d 171, 182–83 (4th Cir. 2017), rehearing granted, 714 Fed Appx 289 (4th Cir. 2018) (Unpublished).

43 Aubrey Whelan, "Police begin probe of teenager's arrest," *Philidelphia Inquirer*, January 18, 2014, www.inquirer.com/philly/news/20140118_Police_begin_probe_of_teenager_s_arrest.html. From January 7 to May 14, 2014, Darrin Manning faced charges in juvenile court for reckless endangerment, simple assault, and resisting arrest; eventually his lawyer worked out a plea deal that avoided a trial, most likely for "diversion" so the charges could be dismissed.

44 Aubrey Whelan, "Grand jury exonerates Phila. Police officer," *The Philadelphia Inquirer*, July 17, 2014, www.inquirer.com/philly/news/20140718_Grand_jury_exonerates_Phila__police_officer.html. ("The grand jury noted that there was no Police Department directive prohibiting female officers from conducting searches on male suspects." Also, the urologist at the Children's Hospital testified to the grand jury that he found no medical evidence that Manning's testicle had been ruptured.)

45 Chase Strangio, "Arrested for Walking While Trans: An Interview with Monica Jones," *ACLU*, April 2, 2014, www.aclu.org/blog/criminal-law-reform/arrested-walking-while-trans-interview-monica-jones.

46 Kara Fox, "Maryland Lesbian Alleges Metro Police Abuse in Arrest," *Washington Blade*, April 26, 2002, recorded in *Stonewalled: Police abuse and misconduct against lesbian, gay, bisexual and transgender people in the U.S.* 68 & fn 285 (Amnesty International, 2005), www.amnesty.org/en/documents/AMR51/001/2006/en/ ("AI interview with Anonymous, San Antonio AIDS Foundation, 5 December 2003).

47 *Stonewalled: Police abuse and misconduct against lesbian, gay, bisexual and transgender people in the U.S.* 83–84, n. 364.

48 Ibid., 84.

49 Catherine Hanssens, Aisha-Moodie Millis, Andrea Ritchie, Dean Spade and Urvashi Vaid, *A Roadmap for Change*, 12 (Center for Gender & Sexuality Law Policy, 2014).

50 https://mafiadoc.com/federal-policy-recommendations-for-addressing-the-criminalization-of_5c2e8d1a097c47fb128b45be.html.

51 Susan Estrich, *Real Rape*, 13 (Harvard University Press, 1987).

52 In 2015, a jury convicted Oklahoma City police officer Daniel Holtzclaw of multiple counts of sexual assault and rape committed while he was on duty. Melissa Jeltsen, "Oklahoma Ex-Cop Convicted of Serial Rape," *Huff Post*, January 11, 2017, www .huffpost.com/entry/daniel-holtzclaw-verdict_n_566591ade4b08e945feff52b; "Daniel Holtzclaw Sentenced to 263 Consecutive Years in Prison for Raping Black Women," *DEMOCRACY NOW!*, January 21, 2016, www.democracynow.org/2016/1/22/headlines/ officer_daniel_holtzclaw_sentenced_to_263_years_in_prison.

53 Matt Sedensky, "AP: Hundreds of Officers Lose Licenses Over Sex Misconduct," *AP News*, November 1, 2015, https://apnews.com/fd1d4d05e561462a85abe50e7eaed4ec/ap-hun dreds-officers-lose-licenses-over-sex-misconduct.

7 INVISIBLE SCARS: *TERRY'S* PSYCHOLOGICAL TOLL

1 Rebecca Solnit, *Wanderlust: A History of Walking* 67 (Penguin Books, 2001).

2 James Baldwin, *The Fire Next Time*, 142 (Dial Press, 1963).

3 Giving police this power, the Court explained, furthers the goal of "effective crime prevention and detection," *Terry v. Ohio*, 392 U.S. 1, 22 (1968).

4 "Final Report of the President's Task Force on 21st Century Policing" (President's Task Force on 21st Century Policing, 2015), https://cops.usdoj.gov/pdf/taskforce/taskforce_ finalreport.pdf.

5 John Hagan, Carla Shedd and Monique R. Payne, "Race, Ethnicity, and Youth Perceptions of Criminal Injustice," *American Sociological Review*, 70 (2005): 381–407 at 390.

6 Amanda Geller, "Policing America's Children: Police Contact and Consequences Among Teens in Fragile Families," Working Paper WP18–02-FF (2017).

7 Allen E. Lipscomb et al., "Black Male Hunting! A Phenomenological Study Exploring the Secondary Impact of Police Induced Trauma on the Black Man's Psyche in the United States," *Journal of Sociology and Social Work*, 7 (2019): 11–18, at 13; Amanda Geller, Jeffrey Fagan, Tom Tyler and Bruce Link, "Aggressive Policing and the Mental Health of Young Urban Men," *American Journal of Public Health* 104 (2014): 2321–27 at 2321.

8 James D. Unnever, *A Theory of African American Offending*, 98–99 (Routledge, 2011); Amanda Geller et al., "Aggressive Policing" (describing stress, stigma and anger). One study that looks at police officers' use of debasing language is Jacinta M. Gau and Rod K. Brunson, "Procedural Justice and Order Maintenance Policing: A Study of Inner-City Young Men's Perceptions of Police Legitimacy," *Justice Quarterly* 27 (2010): 255–79.

9 James D. Unnever, *A Theory of African American Offending*, 139 (citing Leana A. Bouffard and Nicole L. Piquero, "Defiance Theory and Life Course Explanations of Persistent Offending," *Crime & Delinquency* 56 (2010): 227–52; Edwin M. Lemert, *Human Deviance, Social Problems and Social Control*, 2nd ed. (Prentice-Hall, 1972); Edwin M. Schur, *Labeling Deviant Behavior: Its Sociological Implications* (Harper and Roe, 1971); Terri A. Winnick and Mark Bodkin, "Anticipated Stigma and Stigma Management Among Those to be Labeled 'Ex-con'" *Deviant Behavior* 29 (2008): 295–333.) For other race-based research on police stops and children, see Arthur J. Lurigio, Richard Gary Greenleaf and Jamie L. Flexon, "The Effects Of Race on Relationships With The Police: A Survey of African American and Latino Youths in Chicago," *Western Criminology Review* 10 (2009):

29–41 (finding that in African American and Latino boys in Chicago, being stopped and mistreated by police had a negative impact on youths' legal socialization); Juan Del Toro et al., "The Criminogenic and Psychological Effects of Police Stops on Black and Latino boys," *PNAS*, 116 (2019): 8261–68.

10 James Baldwin, *The Fire Next Time*.

11 Unnever, *A Theory of African American Offending*, at XVII, 98–99 (and discussed throughout chapter 3, 52–72).

Other researchers confirm that aggressive policing leads to legal cynicism, which increases the likelihood that these individuals will later commit crimes, including: Jeffrey Fagan and Alex R. Piquero, "Rational Choice and Developmental Influences on Recidivism Among Adolescent Felony Offenders," *Journal of Empirical Legal Studies* 4 (2007): 715–48; Tom R. Tyler and Jeffrey Fagan, "Legitimacy and Cooperation: Why Do People Help the Police Fight Crime in Their Communities?," 6 *Ohio State J. Crim. Law* 231 (2008) (perceptions of police legitimacy influence people's willingness to cooperate with police); Tom R. Tyler, Jeffrey Fagan, and Amanda Geller, "Street Stops and Police Legitimacy: Teachable Moments in Young Urban Men's Legal Socialization," *Journal of Empirical Legal Studies* 11 (2014): 751–85 (finding widespread use of investigative stops undermined people's perceptions of police legitimacy, which influenced law abidingness).

12 In a survey of children from large US cities, 45 percent of black boys reported stops, 18 percent of black girls; 26 percent of white boys and 8 percent of white girls were stopped. Amanda Geller, "Policing America's Children: Police Contact and Consequences Among Teens in Fragile Families," Working Paper WP18–02-FF (2017).

13 Ibid. Juan Del Toro et al., "The criminogenic and psychological effects of police stops on black and Latino boys," *PNAS*, 116 (2019): 8261–66; Arthur J. Lurigio, Richard Gary Greenleaf, Jamie L. Flexon, "The Effects of Race on Relationships with the Police: A Study of African American and Latino Youths in Chicago," *Western Criminology Review*, 10 (2009): 29–41 at 31.

14 *The Wire*, "Misgivings" HBO, November 19, 2006, written by Ed Burns and Eric Overmyer, directed by Ernest Dickerson. "They're not fools, these kids. They don't know our world, but they know their own. They see right through us."

15 Paul Butler, "The System is Working the Way it is Supposed to: The Limits of Criminal Justice Reform," 104 *Geo. L. J.* 1419 (2016); Devon Carbado, "What Exposes African Americans to Police Violence?," 51 *Harv. Civil Rights Civil Liberties L. Rev* 159 (2016); Rose M. Brewer and Nancy A. Heitzeg, "The Racialization of Crime and Punishment," *American Behavioral Scientist*: 51 (2008): 625–44.

16 Leslie Feinberg, *Stone Butch Blues* (Firebrand Books, 1993). In her memoir, Feinberg writes that three pieces of gender-specific clothing laws were regularly and brutally enforced in Buffalo in the early 1960s. *See also*, Leslie Feinberg, *Transgender Warriors: Making History from Joan of Arc to RuPaul* 8 (Beacon Press, 1996).

17 *Lawrence v. Texas*, 539 U.S. 558, 567 (2003); *Obergefell v. Hodges*, 135 S. Ct. 2584, 2597 (2015). In Elizabeth Cooper, "The Power of Dignity," 84 *Fordam L. Rev.* 3, 8 (2015), Cooper writes that the harm from criminalizing gay sex was "the harm to the dignity of the person charged." Even when police didn't enforce the laws, they created stigma.

18 "Nation: 'The Root of the Negro Problem,'" *Time*, May 17, 1963, http://content.time.com/time/magazine/article/0,9171,830326,00.html.

19 In one of New York City's gay areas, 90 percent of LGBTQ youth surveyed experienced police harassment or violence, Catherine Hanssens, Aisha-Moodie Millis, Andrea Ritchie, Dean Spade, and Urvashi Vaid, *A Roadmap for Change Federal Policy Reccommendations for Addressing the Normalization of LGBT People and People Living with HIV*, 2014, www .hivlawandpolicy.org/resources/a-roadmap-change-federal-policy-recommendations-address ing-criminalization-lgbt-people-and In San Francisco, a quarter of transgender city dwellers were harassed or abused by police, Joey Mongul, Andrea Ritchie and Kay Whitlock, *Queer (In)Justice: The Criminalization of LGBTQ People in the United States* (Beacon Press, 2011), citing Shannon Minter and Christopher Daley, "*Trans Reality: A Legal Needs Assessment of San Francisco's Transgender Communities*" (National Center for Lesbian Rights, 2003) www.nclrights.org/wp-content/uploads/2013/07/transrealities0803.pdf and Kerith J. Conron, Mario I. Suárez and Lance Keene, "A Research Agenda to Reduce System Involvement and Promote Positive Outcomes with LGBTQ Youth of Color Impacted by the Child Welfare and Juvenile Justice Systems" 52 (Williams Institute, 2019) https://williamsinstitute.law.ucla.edu/wp-content/uploads/LGBTQ-YOC-Social-Services-Jul-2019.pdf. The Williams Institute reports: "An estimated 20% of youth in detention are LGBTQ compared to just 6% of youth in the general population." The report also noted that lesbian, gay and bisexual "youth are more likely than non-LGB youth to be arrested and detained for status offences (e.g. running away, truancy) and other survival strategies, such as selling sex or drugs ... Much less is known about the experiences of trans youth."

20 Michael J. McFarland, Amanda Geller and Cheryl McFarland, "Police Contact and Health among Urban Adolescents; The Role of Perceived Injustice," *Social Science and Medicine* 238 (2019): 26–49.

21 Gaurav Jashnani, Priscilla Bustamonte and Brett G. Stoudt, "Dispossession by Accumula-tion: The Impacts of Discretionary Arrests in New York City," *Race and Justice* (2017): 1–43 at 18.

22 *Stop and Frisk: The Human Impact Report* 6 (Center for Constitutional Rights, 2012), https://ccrjustice.org/sites/default/files/attach/2015/08/the-human-impact-report.pdf; Sarah Brayne, "Surveillance and System Avoidance: Criminal Justice Contact and Institutional Attachment," *American Sociological Review*, 79 (2014): 367–91 at 367 (finding individuals who have been stopped, arrested, convicted, or incarcerated are less likely to interact with institutions that keep formal records, including hospitals, banks, employment, and schools, than their counterparts without criminal justice contact.)

23 *Utah v. Strieff*, 136 S. Ct. 2056, 2070–71 (2016).

24 Amanda Geller and Jeffrey Fagan, "Police Contact and the Legal Socialization of Urban Teens," *Russell Sage Foundation Journal of Social Sciences* 5(1) (2019): 26–49 at 27–28. Other articles on point include: Jamie L. Flexon et al., "Exploring the Dimensions of Trust in the Police Among Chicago Juveniles," *Journal of Criminal Justice* 37 (2009): 180–89 at 188; Amy E. Lerman and Velsa Weaver, "Staying out of Sight: Concentrated Policing and Local Political Action" 651 *The ANNALS of the American Academy of Political and Social Science* 651 (2014): 202–19 (finding that concentrated policing, includ-ing aggressive stop-and frisk practices in urban communities, negatively impacts civic engagement in the affected communities); Joe Soss and Velsa Weaver, "Police Are Our Government, Politics, Political Science, and the Policing of Race-Class Subjugated

Communities" *Annual Review of Political Science* 20 (2017): 565–91 (arguing that inter-actions with the criminal justice system, police, and welfare authorities are often the only experiences that poor people of color have with the American government, therefore police encounters shape their perceptions on "how the government works, what political life is like for them, and how they understand their own political identities"). See J. A. Schafer, B. M. Huebner, and T. S. Bynum, "Citizen Perceptions of Police Services: Race, Neighborhood Context, and Community Policing," *Police Quarterly* 6 (2003): 440, 441–42 (2003); Steven A. Tuch and Ronald Weitzer, "The Polls-Trends: Racial Differences in Attitudes Toward the Police," 61 *Public Opinion Quarterly*, 61 (1997): 642–63; Elijah Anderson, *Streetwise, Race, Class, and Change in an Urban Community* 190–207 (University of Chicago Press, 1996).

25 Amanda Geller, "Aggressive Policing"; Cynthia Golembeski and Robert Fullilove, "Crim-inal (In)justice in the City and Its Associated Health Consequences," *American Journal of Public Health* 95 (2005): 1701–06 ("a more humanistic and community-centered approach to incarceration and rehabilitation may yield more beneficial results" than the current system which features increasingly punitive sentencing guidelines and privatized prisons).

26 *Terry*, 392 U.S. at 17.

27 Rod K. Brunson, Ronald Weitzer, "Police Relations with Black and White Youths in Different Urban Neighborhoods" *Urban Affairs Review* 44 (2009): 858–85 (2009). ("Black respondents expressed hopelessness … because they felt that officers would never see them as anything other than symbolic assailants even when they were engaged in entirely lawful activity.")

28 Carla Shedd, "What About the Other 99%? The Broader Impact of Street Stops on Minority Communities," in Nancy La Vigne, Pa,ela Lachman, Andrea Matthews, and S. Rebecca Neusteter, eds., *Key Issues in the Police Use of Pedestrian Stops and Searches: Discussion Papers from an Urban Institute Roundtable* (Urban Instituite Policy Center, 2012) ("Youth who must navigate these spaces are inevitably at high risk of negative police contact, which may lead to frustration, disengagement, and perhaps even delinquency.") See Shedd, *Unequal City* (Russell Sage Foundation, 2015).

29 George L. Kelling and William J. Bratton, "Why We Need Broken Windows Policing" *City Journal* (2015)
www.city-journal.org/html/why-we-need-broken-windows-policing-13696.html.

30 Rod K. Brunson, "'Police Don't Like Black People': African-American Young Men's Accumulated Police Experiences," *Criminology and Public Policy* 6 (2007): 71–102, at 95–96.

31 Jason N. Houle, J. Staff, and J.T. Mortimer, "The Impact of Sexual Harassment on Depressive Symptoms During the Early Occupational Career," *Society of Mental Health* 1 (2011): 89–104. Recurring incidences of sexual harassment are also associated with anxiety, posttraumatic stress, and increased substance abuse, Lilia M. Cortina and Emily A. Leskinen, "Workplace Harassment Based on Sex: A Risk Factor for Women's Health Problems" *Key Issues in Mental Health* 178 (2013) in Claudia Garcia-Moreno, Anita Riecher-Rössler, eds., *Violence Against Women and Mental Health* 139–47 (Karger, 2013); Heather Littleton et al., *Sexual Assault, Sexual Abuse, and Harassment: Understanding the Mental Health Impact and Providing Care for Survivors* (International Society for Traumatic Stress Studies, 2018) (citing, Emily R. Dworkin, S. V. Menon, J. Bystrynski, and

N. E. Allen, "Sexual Assault Victimization and Psychopathology: A Review and Meta-Analysis" *Clinical Psychology Review* 56 (2017): 65–81.

32 Geller et al., "Aggressive Policing."

33 Geller, "Policing America's Children."

34 Abigail A. Sewell and Kevin A. Jefferson, "Collateral Damage: The Health Effects of Invasive Police Encounters in New York City," *Journal of Urban Health* 93 (2016): S42–S67 at S43. (citing Michelle Billies, "Surveillance Threat as Embodied Psychological Dilemma," *Journal of Peace* 21 (2015): 168, 168–86 (2015); Hannah Cooper, Sofia Gruskin, and Lisa Moore, "Characterizing Perceived Police Violence: Implications for Public Health," 94 Am. J. Pub. Health (2004): 1109–18 ; Arline T. Geronimus, Margaret Hicken, Danya Keene, and John Bound, "'Weathering' and Age Patterns of Allostatic Load Scores Among Blacks and Whites in the United States," 96 *American Journal of Public Health* 96 (2006): 826, 826–33. Similarly, hypervigilance "produce[s] harmful physiological responses, such as elevated blood pressure, heart rate, and stress biomarkers," Vickie M. Mays, Susan D. Cochran, and Namdi W. Barnes, "Race, Race-Based Discrimination and Health Outcomes Among African Americans," *Annual Review of Psychology* 58 (2008): 201–25 at 204.

35 Dawne M. Mouzon, R. J. Taylor, and A. T. Woodward, "Everyday Racial Discrimination, Everyday Non-Racial Discrimination, and Physical Health Among African Americans," *Journal of Ethnic & Cultural Diversity in Social Work* 26 (2016): 68–80 (concluding that among African Americans racial discrimination is associated with negative health outcomes). Kathryn Freeman, "Diagnosing Discrimination: Stress from Perceived Racism and the Mental and Physical Health Effects," *Sociological Inquiry* (2012): 1–27 (finding that experiencing emotional and physical stress from perceived racist treatment is "an important factor in predicting the number of poor mental and physical health days); P.J. Sawyer, Brenda Major, Bettina J. Casad, Sarah S. M. Townsend, and Wendy Berry, "Discrimination and the Stress Response: Psychological and Physiological Consequences of Anticipating Prejudice in Interethnic Interactions," *American Journal of Public Health* 102 (2012): 1020–25 at 1020; Nancy Krieger and Stephen Sidney, "Racial Discrimination and Blood Pressure: The CARDIA Study of Young Black and White Adults," *American Journal of Public Health* 86 (1996): 1370–78 (finding that perceived racial discrimination is associated with raised blood pressure and poorer self-rated health).

36 Sirry Alang, Donna McAlpine, Ellen McCreedy, and Rachel Hardeman , "Police Brutality and Black Health: Setting the Agenda for Public Health Scholars," *American Journal of Public Health,* 107 (2017): 662–65 at 663 (racialized police brutality is particularly heinous because it, "is a constant reminder of the historic and current devaluing of black lives," and "it sends a signal that there is little hope for justice").

37 W. E. B. Du Bois, *The Souls of Black Folk,* (A.C. McClurg & Co., 1903).

38 Mays et al., 201, 204.

39 Priscilla Bustamante, Gaurav Jashnani and Brett G Stoudt, "Theorizing Cumulative Dehumanization: An Embodied Praxis of 'becoming' and Resisting State-Sanctioned Violence," *Social Personal Psychology Compass* 13 (2019): 1–13 at 7, 13.

40 Hypervigilance has been paired with "anticipated racism," Margaret Hicken, "Racial/Ethnic Disparities in Hypertension Prevalence Reconsidering the Role of Chronic Stress," *American Journal of Public Health* 104 (2014): 117–23; Jessica Forsyth and Robert T. Carter,

"The Relationship Between Racial Identity Status Attitudes, Racism-Related Coping, and Mental Health among Black Americans," *Cultural Diversity & Ethnic Minority Psychology* 18 (2012):128–40 at 136; Amanda Geller et al., "Aggressive Policing"; Rod K. Brunson, "Police Don't Like Black People;" Bruce G. Link and Jo C. Phelan, "Conceptualizing Stigma," *Annual Review of Sociology* 27 (2001): 363–85.

41 *World Report on Violence & Health Summary* 4, 9 (World Health Organization, 2002), www.who.int/violence_injury_prevention/violence/world_report/en/summary_en.pdf

42 Julia Lurie, "10 Hours in Ferguson: A Visual Timeline of Michael Brown's Death and Its Aftermath," *Mother Jones*, August 27, 2014, www.motherjones.com/politics/2014/08/time line-michael-brown-shooting-ferguson. Mike Jones, an African American chief aide to the St. Louis County Executive, explained "[y]ou'll never make anyone black believe that a white kid would have laid in the street for four hours," Richard Prince, "Why Michael Brown's Body Was Left on the Street for So Long," *The Root*, September 17, 2014, www .theroot.com/blog/journal-isms/why_michael_brown_s_body_was_left_on_the_street_ for_so_long/.

43 Cobb, Jelani, "Lena Waithe on Police Violence and *Queen & Slim*." *The New Yorker Radio Hour*. Podcast audio, December 16, 2019, www.newyorker.com/podcast/political-scene/lena-waithe-on-police-violence-and-queen-and-slim.

44 Daphne Blunt Bugental, Jay Blue, Victoria Cortez, Karen Fleck, and Alina Rodriguez, "Influences of Witnessed Affect on Information Processing in Children," *Child Development*, 63 (1992): 774–86; C. Daniel Batson, J. Fultz, and A. Schoenrade, "Distress and Empathy: Two Qualitatively Distinct Vicarious Emotions with Different Motivational Consequences," *Journal of Personality*, 55 (1987): 19–39.

45 Rod K Brunson and Ronald Weitzer, "Negotiating Unwelcome Police Encounters: The Intergenerational Transmission of Conduct Norms," *Journal of Contemporary Ethnography*, 40 (2011): 425–56 at 429; Dennis P. Rosenbaum et. al., "Attitudes Toward the Police: The Effects of Direct and Vicarious Experience, *Police Quarterly*, 8 (2005): 343–65. Vicarious experiences with police can also lead to greater criminality in communities. Tom R. Tyler, Jeffrey Fagan, and Amanda Geller, "Street Stops and Police Legitimacy: Teachable Moments in Young Urban Men's Legal Socialization, *Journal of Empirical Legal Studies* 11(4) (2014): 751–85 (finding that widespread use of investigative stops undermined people's perceptions of police legitimacy, which influenced law abidingness).

46 Allen E. Lipscomb et al., "Black Male Hunting! at 16.

47 Abigail A. Sewell and Kevin A. Jefferson, "Collateral Damage: The Health Effects of Invasive Police Encounters in New York City," *Journal of Urban Health* 93 (Supp. 2016): S43.

48 Abigail A. Sewell, Kevin A. Jefferson, and Hedwig Lee, "Living Under Surveillance: Gender, Psychological Distress, and Stop-Question-and-Frisk Policing in New York City," *Social Science & Medicine*, 159 (2016): 1–13 at 1–2. This study uses similar data to that reported in her paper, titled "Collateral Damage." ("Our findings show that living in aggressively policed communities is of detriment to the health of male residents in the neighborhood.")

49 Sewell and Jefferson, "Collateral Damage," S55; Sewell, et al., "Living Under Surveillance," 10 ("Our findings show that living in aggressively policed communities is of detriment to the health of male residents in the neighborhood.").

50 Tori DeAngelis, "The Legacy of Trauma," *American Psychological Association* (February 2019), www.apa.org/monitor/2019/02/legacy-trauma.

51 Rachel Yehuda, "Intergenerational transmission of trauma effects: putative role of epigenetic mechanisms," *Journal of the World Psychiatry Association* 17 (2018):243–57.

52 Amy Bombay, Kim Matheson, and Hymie Anisman, "Intergenerational Trauma: Convergence of Multiple Processes among First Nations peoples in Canada," *Journal of Aboriginal Health* 5 (2009) 6–47.

53 Tori DeAngelis, "The legacy of Trauma.

54 Ibid, (citing, Yael Danieli and Brian E. Engdahl, "Multigenerational Legacies of Trauma: Modeling the What and How Transmission," *American Journal of Orthopsychiatry* 86 (2016): 1–15.)

55 Dr. Joy DeGruy, *Post Traumatic Slave Syndrome: America's Legacy of Enduring Injury and Healing*, (Uptone Press, 2005).

56 Lipscomb et al., "Black Male Hunting! at 13.

57 Rod K. Brunson and Ronald Weitzer, "Negotiating Unwelcome Police Encounters" at 440 (quoting a 55-year-old black father.)

58 Tori DeAngelis, "The Legacy of Trauma." A 1994 study found that "a black victim frequently shares the account with family and friends, often to lighten the burden, and this sharing creates a domino effect of anguish and anger rippling across an extended group." Rod K. Brunson, "'Police Don't Like Black People': African-American Young Men's Accumulated Police Experiences," 73; Joe R. Feagin, and Melvin P. Sikes, *Living With Racism: The Black Middle-Class Experience*, 16 (Beacon Press, 1994).

8 HIGH COURT CAMOUFLAGE: HOW THE SUPREME COURT HIDES POLICE AGGRESSION AND RACIAL ANIMUS

1 *Kentucky* v. *King*, 563 U.S. 452, 456 (2011).

2 In *Florida* v. *Jardines*, 569 U.S. 1, 8 (2013), the Supreme Court explains that "the knocker on the front door is treated as an invitation" to "solicitors, hawkers and peddlers," that the implicit license to knock "is generally managed without incident by the Nation's Girl Scouts and trick-or-treaters" so when officers approach and knock, this is "no more than any private citizen might do." This sentiment is repeated in *Kentucky* v. *King*, 563 U.S. at 769. ("When law enforcement officers who are not armed with a warrant knock on a door, they do no more than any private citizen might do.")

3 "There is no evidence of a "demand" of any sort, much less a demand that amounts to a threat to violate the Fourth Amendment." *King*, 563 U.S. at 468.

4 *Ibid.*, at 457. Mr. King was charged with trafficking in marijuana, first-degree trafficking in a controlled substance, and second-degree persistent felony offender status. After losing his motion to suppress the evidence seized during the warrantless search, Mr. King pled guilty but retained his right to appeal the motion.

5 Josephine Ross, "Blaming the Victim: 'Consent' within the Fourth Amendment and Rape Law," 26 *Harv. J. Racial & Ethnic Just.* 1, 61 (2010).

6 *King*, 563 U.S. at 470.

7 Michael D. White and Henry F. Fradella, *Stop and Frisk: The Use and Abuse of a Controversial Policing Tactic* 147 (NYU Press, 2016).

8 Devon W. Carbado, *From Stopping Black People to Killing Black People: The Fourth Amendment Pathways to Police Violence*, 105 Cal. L. Rev. 125, 160 (2017) ("That people seemed to consent to searches in the context of traffic stops because they think they have to, and that police officers seem to employ traffic stops to target African Americans for consent searches, does not matter under current Fourth Amendment doctrine.")

9 *Florida v. Royer*, 460 U.S. 491, 501 (1983).

10 *Michigan v. Chesternut*, 486 U.S. 567, 569 (1988).

11 *Ibid.*; *Michigan v. Chesternut*, 1987 U.S. S. Ct. Briefs LEXIS 915 at 8.

12 Devon Carbado, "[E]racing The Fourth Amendment," 100 *Mich. L. Rev.* 946 (2002).

13 *United States v. Drayton*, 536 U.S. 194, 198–200, 211 (2002).

14 The agent explained during the motion hearing in the Drayton that he became suspicious because the men were "overly cooperative" in allowing a search of their luggage and that's why he wanted to frisk them. As Devon Cabado explains, blacks and Latinx people generally feel more pressure to disprove their guilt by consenting to searches, but for Mr. Drayton and Mr. Brown, their cooperation backfired. Carbado, "[E]Racing the Fourth Amendment," 100 *Mich. L. Rev.* at 1022, citing *United States v. Drayton*, 231 F. 3d 787, 789 (11th Cir. 2000).

15 *Drayton*, 536 U.S. at 208 (Souter, J., dissenting).

16 Tracey Maclin' "'Black and Blue Encounters' – Some Preliminary Thoughts about Fourth Am Seizures: Should Race Matter?," 26 *Val. U. L. Rev.* 243, 250 (1991); Carbado, "From Stopping Black People to Killing Black People, 125, 142–44 (2017)("When assessing the coercive nature of an encounter, the Court should consider the race of the person confronted by the police, and how that person's race might have influenced his attitude toward the encounter.")

17 *Whren v. United States*, 517 U.S. 806 (1996).

18 Emily Jacobs, "Unruly Airline Passenger Screams Cops 'Treating Me Like a Black Person' During Arrest," *New York Post*, August 17, 2018, https://nypost.com/2018/08/17/unruly-airline-passenger-screams-cops-treating-me-like-a-black-person-during-arrest.

19 Wesley Lowery "Aren't more white people than black people killed by police, Yes, but no," *Washington Post*, July 11, 2016, www.washingtonpost.com/news/post-nation/wp/2016/07/11/arent-more-white-people-than-black-people-killed-by-police-yes-but-no/. From January 1, 2015 through the date that Lowery wrote the story (July 10, 2016), of the 1,502 people shot and killed by on-duty police officers, 732 were white, and 381 were black, with 382 of another or unknown race, according to *Washington Post* statistics.

20 Logan Strother, Charles Menifield and Geiguen Shin, "We Gathered Data on Every Confirmed, Line-of-Duty Police Killing of a Civilian in 2014 and 2015. Here's What We Found," *Washington Post*, August 29, 2018, www.washingtonpost.com/news/monkey-cage/wp/2018/08/29/we-gathered-data-on-every-confirmed-line-of-duty-police-killing-of-a-civilian-in-2014-and-2015-heres-what-we-found/ ("Of the people killed by police in 2014 and 2015, 51 percent were white, 28.1 percent were black, 19.3 percent were Latino, and 1.7 percent were Asian. The remainder came from other ethnic backgrounds.") Most people killed by police were white.

21 Rachel Wetts and Robb Willer, "Privilege on Precipice: Perceived Racial Status Threats Lead White Americans to Oppose Welfare Programs," *Social Forces*, 97 (2018): 793–822; Jazmin L. Brown-Iannuzi, E. Cooley, and S.E McKee, "Wealthy Whites and Poor Blacks:

Implicit Associations between Racial Groups and Wealth Predict Explicit Opposition Toward Helping the Poor," *Journal of Experimental Social Psychology*, 82 (2019): 26–34.

22 *Utah v. Strieff*, 136 S. Ct. 2056, 2060 and 2073 (2016) (Compare trial court considered the presence of an arrest warrant to be an "extraordinary intervening circumstance" to Kagan's dissent.)

23 *Ibid.*, 2063.

24 "South Salt Lake City, Utah," *United States Census Bureau*, (2010) (showing that the city was comprised of 69.5 percent white and 4.4 percent black residents).

25 U.S. Department of Justice, *The Ferguson Report: Department of Justice Investigation of the Ferguson Police Department*, 17–25, 88 (The New Press, 2015), available online as U.S. Department of Justice Civil Rights Division, "Investigation of the Ferguson Department," 47, 55 (March 4, 2015), www.justice.gov/sites/default/files/opa/press-releases/attachments/2015/03/04/ferguson_police_department_report.pdf. The Department of Justice reported that in the town of Ferguson, Missouri, with a population of 21,000, 16,000 people had outstanding warrants against them, ibid., 6, 55.

26 *Ibid.* Out of a total population of 21,000, Ferguson police could illegally stop 16,000 people and find outstanding warrants.

27 *Strieff*, 136 S. Ct. at 2063.

28 Alexes Harris, a sociologist at the University of Washington, states, "Courts across the nation are using warrants to bring non-paying indigent defendants into courts and either forcing them to pay what little money they have or are jailing them." Devin Denvir, "Two Years After Ferguson, Missouri Cops Are Accused of Shaking Down the Power," *Vice*, November 2, 2016, www.vice.com/en_us/article/gqk58q/maplewood-missouri-ferguson-st-louis-county-debtor-prison-poor-arrest-fine. Ferguson, Missouri, is a glaring example of this. The Department of Justice found that the "Ferguson municipal court uses arrest warrants primarily as a means of securing payment." US Department of Justice, Civil Rights Division, "Investigation of the Ferguson Police Department," 55, (March 4, 2015), www.justice.gov/sites/default/files/opa/press-releases/attachments/2015/03/04/ferguson_police_department_report.pdf. With a population of 21,000 – 25 percent of which lives below the federal poverty level – 16,000 people had outstanding arrest warrants as of December 2014.

29 *Strieff*, 136 S. Ct. at 2069 (Sotomayor, J., dissenting) ("one widely followed police manual instructs officers looking for drugs to 'run at least a warrant check on all drivers you stop . . . Discovery of an outstanding warrant gives you cause for an immediate custodial arrest and search of the suspect,'" citing Charles Remsberg, *Tactics for Criminal Patrol*, 205–206 (Calibre Press, 1995); and Charles R. Epp, Steven Mayard-Moody and Donald P. Haider-Markel, *Pulled Over* 23, 33–36 (University of Chicago Press, 2014). "Utah lists over 180,000 misdemeanor warrants in its database," Justice Sotomayor also pointed out. *Strieff* , 136 S. Ct. at 2066.

30 *Strieff*, S. Ct. at136 at 2064 (Sotomayer, J., dissenting) (emphases added).

31 Nikki Giovanni, *The Selected Poems of Nikki Giovanni* (William Morrow, 1996) (Foreword by Virginia C. Fowler).

32 *Strieff*, S. Ct. at136 at 2064 (Sotomayer, J., dissenting (emphasis added).

33 Lani Guinier and Gerald Torres, *The Miner's Canary: Enlisting Race, Resisting Power, Transforming Democracy*, (Harvard University Press, 2002).

34 Anthony Paul Farley, "The Black Body as Fetsh Object," 76 *Or. L. Rev.* 457 (1997); Paul Farley, "The Poetics of Colorlined Space" in Francisco Valdes et al., eds., *Crossroads, Directions And A New Critical Race Theory*, 97–158 (Temple University Press, 2002); Ta-Nehisi Coates, *Between the World and Me*, (Random House, 2015).

35 *Terry v. Ohio*, 392 U.S. 1, 17 (1968) (citing, L. L. Priar and T. F. Martin, "Searching and Disarming Criminals," 45 *The Journal of Criminal Law, Criminology, and Police Science*, 45 (1954): 481–85 at 481).

36 National Advisory Commission, "Report of the National Advisory Commission on Civil Disorders," 206, 299–305, (February 29, 1968), www.ncjrs.gov/pdffiles1/Digitization/8073NCJRS.pdf. The National Advisory Commission ("Kerner Commission") investigated riots in Newark, NJ; Detroit, MI., Cincinnati, OH.; Atlanta, GA and in lesser detail discussed more than a dozen riots in other cities across the United States in the previous decade. "The atmosphere of hostility and cynicism is reinforced by a widespread belief among negroes in the existence of police brutality and in a 'double standard' of justice and protection – one for negroes and one for whites." Note that *Terry* v. *Ohio* was argued before the Supreme Court on December 12, 1968, after the Kerner Report was released. The relationship between the report and *Terry* is discussed in Devon W. Carbado, "From Stop and Frisk to Shoot and Kill," 64 (2017); *UCLA L. Rev.*: at 1516.

The N.A.A.C.P. Legal Defense and Educational Fund urged the Court to require probable cause for police stops because police use it to harass communities of color: "The evidence is weighty and uncontradicted that stop and frisk power is employed by the police most frequently against the inhabitants of our inner cities, racial minorities and the underprivileged," the organization wrote in an Amicus Brief. Brief for the N.A.A.C.P. Legal Defense and Educational Fund, Inc. at 3, *Terry* v. *Ohio*, 392 U.S. 1 (No. 67), 1967 WL 113672.

37 *Terry*, 392 U.S. at 14–15.

38 *Terry*, 392 U.S. at 15.

39 *Strieff* reasoned that the exclusionary rule only stops bad faith policing. The Court refused to keep out drugs that the officer found during a bad stop because the remedy won't prevent future (good) police officers from accidentally running afoul of the Constitution in their effort to ferret out crime, *Strieff*, 136 S. Ct. at 2062 ("favoring exclusion only when the police misconduct is most in need of deterrence – that is, when it is purposeful or flagrant"). Readers might find it ironic that the Court routinely refuses to consider an officer's motives when litigating stops based on racial profiling, yet the *Strieff* Court suddenly develops an interest in an officer's good or bad faith when the objective facts support excluding the drugs found.

40 From *The War on Marijuana in Black and White: Billions of Dollars Wasted on Racially Biased Arrests* (ACLU, 2013), www.aclu.org/report/report-war-marijuana-black-and-white, an extraordinary book-length report released by the ACLU (analyzing 2001 to 2010).

41 Tracey Maclin, "*Terry* v. *Ohio's* Fourth Amendment Legacy: Black Men and Police Discretion," 72 *St. John's L. Rev.* 1270 (1998); Susan Bandes, "*Terry* v. *Ohio* in Hindsight: The Perils of Predicting the Past," 16 *Const. Commentary* 491, 497 (1999); Frank Rudy Cooper, "The Spirit of 1968: Toward Abolishing Terry Doctrine," 31 *N.Y.U. Rev. L. & Soc. Change* 539, 546 (2007); I. Bennett Capers, "Rethinking the Fourth Amendment: Race, Citizenship, and the Equality Principle," 46 *Harvard Civil Rights-Civil Liberties*

L. Rev. 1, 32 (2011); Paul Butler, "Stop and Frisk and Torture-Lite: Police Terror in Minority Communities," 12 *Ohio St. J. Crim. L.* 57, 69 (2014); Carbado, "From Stop and Frisk to Shoot and Kill," 1508, 1551.

42 "Behavioral Health Response Program," n.d., www.portlandmaine.gov/1150/Behavioral-Health-Response-Program and Michael D. Thompson, "When Police Dealt with People with Mental Health Issues," *Scientific American*, August 28, 2016, https://stepuptogether.org/updates/michael-d-thompson-when-police-deal-with-people-who-have-mental-health-issues for more information on Portland's crisis intervention program. Julie Marsh, Tina Moore and Bruce Golding, "Counselors will join NYPD to combat mental health crisis," New York Post, October 21, 2019, https://nypost.com/2019/10/21/counselors-will-join-nypd-to-combat-mental-health-crisis/ (describing NYPD's new approach to crisis intervention). Police departments are increasingly seeking help from mental health and addiction services to respond more efficiently to individuals with mental health needs, *Police-Mental Health Collaborations: A Framework for Implementing Effective Law Enforcement Responses for People Who Have Mental Health Needs*, 1 (CSGS Justice Center, 2019), https://csgjusticecenter.org/wp-content/uploads/2020/02/Police-Mental-Health-Collaborations-Framework.pdf.

43 "An Update on State Efforts in Misdemeanor Reclassification, Penalty Reduction and Alternative Sentencing," The Spangenberg Project and The Center for Justice, Law and Society at George Mason University, September 2010 www.americanbar.org/content/dam/aba/administrative/legal_aid_indigent_defendants/ls_sclaid_def_aba_tsp_reclassification_report.authcheckdam.pdf; "Misdemeanor Sentencing Trends" NCSL, January 29, 2019, www.ncsl.org/research/civil-and-criminal-justice/misdemeanor-sentencing-trends.aspx.

44 "Deep Dive Marijuana," NCSL, n.d., www.ncsl.org/bookstore/state-legislatures-magazine/marijuana-deep-dive.aspx. For a map illustrating which states have passed laws either fully or partially decriminalizing marijuana possession offenses, see "Map of Marijuana Legality by State," DISA, n.d. (last updated January 2020), https://disa.com/map-of-marijuana-legality-by-state.

45 Christian Henrichson, Joshua Rinaldi, and Ruth Delaney, *The Price of Jails: Measuring the Taxpayer Cost of Local Incarceration*," (Vera Institute of Justice, 2015), www.vera.org/downloads/publications/price-of-jails.pdf. (Using DOJ statistics from 2011).

46 Matt Ferner, "The Full Cost of Incarceration in the U.S. is Over $1 Trillion, Study Finds," *Huff Post*, September 13, 2016, www.huffpost.com/entry/mass-incarceration-cost_n_57d82d99e4b09d7a687fde21 citing Michael McLaughlin et al., *The Economic Burden of Incarceration in the US* Working Paper #CI072016 (2016).

47 Jeremy Welsh-Loveman and Samantha Harvell, "Justice Reinvestment Initiative Data Snapshot," *Urban Institute* May 2018, www.urban.org/sites/default/files/publication/98361/justice_reinvestment_initiative_data_snapshot_0.pdf.

48 Some cities have introduced de-escalation strategies and the results appear promising. Salt Lake City police have not initiated a fatal encounter with a civilian since 2015 and some credit goes to the police department's embrace of de-escalation measures. Nick Wing, "Cops in This City Haven't Killed Anyone Since 2015. Here's One Reason Why." *Huff-Post*, May 18, 2017, www.huffpost.com/entry/salt-lake-city-police-de-escalation_n_591c9070e4b03b485cae1129. Similarly, after the Dallas Police Department made a "shift toward de-escalation," assaults on officers declined by 30 percent and shootings by police declined by 40 percent. Complaints against officers using excessive force also declined by 64 percent over 5 years. "Dallas police excessive-force complaints drop dramatically," *The*

Dallas Morning News, November 17, 2015, www.dallasnews.com/news/crime/2015/11/17/ dallas-police-excessive-force-complaints-drop-dramatically/.

The Police Executive Research Forum (PERF) proposes that employing de-escalation strategies during encounters with individuals who are mentally ill or who are unarmed has significant potential for "reducing use of force, while also increasing officer safety." Police Executive Research Forum, *Critical Issues in Policing Series: Guiding Principles on Use of Force* 5 (March 2016), www.policeforum.org/assets/30%20guiding%20principles.pdf. See also Kevin Rector, "Baltimore Police Institute New 'Use of Force' Policy for Officers as Justice Department Report Looms," June 29, 2016, www.baltimoresun.com/news/crime/bs-md-ci-police-use-of-force-20160629-story.html; DeRay McKesson et al., "Police Use of Force Policy Analysis," 7–8 (Campaign Zero Planning, 2016), https://static1.squarespace.com/static/56996151cbced68b170389f4/t/57e1b5cc2994ca4ac1d97700/1474409936835/Police +Use+of+Force+Report.pdf.

49 *We Have a Lot to Lose: Solutions to Advance Black Families in the 21st Century* (115th Congressional Black Caucus, 2017), https://cbc.house.gov/uploadedfiles/2017.03.22_cbc_ we_have_a_lot_to_lose_v5.pdf.

50 Alex S. Vitale, *The End of Policing* (Verso, 2018) at 221–23.

51 Justin Miller, "The New Reformer DAs," *The American Prospect*, January 2, 2018, https:// prospect.org/health/new-reformer-das/.

52 "Charges to be Declined," *Rachael Rollins 4 DA*, n.d., https://rollins4da.com/policy/ charges-to-be-declined/
(detailing the list of charges to be declined, unless supervisor permission is obtained).

53 Mark Fazlollah, Craig R. McCoy, and Julie Shaw, "Under Court Order, District Attorney Larry Krasner Releases List of Tainted Police," *The Philadelphia Inquirer*, March 6, 2018, www.inquirer.com/philly/news/larry-krasner-philadelphia-police-tainted-misconduct-secret-list-20180306.html; Justin George and Eli Hager, "One Way to Deal with Cops Who Lie? Blacklist Them, Some Das Say," *ABA Journal*, January 25, 2019, www.abajournal .com/news/article/one-way-to-deal-with-cops-who-lie-blacklist-them-some-das-say.
In Baltimore, State Attorney, Marilyn Mosby's office has compiled a list of hundreds of officers with credibility issues and has begun investigating at least twenty-five Baltimore police officers for misconduct. Tim Prudente, "Baltimore's State's Attorney Says She Has List of Hundreds of Officers' with Alleged Credibility Issues,"
The Baltimore Sun, October, 18, 2019, www.baltimoresun.com/news/crime/bs-md-ci-cr-mosby-lists-hundreds-of-officers-20191018-cakqslar5rgujp2sc6knwsklpm-story.html; Crime and Justice News, "Should Prosecutors Expand, Publicize 'Brady Lists'?," *The Crime Report*, September 4, 2019, https://thecrimereport.org/2019/09/04/should-prosecutors-expand-publicize-brady-lists/.

54 Police will continue to pressure people to talk as a means to investigate serious felonies, and that seems fair. Even though the evidence will no longer come in against the speaker (under my proposed rules), these involuntary statements might provide leads for ongoing criminal investigations. Most initial interviews and police legwork don't come into trials and under this proposal, on-the-street interrogations would become another form of preliminary investigation.

Index

Made in the USA
Middletown, DE
14 January 2021

31558218R00137